Dear Les,

Best of luck for a healthy & happy 2009.

Enjoy the book!

Play tennis & win in life!

Love,
Mary Pat.

Praise for *Winning in Tennis and Life*:

Success in tennis and in life requires equal contributions from your mind, body and soul and this book is loaded with great ideas that will make you a winner on the court and a champion in life. — Billie Jean King, Tennis Legend

I was thrilled to learn that a far wider audience will now have access to Mary Pat's extraordinary words of wisdom. I am certain that after reading her book, tennis players in schools and clubs and tournaments all over the globe will play at a significantly higher level and while they play, experience a far greater sense of satisfaction. — Leslie Gilbert-Lurie, Author, Lawyer, and President, L.A.County Board of Education

MP sees what other coaches don't. She has a keen eye, the ability to breakdown a swing, body/grip position and quickly pinpoints and fixes mistakes through minor adjustments. It's the minor changes that make a huge difference and provide immediate results, in both tennis and life.
— David P. Kenworthy, NCAA Pole Vault Champion, 1984 & 1988 Olympic Pole Vaulter

Mary Pat Faley's book is perfect for anyone looking to improve tennis skills. Not only has my game improved, my level of enjoyment has soared!
— Chris Bledy, author of *Beating Ovarian Cancer*

Winning in Tennis & Life is a masterpiece; this book shows you how to achieve success on and off the court.
— Cari Buck, Marketing Coordinator of The Tennis Channel; USPTA Professional

Tennis racquet $150. Tennis outfit $85. Tennis balls $5. Mary Pat's knowledge and simplified instruction of the game of tennis...priceless.
— Michele Fischer, student of the game

Mary Pat Faley's 1, 2, 3 program really works. Apply her philosophy to your game today and you will experience a tremendous difference. She taught me how to serve in ten minutes. — Anders Jeleveus, author of *Integrated Sports Massage Therapy*

A true coach is also a mentor who is the one person you want to call when you win or when you lose. Through their words, they inspire passion and determination. For over fifteen years, Mary Pat has taught my children and me life lessons that we will always remember. I will forever be indebted to her. I now play the game, but Mary Pat gave me my game!!" — Linda Beisswanger

I have had the honor of knowing Mary Pat Faley, MP, for over twenty years. Her incredible knowledge, experience, and personality, and her innate ability to teach and relay information in such a fun and exciting way has inevitably produced thousands of tennis lovers of all ages and levels around the country. MP not only teaches tennis while on the court; she never does just that. She teaches many valuable life lessons that leave her students not just knowing, but also believing they can.
— Kirstin "Smitty" Kastor, CA Tennis Professional

If you are lucky enough to get a lesson with Mary Pat, you are also given a life lesson. As a tennis teacher/coach, Mary Pat astounds her students by her knowledge and care. Every aspect of the game is distilled to its intention, whether it is the footwork, swing mechanism or body direction. Every movement and exercise is with the purpose of playing the game well and to protect our bodies, to be aware of our core and supporting muscles and make them more efficient. And—that "aha moment" extends past the tennis court. In our cluttered lives, perhaps "focus" is her greatest lesson."
— Gail Aftergood

Mary Pat notices every detail about your overall game; then she makes small changes that lead to big improvements in playing. We all want to borrow her brain when we're playing tough matches against big opponents because of her ability to see every detail.
— Kristine Grant, Certified Massage Therapist

I first got serious about tennis after reading Tim Gallwey's book *The Inner Game of Tennis*. Mary Pat is the only instructor I know that could convert that book to the practice of tennis and take it beyond. In over twenty years of taking lessons and drills from Mary Pat, I am consistently amazed at how her instruction is constantly evolving and growing in depth. If I had to use two words to sum up Mary Pat, it would be fundamentals and flexibility. That would be the fundamentals of footwork, body motion, and racquet along with the flexibility of the mind constantly to adjust and grow.
— Thomas J. Moss, MD, VP of Medical MT Group, Assoc. Professor UCLA Dept. of Pediatrics

It has been my extreme pleasure to take lessons from Mary Pat for many years. Her teaching methods and lessons in life go hand in hand. It always amazes me how she can solve any tennis problems with such simple remedies. She continues to keep her teaching methods fresh by exploring new and exciting ideas. I have learned such valuable lessons in life as well as in tennis because of her. I value her not only as a tennis professional, but also as a friend. — Bobbie Gibson

Once in a great while you run across an inspirational teacher who not only makes it easy to learn, but also makes you want to do your best whether it be playing tennis or living your life; Mary Pat is such a teacher. When I first met Mary Pat there was no way I was going to play doubles; too much apologizing and guilt. After a few clinics in doubles technique and strategy, I only want to play doubles because it's so much fun. They say you can't teach an old dog new tricks; well, I am here to say that Mary Pat can.
— Jenny Stewart

My daughter is an avid tennis player at eighteen years old and her first instructor was Mary Pat. When someone watches my daughter, they comment on her classic, beautiful strokes and her gift for doubles and net play. Not every tennis player has the skill to be a good teacher but Mary Pat has that. She gave the gift of beautiful strokes and a love of the game to my daughter. — Pat Schulz

Mary Pat is a constant reminder that no matter what one person's craft is and no matter how long one continues at the same profession, there will always be room to improve and develop that craft. She sets a great example of constantly introducing new ideas, and injecting a genuine energy into her work. The result is an extremely large clientele who are ALL overly satisfied with her product, and who ALL seem continually to get better! — Brady Hiete, Tennis Professional at Calabasas Tennis & Swim Center

I have known Mary Pat Faley for thirty-three years. I truly believe she has a special gift for teaching. She can see things others do not, and she can explain things in a unique, clear, and refreshing way. Her techniques were foreign to me, as I was a reactive player…"Old school"…"Can't teach an old dog new tricks" kind of student. She taught me only to think in three's. In simplifying the learning process, she divided the court into three; each stroke into three and this method has totally reduced brain clutter! She has turned me into a proactive player who enjoys tennis more than ever! I am playing at a 4.5 level at forty-eight years old…Thanks Faley! — Janet Klebesadel

MP is an amazing tennis pro who can quickly assess your weakness and clearly show why and how to improve it. There is no one like her with such great teaching skills, humor and level of energy. MP is the goddess of tennis!!! — Kristi Bala

Mary Pat is a master at teaching tennis technique. She explains technical information from a common sense point of view, breaking it down into sequences of three and then puts it all back together. She is easy to understand and has been most instrumental and invaluable in improving my game throughout the years. Everything she has taught me is in this book. — Beth Willer-Horwitz

"MP," as we call her, is the rarest of instructors. She is the perfect combination of kindness, humor and criticism. She is able to pinpoint specific problems with your game and correct them with her concrete methods and solutions. Her positive attitude and her love of the game make her a true teacher. — Randi Haim

We are moving forward faster than imaginable in sports with our equipment. The technology today is making our racquets better and better. Mary Pat is moving forward in her approach to teaching right along with all of this new technology. Not a lot of professionals in our industry have the talent and ability to change and move forward, but Mary Pat does it with her own brand of humor and fun. There are innumerable techniques and ideas I have learned from her over the last year. My students and I are very grateful for what she continues to contribute to the game of tennis. They say the best teacher is the one who can teach the teacher. Thank you MP!
— Lisa Sherman, CA. Tennis Professional

Within a few minutes of my first lesson with Mary Pat, she was able to diagnose exactly what I was doing wrong and showed me how to improve in a way that was clear and precise. Four years later, she still offers effective guidance and tips during every weekly lesson to help me improve. Her suggestions are clear and easy to incorporate into game situations. I hear her voice in my head as I play, and it has made my performance better than ever. — Karen Kurtenbach

With an amazing combination of perception and technique, Mary Pat quickly identifies one or two key areas to focus on and has a huge arsenal of tips and methods to hone your skill. She has vastly improved my game and the confidence I have walking onto the court—and knowing I can always turn things around on the court. It's an approach I like to bring to life off the court, too. She has shown me that attitude can really affect your altitude. — Nick Polo

I learned to play tennis with Mary Pat fifteen years ago. I was forty-six years old. It was the major turning point of my life. Not only was she my coach, she was and is my friend. Learning tennis with Mary Pat has given me such confidence in everything that I do. I will be eternally grateful to her always. — Sheila Rom

Mary Pat has been an inspiration to both my teenage boys throughout the years. Her style, teaching methods, and exuberance have inspired my children to learn, work hard and enjoy tennis. Mary Pat has taught my kids how to set goals, and through hard work and practice, how to achieve those goals. She has brought out the best in my kids, and they continue to enjoy tennis as a sport they will play throughout their lives for both pleasure and physical fitness. — Beth Shumacher

I have taken lessons from Mary Pat for over fifteen years. The thing that always amazes all of us is that week after week she still teaches us something new. We accuse her of holding out on us!!! We have no doubt we still have much to learn from Mary Pat!! — Missy Tobyansen

When I was age eleven, Mary Pat was my first tennis coach. After working with her for six months, I went from beginner player to my first national tennis tournament. There are many tennis pros who can teach you the mechanics of tennis, but there are very few who can help you find such a love for the game. Thank you MP; you inspired me not only throughout my competitive tennis years, but also as a teaching pro today. — Natasha Mucci, Tennis Professional at North Ranch CC in CA

As a student of Mary Pat for the past five years, I have definitely become a different tennis player because of her. Something about her teaching techniques make you feel 1,000 percent improved once you are done with your lesson, and that has helped me with my confidence level, my game, my athletic abilities and my overall well being as a person. Once you have had her as a pro, it is almost impossible to have someone else be your teacher. I cannot wait to get my hands on her book so I can learn and implement everything in it. — Soraya Hostetter

Mary Pat has been teaching me for eight years, and my nine-year-old son for four years. She's brought my tennis level from a 3.0 beginner to a strong 4.5. I truly appreciate her unique and special teaching skills. She has an incredible ability to identify a problem and quickly fix it. She is also doing outstanding coaching work with my son, Ori, who is already participating in USTA junior tournaments. With her individual attention and helpful attitude toward tennis, not only has she helped him improve his technique but also helped him develop a greater passion and confidence for competing at the junior tennis tournaments. — Miri Mizrahi

You have helped improve my game so much. I still hear your comments when I play, such as "Toss the ball to the net post." — Cece Walsh

One of the things I find most amazing about Mary Pat is her unique ability to watch several players at one time and quickly assess their problems. She has a great eye and knows your mistakes even before you make them. Her corrections are simple and easy to incorporate in your game with long-lasting results. She is the drill master!" — Marci Grogin

After double hip replacements, Mary Pat brought me back to tennis with excellent instruction and personal inspiration. — Marty Lapinsky

I have known Mary Pat Faley for over ten years as a tennis instructor, mentor and friend. She brings an extraordinarily high degree of creativity and innovation to the sport of tennis, transforming her tennis lessons into life lessons. On the court, she is able to tap into and bring out the best in a person's physical and mental abilities, then teach how to assimilate those strengths into everyday life. Her singles strategies help empower personal independence, while her doubles strategies concentrate on teamwork and convergent strategy. Mary Pat Faley is a real ace! — Lauren Kurzweil

Both my daughter and I have taken tennis lessons from Mary Pat. I had not played tennis for over twenty years when I started with her. She is able to break it down for each person individually. She understands how each of us processes information and teaches us accordingly. My daughter was a beginner when Mary Pat started teaching her. Her tennis skills improved dramatically in such a short period of time."
— Alaina Bernstein

Mary Pat...teaching pro extraordinaire. With her new book, it will get you up and keep you up playing tennis for fun and health. — Dr. Henry Golden

Mary Pat exhibits professionalism on the tennis court. Her teaching skills are such that one gets the results expected. Her knowledge and skills run the gamut from technical expertise to being prepared to lead and teach others. Her skills also prepare you with self-confidence that helps you on and off the tennis court. All the benefits that a quality instructor such as Mary Pat offers have greatly improved my tennis game and my overall life. — Hilary Fischer, NASM personal trainer & Pilates certified instructor

Mary Pat Faley is the best tennis teacher I have had the pleasure of learning from in all these years of playing tennis. Her back to basics philosophy has helped me to hone my game. I find that when my game feels like it needs a punch, her 1,2,3 philosophy puts me back on track. Men and women find her teaching methods and drills challenging, and she is wonderful with whatever level of tennis you play and lifts it up. I always leave her class feeling invigorated and excited to try the "new/old" lessons I had forgotten. — Kala Paramesh, Ph.D.

Four years ago, I joined a Mary Pat drill class and rediscovered tennis. After eighteen years competing in the corporate world, I wanted to play competitive tennis again. Step-by-step, Mary Pat worked with me and helped me put together my game. Now, I am USTA competitive and my game is better than it ever was! — Celeste Malott

Mary Pat has been a true mentor of mine and has been extremely influential in my tennis career as well as my life. From an early age, she has taught me so many important lessons I still carry with me as a father and coach. Mary Pat's dedication to her students, friends and colleagues is unparalleled in the industry, and I feel extremely privileged to have been associated with her.
— Darren Miller, Director of Tennis, Sherwood Country Club

Mary Pat is a very professional, engaging and astute tennis professional. I have been most impressed with her ability quickly to diagnose a player's problems, and provide suggestions to correct the problem or issue that her tennis student is having. I had heard about her for some time (that she was the best tennis instructor around), and when I had problems with "tennis elbow" I decided to seek her advice. She promptly provided me with ways to address my condition and assisted me with the techniques I needed to prevent further injury and become a more proficient tennis player. As an educator myself, I am most impressed with her knowledge, her demeanor, and her love of the sport. She sets a high bar for her students and is a wonderful role model. I feel so fortunate to be one of her students. — Dr. Bobbi Lincoln

Sometimes it takes an instructor four different ways of saying the same thing to make a student understand. If you're Mary Pat, you only have to say it once because she already figured out how you, as an individual, learn. — Russell Morgan

Mary Pat's clinic is fun, fast and focused. She does not miss a thing—I think she must have eyes behind her head! There is positive reinforcement, attention to detail and no down time—every minute is well spent working on something. She is the best of the best. — Lynn Heckler

Mary Pat taught me things none of my male instructors could—how to work around my female anatomy (specifically my breasts) in making my backhand. Her wisdom in this department has also translated into my personal life, remembering that men (my husband included) don't understand the female anatomy, more than what they want or like about it, so we woman need to have our girlfriends who can help us navigate our lives in this world. Many thanks to MP for her wisdom on and off the court.
— Peggy Jacobs

I just loved (or hated) how she would push me to my limit each time I trained with Mary Pat! It has not only helped with my mental toughness in sports, but with everything in my life as well! I truly feel like a stronger person mentally and physically after all my many, many tennis lessons as an adolescent! I look forward to having my children learn & train from her! — Jenny Mennell

When I first moved to Calabasas, the thing to do was to join the Calabasas Tennis Club and get lessons with Mary Pat Faley. When I finally got in the club, I would sit by the sidelines and watch MP teach, and I could not believe she did not tie her shoelaces! I thought to myself, "When I get lessons from her, she is going to have to tie her shoes!" I thought for sure my artful placing of the ball would have to be the thing that would make her tie her shoe laces so she could run down my ball, but before I even hit the ball she was standing in the place where it was going to land! Well, many clinics and lessons later and in 100 degree plus heat (on some days), she never tied her shoes for me or anyone else...She continues to teach tennis and motivate people to push their limits without regret. She is a true inspiration and a wonderful person who knows no boundaries. — Melinda LeBlanc

Mary Pat is a brilliant tennis instructor. She has this bag of tricks that is so magical. It transforms you from randomly getting lucky in your games to becoming a proactive skillful tennis player. This happens because she makes it so simple to understand the details of each move. It's incredibly helpful when she breaks it down into little steps of simple tennis moves. One of my favorites is to watch the ball bounce, and again when it's in contact with your racquet. — Lena Alexander

Tennis has been an important part of my life. From the red clay courts and white balls in Europe, to the perfect California tennis weather, tennis is what I love to play. Last year, after healing a shoulder injury, I needed help to re-learn a correct serving motion. Mary Pat analyzed the problem and with her 1-2-3 methods—she never introduces more than three changes, one at a time—my serve is back! Actually I have several serves now and I'm very happy!! — Gilla Sundahl

Where other instructors tended to give up on me because they thought I was either not trying or I was not good enough, Mary Pat said nonsense to that. After seven years of lessons with her, I have consistently improved, raising my level and loving tennis.
— Marilyn Lapinsky

Mary Pat Faley is off the charts when it comes to imparting tennis knowledge and strategies. She eats, sleeps, and breathes the game. After fifteen years as student and friend, I have determined the source of all this energy: her incredibly positive attitude. No goal is too high; no skill is out of reach. After the book, it has to be Mary Pat in person. — Linda Finn

Mary Pat Faley is one of the best and most knowledgeable tennis teaching professionals I have ever had the privilege to teach with. She is always trying to learn and teach new methods for her students. Besides learning new techniques, Mary Pat is the epitome of a true teaching professional. She's well dressed, on time, and always personable. Without a doubt, she is one of the best in the U.S.
— Joe Prado, USPTA, Calabasas, CA

For many years, Mary Pat has helped me to improve my tennis game, both mentally and physically. Her philosophy and methods of teaching have taught me not only to be present and focused on the court, but in everyday life as well. I highly recommend this book! — Cathy Justman

I have been a member of Mary Pat's Thursday morning drill class for over eight years and yet every week she has a new challenge. This is due to Mary-Pat's ingenuity and smart way of teaching competitive tennis. — Lina Boardman

When I was four, my mom would bribe me to go to Mary Pat's 'Tennis Training for Toddlers,' and she promised me every time after tennis we would go to Baskin Robbins! Ten years later, I look back and thank my mother so much, because if it were not for Mary Pat's encouragement and intelligence in tennis, I do not know where I would be right now. Tennis has directed me in so many directions that it still astonishes me everyday. MP is the most positive woman I know. I have never seen her in a bad mood, and she has the attitude of a winner, because she is one. I feel absolutely honored to be able to contribute some of my gratitude into her book, and I will thank her till the day I die for how much she has stepped up my tennis game.
— Shelby Sinoway, Ranked junior in the Girls 16's

Mary Pat is a true motivator. She keeps you going, constantly helps you improve, and makes it all great fun at the same time. She brings a combination of spirit and seriousness to the court. There's no doubt that I've learned some great shots from her! More importantly, though, she has taught me that the real game is never to give up but to smile back at the challenge and hold your ground. That's helped me time and time again, in tennis *and* in life." — Karen Stanol

Mary Pat, the tennis doctor...She can diagnose and cure your sick tennis shots.
— Sara Jane Davis

The paths to success in all facets of life share universal truths. It's the different languages that cover those paths and keep them hidden from most. Mary Pat Faley does an excellent job of articulating these universal paths to success in not only the sport of tennis, but life. — Justin C. Fine

I came to tennis late and via the backyard. I developed many bad habits and gave myself tennis elbow and shoulder pain fairly quickly. Mary Pat's private lessons and weekly drill classes taught me the correct techniques and have made tennis one of the most enjoyable parts of my life today. She has completely changed how I think, see, hit and move to the ball and on the court. I'm in my tenth year of drills with Mary Pat, and she continues to challenge me and to improve my game. She is a fabulous teaching pro. — Beverly Bishop

It was a beautiful sunny day and I knew I was in love with LA! Arriving from a Boston blizzard I pondered what activity I could participate in both day and night: "Tennis!" Since the early 1980's, Mary Pat has coached me from a novice to a competitor. MP, I refer to her as "Master Perfectionist," makes small changes that make big improvements, instantly! — Lisa Sinoway

Mary Pat has written a book that not only serves as an essential guide to the fundamentals of tennis but also offers life lessons learned from her many years of teaching and playing the game. Mary Pat describes her experience and success in bringing people together, learning to play the game, advancing skills, creating friendships and having fun. As a student for several years in her weekly drill classes, I highly recommend this book as an inspirational and insightful guide to the sport of tennis.
— Judge Dana Senit Henry (ret)

I have known MP for at least fifteen years, and I have always learned and enjoyed our get togethers whether they are on the tennis court for a lesson or over a cup of coffee discussing life. She brings concepts together for me so they are so easy to see and easy to implement into my stroke or my life. I so appreciate that quality in her.
— Michelle Berteotti, LPGA touring professional

Mary Pat is a coach who is always looking to improve and develop her own self-awareness, which transfers to her awareness of her students so that she is continually redeveloping and refining her teaching strategies, methods, and techniques. M.P. gets it that tennis represents an ever-changing form of energy much like our own lives and the world we live in. — Mary Hale, Schoolteacher; 4.5, USTA player

WINNING
IN TENNIS AND LIFE

How to Execute Your Strategy On and Off the Court

MARY PAT FALEY

Winning In Tennis And Life
How to Execute Your Strategy On and Off the Court

Mary Pat Faley
c/o My Raquet
16836 Bosque Dr.
Encino, CA 91436

www.WinningInTennisAndLife.com

Published by:
Aviva Publishing
2301 Saranac Avenue, Ste. 100
Lake Placid, NY 12946
518-523-1320
www.avivapubs.com

Every attempt has been made to source all quotes properly.

Editor: Jeannine Mallory
Cover Design: Shiloh Schroeder Design
Proofreader: Tyler R. Tichelaar
Typesetting: Kimberly Martin
Illustrations: Rick Evans
Photos: Randi Haim

Printed in the United States of America

ISBN: 978-1-890427-47-4
Library of Congress # 2008939202

For additional copies visit:
www.WinningInTennisAndLife.com

DEDICATION

To my best friend: You are my rock. You make sure I never give up. You stand up for what is right in the world, and you have taught me to do the same. Thank you for being supportive every step of the way on this beautiful journey. I am so grateful you will be in my life forever. I love you tons and more.

To my precious little Rem-Rem: You are the joy of my life. You always have a smile on your face, and you put one on mine. You have inspired me to be a good stepmom, to teach you about life's lessons and to write this book. I hope you will develop a love of this sport, as much as I have over the years. I love you.

To my family: You have traveled this journey with me for such a long time. Thank you for being there through the ups and downs.

To all my students throughout the years: You have made me the person I am today. I, the teacher, have learned more from you, the students, than you have from me. I am the lucky one. You have inspired me and driven me always to strive to be better, always to look for improvement in anything I do and never to be satisfied until I have reached my goals and dreams.

To you, the reader: It is my honor and privilege to help you learn about your health, your tennis and your life's lessons. I hope you always try to be the very best you can be. Never give up!

ACKNOWLEDGMENTS

So many people made this book possible. It has been one of the most awesome journeys I have ever taken. I hope it will help many other people.

Thank you, Billie Jean King. Your love for the game, your passion for life and dedication to equality for all inspired me to set goals that I still strive for every day. Your courage and tenacity have motivated and challenged me since I first saw you playing tennis. You have helped make my life what it is today.

Thank you, Chase Richards, for leading me on my path to a happy, joyous and free life. Your short three years on this earth taught me invaluable lessons. Thank you, Susan Richards, for sharing him with me. I still think of you both often.

Thank you, Rich Francey and Prince Sports Company, for sponsoring me throughout the years with the greatest racquets, shoes and clothes. You have helped many junior players over the years as well in your generosity and wonderful products. Your continued support is always appreciated.

Thank you, Steve McAvoy, Top Seed Tennis Academy, Calabasas Tennis and Swim Center and all the tennis pros I work with currently and have worked with over the years. You've made me strive to achieve more than I ever thought possible.

Thank you, Chris Bledy, for your courage to battle and live through ovarian cancer—and then write a book about it. You helped me to be brave and follow your path of writing to inspire and help others.

Thank you, Bob Collins, my first tennis coach. I appreciate the extra help you gave me during those years I was a junior player learning to play the game, and then when I was learning how to teach the mechanics of the game.

Thank you, Diana Rankin, who is an amazing psychic reader and told me a few years ago that I was going to write this book. I really did not believe you!

Thank you, Patrick Snow, who has been the greatest book coach a person could ever have. Your encouragement and enthusiasm are unbelievable.

Thank you, Randi Haim, for you generous time in taking all the great photos.

Thank you, Sam Martello, another incredible photographer, and a wonderful dad to Rem-Rem.

Thank you, to all the other people who helped me put the pieces of the puzzle together in completing this book: Jeannine Mallory, the wonderful editor who made this book what it is today; Susan Friedmann, Shiloh Schroeder, Rick Evans, Tyler R. Tichelaar, Kimberly Martin and Kathy Brown. Your hard work is greatly appreciated.

Thank you, my past and present clients. You challenge me and make me want to strive to get better every day of my life. You've all brought that gift to my life. Sharing your life's journeys as we play and learn tennis is so important to me.

Thank you to my true friends. I am blessed to have you all in my life. There isn't enough room to list each of you, but you know who you are! You have made a tremendous difference in my life. I am forever grateful to each of you.

Finally, thank you to my immediate family and to my extended family. Thank you to Ilene and my little Rem-Rem; you make my life complete. Thank you for always being there for me with your encouragement, love and support. I could not have done this without you. I love you and I thank you all from the bottom of my heart.

CONTENTS

WINNING
IN TENNIS AND LIFE

How to Execute Your Strategy On and Off the Court

MARY PAT FALEY

INTRODUCTION:
GETTING STARTED

Life's up and downs provide windows of opportunity to determine...
your values and goals...Think of using all obstacles
as stepping stones to build the life you want.
— Marsha Sinetar

Self-awareness is a key to self-acceptance,
which drives self-motivation and self-fulfillment.
— Stedman Graham

A dream is just a dream. A goal is a dream with a plan and a deadline.
— Harvey Mackay

Are you in the best shape of your life? Are you eating healthy most days? Is your tennis game where you want it to be? Are you happy at work? Do you want to get more out of life? Are you doing what your heart is calling you to do, both professionally and personally? Have you fulfilled your dreams? If not, do you have a plan for fulfilling those dreams?

It's through passionate stirring of your soul that you will
be moved and thereby inspired to fulfill your special mission.
— Rusty Berkus

My "special mission" is to be of service to the world. Tennis is the vehicle through which I can accomplish this mission. This book will be your blueprint for exploring all the important areas of your life. It will encompass the game of health, the game of tennis and the game of life. Get ready for the journey of a lifetime.

Billie Jean King said that when they take the surveys of successful women in *Fortune 500* companies, **80 percent** of them say they participated in sports as young women. Clearly, tennis gets individuals ready for the "real world." The skills needed to survive on the tennis court are the same needed to survive in business. If you apply the techniques you will learn in *Winning in Tennis and Life*, then you too will become successful.

Disclaimer

Since this book is broken up into three parts:

1) The Game of Health
2) The Game of Tennis
3) The Game of Life

I'm giving you the option to skip the tennis section, if you aren't a tennis player. You can always come back to that section later.

"Lefty" Disclaimer

Since 70-80% of the population plays tennis right-handed, the tennis section of the book was written for right-handed players. No, I have nothing against lefties. My dad was a lefty, and I played him all the time, which enabled me to figure out how to play lefties!

If the play descriptions in this book do not make sense to you, I will personally show you from a left-hander's point of view, or I will e-mail you the same information as if you were left-handed. Let me know at my e-mail: marypat@WinningInTennisAndLife.com.

Winning in Tennis and Life is your own personal blueprint for healthy living. Healthy living includes putting *YOU* at the top of your game for your own personal health.

If you read this book, you will better understand that, "If you don't have your health, you don't have anything." I've heard that statement for years, but I never really grasped what it meant. Over the past year, my life has been jeopardized. I almost died and now I am writing this book to share some stories with you to help you achieve the best health you've ever had. I hope in reading this book, you will relate to some of the stories and this will be your "call to action" to make some life changes, *NOW*.

SECTION I:

The first part of the book talks about the game of health. You will learn about your health, your nutrition, and your exercise programs. If you follow these specific plans, you will be in the best shape of your life. Your fitness will far surpass any of your dreams to help you live a long and healthy life.

You will see, from stories of my students, how to overcome adversity, how to balance family and life. Then you will see that by following my steps, the sky is the limit, and you can accomplish anything. "Can't" and "Fear" will not be in your vocabulary anymore.

John Addison, an executive of Citibank, said,

> *"I will do today what others don't,*
> *so I will do tomorrow what others won't."*

For me, that includes exercising daily. I was willing to do whatever it took to write this book. I trusted the path set in front of me; I did not worry about the "Hows." Some of the "Hows" included, "How am I ever going to have time to write a book?" "How am I going to duplicate myself so I can teach others all I've learned, including stories about my health, my tennis game, and finally, my life's lessons?"

An Escape

> *"Playing a good tennis match gives you an*
> *overwhelming feeling of elation. Nothing else in the*
> *world matters at that point in time. All the stress and strain of the*
> *mundane, the housework, the nine-to-five job, are buried and forgotten*
> *as you concentrate on the game at hand."*
> *— Lisa Scully-O'Grady*

*"It takes far more than just hitting a tennis ball
to be the very best and to reach your own
highest point, not only in sports but in life."*
— *Nick Bollettieri*

*Whoever said, "It's not whether you win or lose
that counts," probably lost.*
— *Martina Navratilova*

SECTION II:

The second section of the book discusses the game of tennis. It is everything you need to know about tennis and much, much more. If you read this section on how to play tennis, you will play the best tennis you have ever played. You will learn that if you can count to three, you can play tennis!

Every stroke is broken down to its simplest form for you to learn all the basic shots needed for playing your best tennis. Whether you are a beginner, or want your child to start playing, or played many years ago (we do not have to count how many years), and want to take the game up again, this book is for you. This section is guaranteed to improve your tennis game. You will discover that tennis truly is the sport of a lifetime.

You will overcome mental hurdles that have kept you from bringing your tennis game to levels you never thought possible. You will learn strategies for both singles and doubles. The best-kept secret in tennis is learning, understanding and mastering secrets that seem so simple you'll be surprised you haven't thought of them yourself. I will show you the secret to mastering the art of how to focus, on the tennis court, in school and in business. You can achieve any goal if you learn these methods.

The best-kept secret in tennis is learning, understanding and mastering how to "focus." Secrets that seem so simple—you must be surprised that you never thought of them yourself. How many times have you been playing tennis and you say to yourself, "Watch the ball. Watch the ball?" Then, the next shot would come to you and you would miss it, and you would berate yourself because you just told yourself to, "Watch the ball," and you did not see the ball at all? It is a wonder you even made contact with it!

I will show you the secret to mastering the art of how to focus, either on the tennis court, in school, or in business. This is one of life's greatest lessons. You can achieve any goal if you learn these methods. You can also go to my website, WinningInTennisAndLife.com and learn six more "focus techniques" that will further enhance your tennis game.

SECTION III:

The last part of the book talks about the game of life. You'll learn how tennis can teach you lessons you need for a happy and successful life.

> *"Sport strips away personality, letting the white bone of character shine through. Sport gives players an opportunity to know and test themselves."*
> — *Rita Mae Brown*

Tennis is a very forgiving game and can teach you a lot about yourself. The opportunities to improve, take risks and challenge yourself will present themselves time and time again.

Ultimately, it is up to you whether you choose to step out of your comfort zone, step out of what is familiar to you and take the chance to use some of these tools. This book will help you learn, improve and achieve personal triumphs.

Once you decide and choose to practice the skills and strategies presented in this book and commit to using them, you will experience a freedom and level of performance you may have only felt on a few occasions. *Winning in Tennis and Life* will help you achieve your desires, goals and dreams. Come and join me on a trip of a lifetime.

This book will give you more "tools for your toolbox." Every strategy, every focus tip, every new shot you learn how to hit properly, every exercise for fitness that is new for you, is another tool. The more tools you have, the more you can deal with adversity in life, whether you need the toolbox to find a different strategy that works on the tennis court, or you need a different tool to handle a situation at work.

You will accumulate lots of different "tools" and skills from this book. You will have tools to help you in life, in tennis, and in your health.

> *My mother drew a distinction between achievement*
> *and success. She said that "Achievement is the knowledge*
> *that you have studied and worked hard and done the best*
> *that is in you. Others are praising success, and that*
> *is nice, too, but not as important or satisfying.*
> *Always aim for achievement and forget about success."*
> *— Helen Hayes*

> *What is the recipe for successful achievement? To me there*
> *are just three essential ingredients: Choose a career you love.*
> *Give it the best there is in you...And seize your opportunities.*
> *— Benjamin F. Fairless*

> *Practice hope. As hopefulness becomes a habit,*
> *you can achieve a permanently happy spirit.*
> *— Norman Vincent Peale*

SECTION ONE:

The Game of Health

CHAPTER 1:
CHOOSING HEALTH

Plan with your head. Play with your heart.

Your Overall Health

Do you go to the doctor at least once a year for a complete physical check-up? Do you listen to your body when it talks to you? The older you get, the more, it, your body, talks to you. How many times have you heard the saying, "If you don't have your health, you don't have anything?" How well do we really take care of ourselves? On the other hand, are we better at taking care of other people, and ignoring what is going on with our own bodies? It is a great form of denial to focus our attention on someone else, not ourselves.

But if we don't take care of ourselves first, how can we possibly take care of someone else adequately? If we get sick, then who will take care of that other person? It is not selfish, but rather, self love. There is a big difference in those two things. Most people today do not know the difference. Or perhaps I should say they have not practiced it.

This must be your number one goal in starting to bring about a new healthy way to live. We are all living, breathing and getting through day-to-day, but are we really doing it in the healthiest way so that we love ourselves first? Most of us just come to in the morning hours, but do we really wake up excited to start the day's journey?

Do you still have that zest or excitement for life? Did you have it years ago, and now for some reason it does not seem to be there anymore? This book will change your way of thinking. You'll learn simple things to make you appreciate the little things every day has to offer. People will see it in your actions, in your living your day to its fullest; they will see it in your eyes. It will be contagious. So, let us start our journey.

Let me share a story with you about myself that happened in February. I am a very active person, some call it a "Type A" personality. I do not sit still very much; a couch potato to me sounds as if you take a potato and sit on it on the couch. (Is that what makes hash browns?) I have been a USPTA tennis professional for thirty years. I still teach about thirty to thirty-five hours a week. I ride a bicycle about 100 miles a week. I am a National Academy of Sports Medicine certified personal trainer; I play golf, hike, swim, do Pilates, work out three to four times a week, spin indoors on a bike trainer and take my dog for walks three to four times a week. That's a typical week for me. Therefore, I am very active. I must admit that sitting on the couch eating cherry bon-bons does sound like a fun treat, though.

I had been working out extremely hard, since I was developing some new techniques for my tennis clients to incorporate training with weights, medicine balls, stability balls and exercises to strengthen their core that would directly improve their performance on the tennis court.

Therefore, when my calf muscle hurt a little bit, I just thought I had strained it since I had been working out so much more with all the new exercises. My leg was quite a bit swollen, but I assumed it was just from the strain. The pain did not hurt as much once I walked on it. It was extremely sore when I walked on it after a night's sleep or after I had been sitting for a little while. However, within fifteen to twenty minutes, the pain subsided for the most part, so it just seemed like a strained muscle.

My typical day on that Saturday in February was a forty-mile bike ride, then a Pilates class, then a hike with my dog for about four miles. That was a great day for me! My leg was sore starting the exercises, but warmed up as we were well into the activity. With much prodding from friends all weekend to call the doctor because the pain was still there and the swelling had not gone down, I said I would call on Monday. Of course, I did not want to bother him on the weekend, for goodness sake.

Oh, a quick side note—in December 2007, I suddenly had a pain in that same leg one day. But that time, it swelled up much, much more than it did in February. The pain in December was absolutely crippling so I could not even walk on the leg. I looked in my Blue Cross directory for a vein doctor in my area (on a friend's recommendation) and saw the name of a doctor, whose wife and children had been my tennis students ten years ago. Thank goodness, the memory is still there.

I called that day, and the doctor's secretary squeezed me in. I went to see him, barely able to walk on the leg. He looked at it and immediately set up a Doppler test. The Doppler test is done in the hospital (which I did not know until then), and a technician waves a wand over your veins and gets a reading on the computer to see whether there are any blockages in your veins.

He found one immediately. I almost kicked the tech as he touched the area with the wand…I had told him how much it hurt. He didn't believe me…so he almost had a bloody nose from my foot jumping so much from the pain. It was a superficial clot in the calf area. He said there was no danger; the clot was just very painful.

The doctor then recommended lots of Advil and anti-inflammatory medication, along with elevating my leg as much as possible for most of the day for the next few weeks. Thank goodness, it was around the holidays, so missing work wasn't so bad since it is a slow time anyway. I went back to work full-time by the middle of January, with no more pain.

That is until February 11, 2008, which was a Monday. I called my vein doctor again to tell him I had a little pain in my calf, but it was nothing like the episode I'd had in December. I told him about my weekend adventures with biking, Pilates and hiking. He said that if the leg were not severely swollen, he wouldn't be able to see too much in his office anyway, so the best idea was to go and have a Doppler test again on the leg. His secretary called me, set up the appointment, and told me to have a nice day. The test was scheduled at the hospital that evening at six o'clock. I decided rather than to exercise that day just to make it a paperwork day. In hindsight, that might have been a very good decision.

I cooked dinner that night, put it in the oven and left to have the test done, intending to be home within the hour. I drove myself to the hospital, checked in at admitting and went for my Doppler test. My friend, Jose, the tech who'd administered the test in December, was there. "What are you doing back here?" he said. "Didn't I just see you a couple of months ago?" We chatted about how our holidays had been, and I promised not to kick him when he gave me the test again. I assured him that it did not hurt half as much as last time. He remembered that he'd made me cry.

So, as he ran the wand over my leg, he said, "Oh no, this is not good. You have a DVT in your vein."

When, I asked what that meant, he explained, "Deep vein thrombosis; a blood clot in the deep vein. It is very dangerous. We have to admit you to the hospital right now."

"What?" I exclaimed. "I have a chicken in the oven, and my kid is waiting for me to come home. I can't go into the hospital. I have eleven hours of teaching tennis tomorrow. It doesn't even hurt that much and I feel fine!"

Jose calmly said, "I'm afraid not. I'll call your doctor and you can talk to him." I talked to my doctor and told him, "I have a chicken in the oven and my kid is waiting for me at home." He replied that I had to be admitted immediately.

He asked who had driven me to the hospital. I told him I'd driven myself because I never thought I was going to stay. That would be crazy. Anyway, because I had known him for so many years, and was very persuasive, my doctor let me drive home. It was just a few miles away. I could get a few things as long as I had promised to have someone drive me back to the hospital for admittance immediately. I agreed.

I did drive home rather cautiously, shocked at the news I had just received. I got the chicken out of the oven and my little girl helped me pack a bag for the hospital. I assumed I might be there for one day, no more than two. I packed strange things that I later discovered…sweats, workout clothes, a heart rate monitor and a movie. I must have thought I was going to a spa or something. I could not really tell you. I think they call that "denial."

Anyway, I called a friend to take me to the hospital. Once I was admitted, I went up to my room. Remember, this entire time, I really felt absolutely fine—the specimen of perfect health. How could I be in a hospital bed? Of course, I refused to wear the hospital gowns so nicely provided by the hospital and immediately got into my sweat outfit. I even looked fine in the hospital.

The nurse came in and said, "I have specific instructions for you not to leave the bed, one-hundred percent bed rest." I said, "Are you kidding me? You mean to tell me I cannot even get up and go to the bathroom, which is seven steps from my bed? It's right there," I said pointing to the beautiful hospital bathroom. She said again that I was not to get out of the bed and showed me the picturesque, one-of-a-kind, made especially for you, pink bedpan. Ugh! *What am I doing here?*

Needless to say, I didn't sleep very much, even though I felt fine. Rolling in the next morning came breakfast. It was pancakes, one of my favorites. I felt like queen for the day; for a moment, breakfast in bed was a treat. Oh yeah, I was in the hospital, not at home in my cozy bed.

I love spreading on the butter, just a little, cutting everything up into bite-size pieces, slowly pouring the Aunt Jemima syrup (low fat, I'm sure) on the pancakes and getting them perfectly ready to eat. How can you ruin pancakes? I am not a fussy eater, either.

Then reality hit as I was wheel-chaired down to run some more tests. I sweet-talked the attendant into wheeling me into one of the hall bathrooms so I didn't have to use the glamorous pink bedpan. It is the little things that make life bearable, right? I was in CAT scan machines, chest x-rays, pulmonary machines; I couldn't even tell you the entire battery of tests that were run my first full day in the hospital.

My internist, Dr. Richard Wulfsberg, who is the most wonderful man, as well as my doctor, came in that morning and stood by my hospital bed.

He said he had some bad news. I had four pulmonary embolisms. Not one, or two, or three—but four clots in my lungs. That's typical for me; I've never been known to do things halfway. It's all or nothing with me! He said, "You shouldn't be alive right now." How was it that I was not dead, especially with the size of the clots in my lungs? The only reason I was alive was because of my fitness.

The lung capacity I have from years of being an athlete and being physically active saved my life. One clot in particular was massive. Dr. Wulfsberg asked, "Haven't you had any trouble breathing at all? I can't believe you haven't felt any pain, because they are so substantial."

I replied, "Well, I guess now that I think about it, for a couple of months, I have felt like when I train at a very high heart rate, I couldn't really catch my breath and breathe correctly. I thought it was just because I was out of shape, or maybe just getting old."

That's why I'd started training more. Never once did it occur to me that something was really wrong with me. Again, is that denial in its strongest form? I never felt it day-to-day, or just during my regular teaching days.

Then they gave me massive amounts of blood thinners—heparin and coumadin. Many doctors came to talk to me about my condition. Every one of them, and there had to be ten different doctors, said I should not be alive. Anyone else would have died. Every doctor agreed it was only because I was in such good health—in such good shape and so active—that I was still alive.

That was a real wake-up call. Especially when you are in the hospital at night, when it is quiet (Well, not really; alarms go off all night long and the patient next door to me thought it was the middle of the day, yelling at the game of Jeopardy on the blaring TV) and you're alone with your thoughts about what has happened.

I was in the hospital for eleven long days. Luckily, I felt fine; I just could not get out of the bed until my blood levels were "heparinized." That means my blood needed to be thin enough that it was in the range of

2.0-3.0. Everyone reacts differently to the medication. Some people take longer to get to that level.

On this medication, you must pay attention to your diet; there are certain things you can and cannot eat. My blood levels had to be checked regularly, weekly, when all this first happened. Every doctor I saw in the hospital told me my motto while on this medicine needed to be, "Just don't fall." Therefore, that meant bike riding, snow skiing and water-skiing were out of the question. It was precautionary so that if I fell, I would not bleed in my head. Therefore, my workout schedule has had to change.

This big change for me is having the time to write this book. I have been thinking about writing for a couple of years now. It has given me time to review my priorities and realize what is really important in life. "Things" in life do not really matter. What matters are your relationships with other people, your family and your friends. How many people can you help on a daily basis? Have you ever walked by someone and just said "Hi" to that person? Just a simple little hello like that can absolutely change someone's day. It has been said for years, "It's the simple things that matter." You really should not sweat the small stuff. You find out that your real friends are those who were there in your time of crisis. You thank people for being there when you needed them most. Tell people that you love them before it is too late. Go to sleep never having any regrets.

"Tennis...Play for the Health of It!"
United States Professional Tennis Association

EXERCISE:

If you've had a life-threatening disease, accident or incident in your life that changed your priorities, write down what priorities changed in your life:

1._____

2._____

3._____

4._____

5._____

If you have not had any life-threatening incidents in your life, what priorities would you like to change in your life now?

1._____

2._____

3._____

4._____

5._____

I believe you can have whatever you really want in this life, in one form or another, sooner or later. All you have to do is take care of your health and be lucky enough to live for a while. But you can't have it all at once and you can't have it forever.

No life has the room for everything in it, not on the same day.
— Barbara Sher

10 Ways to Add Years and Balance to Your Life

1. Eat Right. Start with making small changes in your diet.

■ *Drink more water* instead of soda or other sugary drinks. Drink at least eight glasses of water a day. Water helps your metabolism. If you feel tired at the end of the day, it's often a sign of dehydration. Drinking sodas when you are thirsty can really add to the calories that you are putting in your body, and those calories add up fast.

■ *Avoid soft drinks.* Soft drinks are loaded with sugar—about ten teaspoons per can—and are among the worst beverage choices you can make. Even if you drink diet soda, the artificial sweeteners in it, according to research, confuse your body. For some sugar-sensitive people, diet sodas may stimulate cravings for more sweets. They may also elevate blood sugar in the same way regular soda does. When your blood sugar goes up sharply, your body releases insulin, a hormone that tells your body to store calories as fat.

■ *Limit the amount of caffeine you consume daily.* Caffeine is a powerful stimulant found in coffee, tea, soft drinks and many over-the-counter medicines. If you have trouble falling asleep, then limit your caffeine intake to one of two cups of coffee in the morning or eliminate caffeine altogether. Anyone with a heart disease, an irregular heartbeat or high blood pressure should avoid caffeine altogether. It can elevate stress hormones that can have harmful effects on the cardiovascular system. If you want to reduce your intake of caffeine, switch to green tea. It is loaded with disease-fighting, anti-aging oxidants.

■ *Try to avoid sugar and processed foods.* Sugar and processed foods are hard on your metabolism. You are apt to feel tired and hungry because these foods make your blood sugar levels go up and down. These foods have very little fiber in them; therefore, you may still feel hungry.

■ *Put fiber in your diet.* Fiber is a great complex carbohydrate. Higher intake of dietary fiber is associated with a lower incidence of heart disease and certain types of cancer. It may also reduce your risk of heart and artery disease by lowering blood cholesterol. You should have at least twenty-five grams of fiber daily.

■ *Try to avoid too much red meat.* Too much red meat is hard for your body to digest. The digestive system slows with age. Meat is high in saturated fat, which can contribute to blocked arteries and a diet overloaded with red meat has been seen in many cases of colon cancer. If you really enjoy red meat, try to limit your intake, especially as you get older, to a few times a month.

■ *Buy organic fruits and vegetables.* Any foods that are organic have been shown to be higher in nutrients, and are a better all-around choice for ensuring the quality of your diet. These foods are produced without pesticides, hormones or antibiotics.

2. Stay at a Healthy Weight. Eat three balanced meals a day, plus two to three snacks. Eat five servings of fruits and vegetables a day. Green veggies are especially loaded with folate, a nutrient that reduces the risk of common aging-related diseases. For great health and rejuvenation, fruits and vegetables need to be at the core of your diet. If you are not happy with your weight, maybe you are overweight and perhaps at risk of obesity. Being heavy is more than an appearance issue. Obesity puts you at risk for developing one or more serious medical conditions, which can cause poor health and premature death. In fact, obesity is associated with more than thirty medical conditions. Among them are heart-disease, type 2 diabetes, certain cancers and kidney disease.

3. Make Activity a Must. We all feel better after participating in some type of workout, whether it is walking the dog, going to the gym, going for a bike ride or playing tennis. Make sure you have fun. If you enjoy what do, you are much more apt to continue for years to come. Exercising on a regular basis cuts the risk of high blood pressure and stroke. It also helps you lose weight and maintain that weight loss. Regular exercise slows bone loss, boosts immunity, improves sleep, eases anxiety and stress and lowers the risk of type 2 diabetes.

4. Flex your Mental Muscle. Studies now show that the progression of Alzheimer's disease is slowed according to the amount of mental activity you get. Tennis is a great sport because you must think while you are doing the activity.

5. Ditch the Habit. Yes, habits are hard to break, but that smoking habit is just killing your body, slowly, one day at a time. I have read that quitting smoking can add nearly nine years to your life. I believe it. Smoking is estimated to cause one-third of all cancer deaths and one-fourth of fatal heart attacks in the United States alone. Approximately, 440,000 Americans die each year from diseases related to smoking, according to the American Lung Association. Please, think about living for yourself by living a healthier lifestyle. Be an example to your kids by living a long and healthy life.

Have you ever looked at a picture of the lung of a non-smoker and the lung of a smoker? It's amazing and should be enough incentive to quit. Please, quit NOW. Drinking is another very nasty habit. Try to limit your alcohol intake to special occasions. If it is a nightly or daily habit, then you may want to take a good look at why you have to drink alcohol every day. Medical help and support groups are everywhere. Please seek help if you think you may have a problem.

6. Stop Stressing. More studies now show that stress can contribute to various forms of disease; cancer is the big one. We all have cancer cells in our body, and when we are under great amounts of stress, something is triggered and is released. Stress shows up in many different ways in our body. If you can at least reduce stress in your daily activities, your body will thank you. Rest and relaxation will keep you young.

7. Get Your Rest. How many times have you heard, "You need to get your beauty sleep?" There's a reason for this saying. Anti-aging hormones such as melatonin, human growth hormone and testosterone are produced in greater amounts at night during sleep. When you don't get enough sleep, then your body is not able to make these hormones in the amounts it needs. In addition, lack of sleep can cause the release of a stress hormone called cortisol, which, according to many studies, is directly related to weight gain. To feel and look your best, you need seven to nine hours of good sleep each night.

8. Slather on the SPF. It still amazes me how many people don't use sunscreen. The sun's rays are stronger now than they were ten or fifteen years ago. We all used to sit on the beach with baby oil slathered all over our bodies, holding aluminum foil-covered cardboard under our chins to get more sun on our faces to get a quicker, darker tan. Oh, now we look back and cringe at the thought. Each day, just get into the habit of putting sunscreen on as a moisturizer before you start your day; at least you'll be somewhat protected. Studies show that if you are exposed to the sun, you should re-apply sunscreen at least every few hours. There are now so many more deadly cases of skin cancer; just start your new good habit today.

9. Screen for the Big Three: Breast, Cervical, Colorectal. Be good to yourself and get tested for all three of these cancers annually. So many conditions can be avoided or treated with early detection. Most people admit they get tested yearly because they are scared of what the doctors might find, especially if cancer runs in their family. What is the alternative? They find it a few years later, and then the doctors cannot do anything because the disease was not detected and treated early enough.

10. Become a Social Butterfly. When you are active with your peers in an activity you enjoy doing, it is much better mentally. You have fun; you laugh; you talk and you feel alive. People who get older and keep more to themselves often have more signs of depression and loneliness. Therefore, whatever activity you do...call a friend. Be social. Studies have shown that staying connected with friends, loved ones and having close relationships into old age has a positive impact on your health.

Exercise:

Take this inventory of your personal health and fitness, and answer the questions honestly:

Circle YES or NO for each question.

1) Do you try to eat at least five servings of fruits and vegetables each day?

   YES   NO

2) Do you eat mostly natural carbohydrates, such as whole grains, instead of processed carbs, such as sweets?

   YES   NO

3) Do you try to limit your consumption of red meat to a few times a month?

   YES   NO

4) Do you try to limit your intake of foods containing additives, preservatives, or artificial colors?

   YES   NO

5) Do you ever buy organically grown foods?

   YES   NO

6) Do you drink at least eight cups of pure water daily?

   YES   NO

7) Do you try to limit your consumption of soft drinks, including diet soda?

   YES   NO

8) Are you happy, or comfortable, with your present weight?

   YES   NO

9) Do you limit your intake of alcoholic beverages to one or two drinks daily or have none at all?

YES   NO

10) Do you limit your intake of coffee or caffeine-containing beverages to one serving a day or have none at all?

YES   NO

11) Do you exercise for at least thirty minutes or more at least three times a week?

YES   NO

12) Are you a nonsmoker, or if you used to smoke cigarettes, have you quit?

YES   NO

13) Do you regularly participate in stress-reducing activities, such as relaxation, meditation, reading, exercise, yoga, hobbies, or other fun hobbies?

YES   NO

14) Do you get enough satisfying sleep most nights?

YES   NO

15) Do you have a supportive network of friends and family?

YES   NO

For every yes, give yourself credit for your healthy habits and congratulate yourself. You have a great basis for a healthy life. Reflect on all the things you are doing, and agree to continue doing them. If you circled a "NO," it simply means that is an area in your life where you need to do some work. We all do. No one is perfect.

I consider my life a work in progress. It gives me something to strive for, to better my life. There is always room for improvement, from improving my tennis game, to improving my mental wellbeing, to improving my good physical and emotional health. Take it one day at a time.

Medical Doctor Visits and Regular Tests You Need:

The American Cancer Society recommends these visits and screenings:

1) Physical with your doctor—once a year

2) Dental exam—once a year

3) Dental hygienist visit—twice a year

4) Gynecologist (women) —once a year

5) Dermatologist—once a year

6) Mammogram (women)—once a year, starting at age forty

7) Prostate exam (men)—once a year, starting at age fifty

8) Colonoscopy (men & women) tests that find polyps and cancer starting at age fifty:

   - flexible sigmoidoscopy—every five years

   - colonoscopy—every ten years

   - double contrast barium enema—every five years

   - CT colonography—every five years

OPTIONAL:

1) Acupuncturist—at least once a month

2) Massage—every day (just kidding). At least every two weeks. Or minimum, monthly.

Massages are one of the best things ever invented. They help with muscle soreness; they keep the blood flowing and they get rid of the lactic acid.

The Physical, Emotional, Mental and Spiritual Way to Live

It is a great way of life: A balanced life with your physical, mental, emotional and spiritual life all working in harmony.

Balanced energy fields could be represented as feeling:

- Physical = Energized
- Emotional = Connected
- Mental = Focused
- Spiritual = Aligned

As you get older, your mind, body and spirit become more in balance, which helps you become a better person, someone who makes a positive difference in the world.

Overcoming Adversity

All of us face adversity in our lives. It is a part of life. Everyone goes through adversities. The challenge is how well you handle adversity, no matter what it is.

Here are some tips for dealing with adversity:

- Know in your core that you have what it takes to persevere. You have done it before; you will do it again.
- Be thankful for your life. Even if something bad happens, try to focus on the positive things in your life—your family, your health, your freedom, etc. If you stay focused on the positive, the adversity will not seem as big.
- No matter what adversity you are trying to overcome, there is always someone else who has it worse. Talk with others; your perspective will soon change.

Adversity comes in many shapes and sizes. Another adversity I faced in my life came in the form of addiction.

Here are some suggestions for coping with addiction:

- Acknowledge the fact that you have a problem. Admitting that you have a problem is the first step. And this is usually the hardest part.
- Seek professional help. No matter where you live, there are support groups out there and there's a support group that is right for you. There is no shame in asking for help. Think of it as "your badge of courage."

Live one day at a time. If you adhere to that principle, your life will change in ways you never thought possible.

Second Chance

You need to take care of yourself and your health first. In dealing with an addiction, if you have been living with an addiction, then you have deprived yourself mentally, emotionally, mentally and spiritually for quite a long period. You may be sicker than you think. You have affected everyone around you, negatively, in ways you may not even know. Therefore, if you have adversity, especially addictions, please seek help right away. Your life will be so fulfilling, and you will come actively participate in your life. Here is my personal story:

Have you ever had a problem you thought no one else would understand if you told anyone about it? Have you ever had a secret so deep that you knew if anyone ever found out, you might as well just die? Have you had thoughts that you were different, you couldn't tell anyone how you really felt, or what you really did? I have heard many times, secrets will kill you...eventually.

Have you ever hidden things that were buried deep in your core and thought they would never be exposed? If they were uncovered, you felt like you might die? You continually did things you knew were not healthy for you—just to keep the secret hidden. But despite your best efforts, somehow you had no control over it. Something inside you had control over you; you were powerless over "it."

I always thought I put my health first. I was an athlete all my life. I made my living from being an athlete. I encouraged and taught people about the importance of health. I stressed how important health is for all of us. I drove and flew all over the country to national junior tennis tournaments almost every weekend.

I had to make sure all my junior players had the right nutrition, the right amount of rest and the right amount of preparation before matches. That was my job. Those tournaments took over most of my waking hours. Little did I realize I was slowly killing myself. I was an alcoholic. I never, ever drank on the tennis court. But I stayed up at night, drinking until I finally went to sleep—or passed out.

Then, I got up at the crack of dawn, warmed-up all the kids, made sure they had a good breakfast, mentally prepared them for who they were playing that day, etc. But over the years, I was slowly killing myself. For quite a long time I was in a deep, dark hole. I knew I was an athlete and I had great determination and willpower. I knew I could stop at any time. It was incomprehensible to me that I could not just put my mind to it and stop drinking.

Why would this be different from any other goal I'd set in life? I knew what I had to do to stop drinking. I hid my keys from myself so I wouldn't drive after I had been drinking at home. I knew I could never forgive myself if I hurt someone while I was behind the wheel of a lethal weapon—my car. I just made sure I bought enough booze so I wouldn't have to go out again once I came home and started drinking. Needless to say, when my behavior started changing, as the years went by and I couldn't stop, no matter what I tried—no matter how much willpower I had—I knew I had to look at what was really going on.

As the years progressed, I had to drink daily. At the time, it seemed very normal to me. But, when I started to forget whom I'd talked to the night before last, I realized this might be a much bigger problem. One of my clients took me to AA for the first time. Nevertheless, I thought, I was certainly NOT an alcoholic.

I had a great job; I was well-known throughout the country as one of the top junior coaches; I had a nice house, a tennis court in my backyard, a nice car, money in the bank and a retirement account. I was very successful, or so I thought. I didn't drink when I worked. Drinking did not affect my work since I was not drinking when I was on the tennis court. I was in and out of AA for three years. I couldn't stop drinking for longer than about three months. That was about my limit during those three years. I do call that time in my life my three-year nightmare.

Now, in my mind, I knew I had a problem; **I was an alcoholic**. However, I always thought I could control it if I just tried a little harder. If I tried harder, things would be different this time. Problem was, I just could not possibly think of not drinking for the rest of my life. Going to AA really does ruin your drinking, though, because now you really know you shouldn't be doing this.

That was always buried inside of me. Before, I thought it was normal behavior, to have a few drinks just to relax. Now, I knew I was far from normal. It was not normal if I had to ask myself if I were an alcoholic. They say most normal drinkers never ask themselves that question— "Am I drinking too much? Do I think I'm an alcoholic?" Therefore, AA does get your mind thinking differently about the actions you can control.

I learned that alcoholism is a disease. My problem was that I went to AA meetings and sat and listened to all the stories and thought to myself, "Well, surely, I'm not *that* bad. These people are *really* alcoholics, but I still have a job. I haven't had a DUI yet. I can still get out of bed in the morning, go to work and work for twelve to fourteen hours." Every time I thought that, I went back out to see if I could "control" my drinking this time. I told myself it would be different because I knew better. I had more knowledge, I told myself. I was very smart; it shouldn't be that hard to figure out.

Anyway, this cycle went on for my three-year nightmare. In that time, I had a family intervention, which did not go very well; I also was in rehab for two days. I went to meetings; I tried to get involved in the program, but it still did not work for me. How could something like this be controlling my life? By that time, my drinking had progressed since I now knew I was drinking and should not be. Therefore, I had to numb out the pain of being a "loser" who could not control her booze.

Finally, after being at a junior national tournament in January, I came home and felt humiliated by the national kids at the tournament. In my mind, they knew I must have been hung over, because I was not myself at the tournament. I was late getting there; I did not warm them up properly, etc. They didn't listen to me when I talked to them. They split sets in the tournament, and they wouldn't look at me, never mind listen to my strategy for them to win the match in the third set.

I left that tournament feeling as though my life had really gone down the tubes. Especially when I felt like I had lost the respect of the kids. That was my only love and escape at the time. To me, if I had lost their respect, what was left?

It was Super Bowl Sunday, so I stopped at the liquor store on the way home from the tournament and bought enough alcohol for a huge party. However, there was no party; it was just me, alone, sitting in my own living room, feeling as if I had nothing left to live for. Life had no meaning for me anymore. I had never felt that lonely and desperate. I knew I had to stop drinking, no matter what it took. I had no choice. There were no options left.

The next morning, I woke up (or came to) and decided I was going to stop drinking that day. I had woken up many mornings and told myself that same thing—thousands of times over the last three years, in fact. I drove to work, and while I was in the parking lot, I received a telephone call from one of my good clients. She said she had some bad news to tell me.

Chase, the three-year-old boy of one of her best friends, another one of my clients, had died. He always came onto my tennis court full of life and boundless energy. He had the most beautiful olive skin, with very blond, curly locks of hair, always bouncing around. His favorite thing was to run and pick up all the balls from my tennis court, while his sister had a tennis lesson.

Over the last two months or so, Susan, his mother, had noticed he was not walking in a straight line anymore. She took him to the doctor, just to be safe and get him checked out. They did many tests and concluded that he had a brain tumor. He died within three months.

I cried so hard that morning in my car; I could not go to work. I felt that was one of the saddest things I had ever heard. Chase was so full of life, and he gave so much during his little short life, and here I was consciously and slowly killing myself. I was really living and breathing my way to a slow death. God gave me the choice to live my life to the fullest, and Chase did that, too, even though he was just here for three short years. That little boy saved my life. I felt I was given a second chance.

I now had a choice—to live or to continue dying. I went to an AA meeting later that morning. I went to different meetings than I had been going to for the last three years, when I was going in and out of the program. I did not want anyone to know who I was. I wanted to try to do it differently this time. I felt I had a chance to live, and Chase hadn't had that choice. I was given another chance to live and I had not been doing a very good job of taking it. This was my "moment of clarity." I had a disease. Now I needed to take control and realize I had a problem, and I needed help.

Since that day—January 27, 1992—I have not taken another drink. I try to work "my program" every day. I get up every morning and thank God for another sober day. My life has gotten 100 percent better since being in AA. I would not trade my life now for anything. Overcoming my alcoholism was one of the best things that ever happened to me.

I am not ashamed of being an alcoholic anymore; I now consider it my "Badge of Honor." Moreover, I can help other alcoholics along the way, or other people with addiction problems. So, if you think you have a problem with something, please seek professional help and do not let the problem linger. It does not get any better, only worse, unless you do the work. Realize you have a problem and you need help. There is no shame in it—there is only help.

Your health is something you can control. If there is an area where you may have a problem, or if you have an addiction, please seek help. It is the best thing I ever did. My life is so great now since I recovered from those terrible, lonely, dark days. We all have much to give to each other just by showing up and being present. You never know whose life you may touch by sharing your story. If you have an addiction problem, I hope my story inspires you to do something about it. Addiction does not go away by itself; it just gets worse. That has been a fact for many, many centuries.

Addictions can come in many forms—alcohol, prescription drugs, street drugs, smoking, overeating, gambling, shopping—the list could go on and on. There are many programs available today for any form of addiction. Please start your process today, for you. You are the most important person in your life. If you do not love yourself first, you have nothing left to give anyone else. Life is too precious not to be fully present and engaged in all of your daily activities, and with all of the people who come into your life.

Thank you for listening to my story. I hope it touched someone's life today.

Exercise:

List any addiction you think you may have trouble with in your life:

_____

_____

List whom you will contact to help you overcome this problem:

_____

_____

_____

_____

"How could I have cancer?"

Louise Kohan is a psychologist with a thriving practice. She has been my student for at least six years. She is one of those people whose tennis lesson I look forward to very much. She is always willing to learn something new and try it. She'd improved so much in the last few years that she became our club's secret weapon to put into the line-up in our tournaments when we played other clubs. She was in great physical shape and could last for three sets. No one from the other clubs knew who she was, or how she played.

I gave her a lesson one week, and the next week I had a weird message on my answering machine from her telling me that she would have to cancel her lesson for the next week and for a long time because she had just been diagnosed with cancer. Here is her story:

"Getting a cancer diagnosis was staggering. At 51, fit and feeling like my life was rolling along, I had the same reaction as everyone else who heard the news: 'How could I have cancer?' I had just played USTA Nationals and made it to the finals—something that will always be on my top 10 list of lifetime best events. This could not be true.

"Nevertheless, I did have cancer, and a stage 3, eight-centimeter tumor that had metastasized was terrifying. Surgery wasn't an option, so I started an aggressive overlapping regime of chemotherapy and radiation. I made it through the first five days of treatment with no problem. Then, on day six, I started a long slow slide into an altered universe. As my treatment progressed, my days became a routine of getting myself to treatment, trying to eat, sleeping many hours and devoting any energy I could rally to being with my 11-year-old daughter.

"Watching the majors on the Tennis Channel became my respite. I am an avid reader, but my brain could not focus as it normally would. Watching matches provided motivation and distraction from the pain, isolation and sense of loss of my life and me. I used over-identification (I am a psychologist after all) with the tournaments, and especially Roger Federer's striving for his fifth Wimbledon, as a parallel of my own struggle and suffering. The idea of profound sacrifice to attain a goal of physical and mental ability was a model of endurance I embraced. When he won Wimbledon, I cried, and told myself I could do it, too. I could fight, endure and survive.

"My battle had help from so many sources. My husband and mother, friends who cooked, drove, took my daughter, kept me in mind. Nothing comes close to the power of my drive as a mother to survive, but after my family, the joy of striving is what I value in life. I am so lucky that I have a career that allows me to do this every day, but also that I have a court to play on with friends including Mary Pat as friend and coach to return to day after day.

"I am back to work and tennis. One year out, I am clear of cancer. It always looms over me and the fear is not gone, but the joy is returning. I'm playing my first USTA match in a week and will get back on the ladder. The fun and striving are always there to grab onto. The learning is always there to pursue."

Spinal Meningitis and Polio

My first tennis lesson with a tall, slender, wild redheaded woman (her hair was not wild, she was) was at seven in the morning. This woman was full of life and energy, even at that hour. She talked even more than I did, early in the morning. She gave me her background. She had never held a tennis racquet in her hand and she told me that she'd had spinal meningitis and polio as a child. Therefore, she had never really played sports while growing up. She wasn't sure whether she could play tennis, but she couldn't wait to try. Talk about energy at its utmost! She was so much fun to teach. She has become a very good friend over the years. I did have to tell her what "tennis attire" was appropriate when she first started coming to the tennis courts. I knew I would have to demonstrate many more things with her because of what she had been through in her younger years.

I have been teaching Patte Yungfleisch for twenty-one years (That hardly seems possible since we are both twenty-nine years old). During this time, she has gone from being a total beginner to one of the top players at the Calabasas Tennis and Swim Center Club. She has won the club championship numerous times. She has won tournaments all over Southern California and has great ability to find an opponent's strengths and weaknesses quickly so she and her partner can exploit them right away.

Because of knee problems, Patte recently had to change sports to golf, but she has transferred the skills learned from the tennis court to the golf course. I am sure she will be as successful at golf as she was at tennis. She knows "the secret to focusing." Here is Patte's story:

"As a child I suffered with spinal meningitis and polio, which affected my legs. Needless to say, my parents were very protective of me ever participating in any sports. After working for twenty years, I decided to change things up, take some time off and enjoy myself. After many discussions with my family, who were big tennis players, I decided to explore this great sport at thirty-eight years old.

"I was very fortunate enough to meet Mary Pat Faley, who was the first person to put a racquet in my hands. She has the ability to assess an individual's needs and get to the source of the problem in a very short time with excellent results. She was able to bring out my competitive nature over many years of training—and the rest is history.

"Mary Pat has been a wonderful teacher, mentor and friend, who gave me the courage and strength to believe in myself. The lessons I have learned through her teaching, especially concentrating and focusing, have helped me in other sports as well."

32 Skull Fractures

I received a phone call one day from another client asking if I could teach her son. She said that he used to play baseball, but a few months before, he'd been hit in the head with a baseball, resulting in thirty-two skull fractures. *What!?* I had never heard of such an injury. The doctors told him he could not play contact sports, or sports that would put him in danger of being hit in the head. She told me he was a very good athlete and would learn quickly. She'd heard I had taught many of the ranked juniors at that time. Would I consider teaching him?

How could I say no to a family that had just been through such adversity? Therefore, I began teaching Jason Weiss. Jason was a great kid. He was funny, fun to be around and he had a heart of gold. He was one of the quickest students I ever taught. He was like a sponge. I showed him how to do a stroke and he understood and hit the shot instantly.

Jason was a perfectionist. That was one of his biggest downfalls, though, because if he missed a shot, he had a temper tantrum. I did not put up with that, so we had many discussions about his attitude. If he'd been able to curtail his temper, he would still be playing on the men's pro tour. Many of his friends are still on the tour. He played with all of them, Mike and Bob Bryan, Justin Gimelstob, Kevin Kim and Jan Michael-Gambill, just to name a few. We traveled all over the country, playing all of these same kids at all the national tournaments. Jason hurt his back in college, so that didn't help. Jason had such talent as a junior. If he'd continued playing and training, who knows where he would be now?

Now he is a happy person. In fact, he is a real estate mogul. He stayed with his fitness regime and he is in great shape. I am so happy to see him thrive in his business and personal life. He is still a good friend. Here is Jason's story:

"My life experience has taught me many things over the past thirty years and has been a major factor on whom I have become. As a youngster, I lived to play baseball, but after a freak accident that left me with thirty-two skull fractures, the doctors told me I could not play any contact sports for one year, which left me with tennis, golf or swimming. I was not happy about any of these options because I was a team sports kid. That being said, I chose to pick up tennis, and it was the best thing I ever did.

"When I walked on the court for my first lesson with Mary Pat, she watched me hit for a little while, then proceeded to put me in a chair on the court and have me hit like that. I thought she was nuts, but I did it anyway. As usual, her "back to basics" teaching methods worked wonders. After a short stint of lessons, I was ready to start playing tournaments. I expected to beat everyone because I was a baseball player and these people were tennis players. Wimps!

"I was in for a real surprise because as talented as I was, I did not know what it was like to be the only guy out there, all alone without a team behind me. I had a bad temper and did not like to lose points, let alone matches! But, the lessons I learned through competing in this individual sport were life changing.

"I was an underdog in the beginning of my junior career because I played against kids who had been playing tournaments for years, but I didn't care. I was so competitive that I would do anything to win, and I fought for every point. Throughout the early years, I regularly beat people whom I was "not supposed" to beat, simply because I knew I could win. That being said, my mental game and attitude became a problem for me, because as I got used to winning, I thought I should beat everyone When I didn't, I completely lost it—throwing and breaking racquets, cursing all over the place, yelling at everyone within earshot, etc.

"In one match, I was so outlandish that Mary Pat threatened to pull me off the court if I threw my racquet one more time. So just to test her, I did exactly that. To my surprise, she stuck to her word and pulled me off the court from the finals of the tournament. I was livid, but I learned a very valuable lesson, which was that my ranting and raving not only made me look like an idiot, but the end result was usually a loss of the match and a loss of respect from other players.

"However, instead of learning the lesson, I tricked myself into believing that I liked being "the bad boy," and in a weird way I tried to use it to my advantage to intimidate people, which actually worked some of the time. As I got older and more successful in tennis, the thought of playing in college and as a pro were on the agenda. Nevertheless, because I never chose to learn the lessons Mary Pat tried to teach me, I talked myself out of any chance at playing at the pro level. I was scared to try and fail, so I figured I would "half-ass" it and make sure people knew that if I really wanted to, I could be great. I was content with just getting by, which was total crap!

"The point is that it has taken me thirty years really to look inside myself to figure out what I really wanted; and to be truthful about my fears and insecurities in life, business, relationships, etc. When I started to dissect myself, a lot of my thinking related to tennis and the things MP told me—keep a cool head, believe in myself, put the work in and the results will come. Don't fear anyone or anything and always fight until the end. All of that has finally kicked in, and I use that advice in my everyday life. When I get down or fearful or insecure, I pull from those experiences and remember the consequences of not doing what I'm supposed to or was taught, and try to take contrary action in order to get the results I want.

"It has worked, because I have become a pretty successful young man, but I will not get cocky because there is always more to learn. I can always become more successful, and there will always be someone just as successful or more successful. Instead of running from those people, I know I need to embrace them, take them on, learn from them, and I will get to that level and beyond.

"Although I still wonder whether, had I never been hit in the head, would I have become a pro baseball player, tennis was the greatest thing I could have ever done for my life. Almost every business contact I have is a result in some way, shape or form of my tennis accomplishments or skills, and that is priceless.

"It is tougher to become successful at an individual sport because it is "just you out there," but it prepared me for the real world more than any other sport or any school could have even come close to doing. Mary Pat was my basis and foundation for tennis and for many lessons in life, and a big part of who I am today is because of who she was as a friend, coach and mentor to me at a very early age."

> *I make no distinction between the mind and the spirit,*
> *and therefore no distinction between the process of*
> *achieving spiritual growth and achieving mental growth.*
> *They are one and the same.*
> — *M. Scott Peck*

HEALTHY LIFESTYLE

Balancing Family Life and Work

Do you enjoy a healthy, well-balanced lifestyle, doing work that you love, work that gives you excellent financial returns and allows you to have significant time off to pursue your other interests?

Bickering and fighting is becoming more common in family households as people struggle to create a healthy balance between their careers, personal and family lives. Often the greatest pressure is on women who work full-time building a career and are still expected to cook, clean and somehow cater to most of the family's needs at the same time.

In fact, these pressures are one of the biggest reasons for divorce today. People end up with the "ships passing in the night" routine. Eventually something has to give, and it will probably be sooner rather than later.

The one thing that separates winners from losers
is that winners take action.
— Anthony Robbins

There are essentially two things that will make you wiser—
the books you read and the people you meet.
— Charles Jones

I teach Burt and Helene, a husband and wife. They're both very nice people and seem very happy. They spend a lot of time with their three children, and their children adore them. Both of them work, and they don't have a nanny to take care of their children. One day I asked them if they'd share their secret to achieving balance in family, life and work. They chuckled to each other and replied, "A lot of planning and working at it."

Burt runs his own company, and they told me they make sure that they take annual vacations with the kids. Their secrets included:

1) Strong work ethic and values. Each agreed, "If you are going to do a job, then do it to the best of your ability."
2) Saving and investing money. Always pay yourself first. Always put something in savings. Maximize your 401k plans.
3) Establish an education fund to pay, or help pay, for the kids' college expenses. 529 investment plans are specifically for that.

Because of Burt's ability to be well-organized, he enjoys most weekends off. Burt rarely gets home later than 6:00 p.m., which allows him to spend quality time with his family.

At the beginning of the year, Burt and Helene plan their personal and family goals for the year. This includes scheduling specific time for vacations, including one major holiday together as a family and mini-breaks for three or four days for just Burt and Helene—no kids. Twice a year, Burt enjoys a long weekend with his tennis buddies at a tennis resort. Helene also has a couple of tennis getaways with a group of her women friends.

They seem to have found a good balance in their lives. They have not fallen into the "workaholic" mode, which is where so many people are today. Besides that, *USA Today* recently reported that more than fifty percent of working people are unhappy at their jobs. If you are that unhappy at work, it is hard to come home and have energy to spend any quality time with your family.

Burt doesn't feel guilty for taking time off. He believes he works hard when he's at work, so he deserves some time for fun. As a result, he generates a high income, and he and Helene consistently invest their hard-earned money, which minimizes their financial pressures.

They don't spend money they don't have. They pay their credit cards on time. Their mortgage is manageable. They don't spend money on things they don't need. They would rather save their money and go on their yearly, memorable vacations. They're teaching these strategies to their children, too.

Exercise:

Name six things that you can spend less money on.

1._____

2._____

3._____

4._____

5._____

6._____

What three things can you do or eliminate in order to spend more time with your family?

1._____

2._____

3._____

How Tennis Benefits
Your Physical and Mental Health

- It can be a life-long game. People can play tennis from ages four to ninety-four. There are no limits.
- "The only possible regret I have is the feeling that I will die without having played enough tennis." — Jean Borotra
- Baby Boomers can take control of their health, play tennis and stay active to increase their longevity—Tennis can change lives!
- You can be in charge of your future. Playing tennis keeps your mind sharp. Playing tennis lowers your cholesterol and your blood pressure because you stay more active and healthy.

- Why not do what you love to do? When you love playing tennis, you will be more inclined to go and do it, and not make excuses to yourself about why you do not want to go.
- You can create better choices. When you play tennis, you *will* create better choices. You'll create better choices about what food you are going to eat, better choices about not smoking, and you'll make better choices about being a good, healthy example to your children.
- "Scientists and physicians around the world view tennis as the most healthful activity in which you could participate. While other sports can provide health benefits and some can promote mental and emotional growth, none can compete with tennis in delivering overall health, mental and emotional gains to those who play." — United States Tennis Association
- Tennis...the sport of a lifetime. Tennis provides so many benefits when people learn the game early in life. It is the ideal sport for children. In addition, it is never too late for adults of all ages to take up the game. The human system can be trained and improved upon at any stage of life. The key is to start playing now to get the most out of these benefits throughout your lifetime.

Tennis: A Sport for All

Tennis has truthfully given me everything, brought me everything: the people I've met, travel, work, bad times, good times, emotions...I adore this sport: it's technical, physical and mental all at the same time. Tennis is extraordinary because it is played just about everywhere in the world with the same enthusiasm, and by an astonishing variety of individuals: from the very young to the very old, the most clumsy to the most talented...

— Yannick Noah

CHAPTER 2:
EATING HEALTHY FOODS

*It takes far more than just hitting a ball to be
the very best and to reach your own highest point,
not only in sports, but in life.*
— Famed Tennis Coach Nick Bollettieri

Have you ever wondered why, when we are such smart people, we are so challenged about diet? Haven't we read enough self-help books about diet and how to be thin? You know..."Fat-Belly Blasters," or "Think Yourself Thin," or "The Four-Minute Workout," or "How to have a Super-Model Body in Less Than 30 Days," or "Abs Crunch to Fitness," etc., etc., etc.

If someone promised you a million dollars to stick to a healthy diet for a month, could you do it? You would probably figure it out, very quickly. You would probably throw away all the "crap" food in your cupboard and refrigerator. You would tape a picture of a million dollars to the outside of the refrigerator, your bathroom mirror and the visor of your car. You would attach an alarm to your refrigerator door that would go off if you opened it past 8:00 at night.

Weight loss has become a billion dollar industry in our country. We are a nation of obese people. Obesity is an epidemic in our society. Why? How is it that the biggest rate of diabetic growth is in our children? What are we teaching them today to carry them into the future? We need to be in charge of our bodies and our food. There is no magic formula. Calories consumed versus calories expended or burned seems to work. If it's that easy, then why aren't we all in at least average shape?

Why are Americans the most overweight people in the world?
Eighty percent of Americans are overweight and thirty-five percent are
obese. People think that fat itself is the problem, but fat is just the
symptom. The source is lack of lean muscle tissue.

Why do people overeat? The secret to weight loss doesn't have
anything to do with food choice. Change your mind first; your body will
follow.

In a 2006 article from "Bottom Line's Daily Health News," Carole
Jackson interviewed many psychologists, and they all agreed that
people are not dealing with the very real danger that excess weight
presents. "It is not a matter of another diet. Rather, it is about individuals who do not feel proud of themselves in general, be it their bodies or
their station in life, which in turn makes them feel like they cannot
control their lives nor do anything to change the situation," Jackson
concluded.

Keeping a promise about controlling your weight, is developing self-
confidence that you can set a goal to make any of your dreams come
true. Keeping a promise to yourself is important in every aspect of your
life. To thine own self be true.

Having enough self-control not to overeat and to control your weight
can be the first step in finding the perseverance to achieve all your
other dreams as well.

Step 1 in Losing Weight:

Take charge of your own life and lose weight for yourself. Don't do it
for someone else. What makes you happy? Is it how you look and feel
in your clothes? When you do not achieve this goal, it directly reflects
your lack of self-confidence.

Step 2 in Losing Weight:

Accept your body for where it is right now. Acceptance is the key to forgiveness. Forgive yourself for being overweight and take action to do something about it. Remember—you are in charge!

So many times, we are our own worst enemies. This happens in all aspects of our lives. We are our worst critics. We are harder on ourselves than we would be to any other human being. We say things to ourselves we would NEVER say to our best friend.

Try this experiment: For one entire day, pretend you have a little leprechaun on your shoulder (He should be a cute little green man, with black boots, red hair and a stylish black hat). That leprechaun represents your best friend. Think about everything you say to yourself that entire day. After you say it, decide if you would say it to your best friend, the little man on your shoulder.

After just one day, you may discover you would not have a best friend anymore—probably no friends around you at all. Why are we so negative with ourselves? Don't we think we deserve better? Aren't we worth it? Where does this "stinkin' thinkin'" come from? Do you want to pass this onto your children, too? You can make changes right here, right now—*today!*

Step 3 in Losing Weight:

Be patient. It is a process. We are works in progress. It is not about perfection. We didn't become overweight overnight, but yet we expect our results to happen overnight. Think of losing weight as a healthy lifestyle change, not just a "diet." Your nutrition plays an important role in your health, your energy level and your performance.

Thoughts you may have had regarding food:

Negative: You have to eat everything on your plate. There are starving children in Africa who don't even have dinner.

Positive: You do not "have to" eat any particular thing.

Negative: No one is going to tell me what I can and cannot eat.

Positive: I am choosing healthy foods to put into my body for fuel.

Negative: "You sit here until your plate is clean." (Probably a voice from your past)

Positive: I am full. I'm going to stop eating even though there is still food on my plate.

Negative: I hate exercising, it is too hard and I might get hurt.

Positive: I hated exercising in the past because I started too fast, trying to get results right away, and had a tendency to get hurt. I will now start gradually and look for smaller successes. I love the feeling of trying my best. The stronger I get, the less I will get hurt.

Negative: Plain fruits and vegetables are boring.

Positive: Fruits taste like treats and rewards for all the hard work I have been doing in taking care of my body. I now have a great opportunity to look for new recipes for vegetables.

Negative: At the holidays, I should be able to have all of the wonderful treats.

Positive: I can eat a healthy meal before I go to a party, and snack on healthy alternatives such as fresh vegetables. I will not make the focus about the food, but rather spending time with my friends.

Exercise

List three negative things you've said to yourself. Then list three positive things about the same subject.

1. *Negative:*_____
   *POSITIVE:*_____
2. *Negative*_____
   *POSITIVE:*_____
3. *Negative:*_____
   *POSITIVE:*_____

Mentally Shifting How You Think About Diets:

If you've tried one diet before, then you've probably tried hundreds of diets. You now need to shift your mind to think: "I am beginning my new, healthy, fitter way of life." You want this for *yourself.* You are doing this for *yourself.* If it rubs off on people around you, friends and family, for example, then that is an added bonus. You do not want to think of this as, "I'm going to get to my goal weight, so I can pig out on my favorite desserts again." This is a new, stronger, fitter, leaner, healthier you.

Therefore, each day you brush your teeth, have your little leprechaun on your shoulder, and follow your food promises.

If you break any of your food promises, then look at what excuses you told yourself (or what the little leprechaun told you) about why you chose to eat that big dessert or have a second helping of food. Then go back and reaffirm your weight goal and how you are going to get there. Every day is a new beginning. Every meal can be a place to continue to keep your promise. As you continue on your journey, try to stay away from beating yourself up. Just forgive yourself and start again. You do not have to stay on the path of self-destruction for days on end because you didn't make good food choices one day. Simply start with the very next meal.

Once you realize you have the power to change this way of thinking, you're free to construct a new life for yourself. You may be able to dismantle old stories that were never true and create new ones about the role food plays in your life. This will create positive associations about "the right" foods and you will no longer "medicate" yourself with "the wrong" ones.

Embrace the fact that you are in charge! You are ready to move toward achieving your weight loss goal. Be nice to yourself and start out with small goals. An example of this could be that during the first week, you might limit bread and desserts to no more than twice a week. Next, you might eliminate them entirely and add more fruits and vegetables, and so on.

Being in charge of your body, which you've previously accepted as it is, ends up being a win-win situation in every way. People who have succeeded in taking charge of their bodies find that it makes everything better. Besides improving your health, it energizes your confidence and knowledge that you can do better for yourself. Once that starts, it's like a ripple effect that carries over to other areas of your life. If you start to measure how much you suffered because you don't accept the body you have, you'll understand that this is about *happiness*—not dieting. Changing the way you think leads to greater happiness.

Exercise

List your ideal goal weight: _____

How do you want to feel with your new weight loss?

_____

_____

_____

What are three small changes you can make immediately?

1._____

2._____

3._____

Preparation

If you have a big test coming up, do you study your book and study your notes and all the materials? If you have a big tennis match coming up, do you or your coach go out and scout your opponents? If you have a piano recital coming up, do you practice the songs over and over until you can play them in your sleep? If someone offered you a thousand dollars if you could hit your serve into the correct service box ten times in a row, in two weeks, would you practice serving until all hours of the day and night?

If you had to give a speech in front of 500 of your colleagues, would you study your notes night after night until you almost memorized your speech? All these questions have the same answer. Of course you would! Therefore, why not take the same amount of time in preparing your food? It does take a little extra time, but the result is always worth it. You are now in charge of preparing for a healthy productive life-style...start living!

In Martina Navratilova's book *Shape Your Self*, she states that one of her favorite quotes is from Joe Paterno, the great football coach from Penn State. He said, "The will to win is important, but the will to prepare is vital." Top athletes like Martina Navratilova know this and they are willing to put in the time to work hard at their sport. In tennis, for example, it is not an accident when you hit a great shot, because you have done it in practice. You have put in the work. Every great shot you hit, you have already hit a bunch of times in practice.

Things You Can Implement In Your Preparation

1) Clean out your cupboards of unhealthy foods and restock with healthy choices.
2) Go grocery shopping with a list of healthy foods (try not to deviate from the list). Do not go to the grocery store when you are hungry. (Danger, danger...)
3) Plan out your weekly food menu. This helps you get everything for the week during your grocery shopping trip. It also saves you money because you won't go to the grocery store daily.
4) Cut up all the veggies and put them in small baggies that you can grab on the run.
5) Cut up fruit into bite-size pieces and place in individual containers. If you put all the fruit together in one container for a big fruit salad, it tends to spoil much quicker. These also make for great grab-n-go healthy snacks.
6) If you are invited to a party, not a dinner party, eat a healthy dinner before you go so you won't be tempted to indulge in unhealthy "party" foods that have many hidden calories in them.
7) Try to pick restaurants that serve healthy meals. An example of this may be a restaurant that grills entrees, put the sauces on the side, steam vegetables, and uses very little butter if requested.

Exercise:

What three changes can you make to promote a healthier lifestyle?

1._____

2._____

3._____

> *"This is the body you have been given, love what you got."*
> — *Oprah Winfrey*

Foods that Fight Cancer

Do you eat foods daily that help prevent cancer in your body? Do you know what some of those foods are? Would your lifestyle be healthier if you made those changes in your diet? There is more and more research that comes out everyday on what foods can help fight cancer, or what foods have been tested to cause cancer.

David Grotto, author of *101 Foods That Could Save Your Life*, says, "Up to one-third of all cancers could be prevented if people adopted healthier lifestyles, including eating healthier foods."

Grotto goes on to give as examples some of the foods that fight cancer and how often we should include them in our nutrition plans:

- mushrooms, ½ cup, three-four times weekly
- cabbage, ½ cup, three times weekly
- flaxseeds, one-two tablespoons, daily
- onions, ½ cup, three times weekly
- olives, eight daily
- raspberries, 1 ½ cups, two-three times weekly
- pumpkin, ½ cup, three times weekly

Students of mine who have had cancer, and have fought cancer, using every source that they could possibly imagine, have come back strong by beating their particular cancer. They had cancer, beat cancer, and are back playing tennis and enjoying their lives. It shows that even if you have cancer, you can get back to your normal life. Playing tennis was a great way for all three of my clients to look forward to an active life again. Exercise helps build your body back to where it was, and exercise is one of the best things for your outlook on life, even while battling cancer.

Here are two examples of my heroes who are also my clients. They are an inspiration to all who meet them, both on and off the tennis court.

A student of mine was taking a tennis drill class from me at 8:30 in the morning. It is a tennis class with about six people and we do various tennis strokes for ninety minutes. The students work on their fore-hands, backhands, volleys, overheads and serves. They get a great workout at the same time. They are in constant motion during the entire class.

We were all picking up the balls and I asked my student, Chris Bledy, how she was doing that day. I hadn't seen her in about a year. I just thought that maybe she'd gone back to work and couldn't make tennis class on Thursday mornings anymore. Chris replied, with the biggest grin on her face, "I am so happy to be out here today hitting tennis balls. I can't even tell you how excited I am to be here." She couldn't stop smiling. I said, "Are you done working? I know I haven't seen you in a while." She replied, "I just finished all my chemotherapy and radiation treatments and I am in remission. Finally, my doctor let me come back and play tennis."

Now, everyone's jaw dropped to the ground. I apologized to her and said I had not known she had gone through all that. I told her I thought she'd gone back to work. She said she was going to go back to work, but her cancer had come back. I was now in more shock. "Did you have cancer before?" She replied, "Yes, I had it three years ago. It was in remission, and then it came back in another part of my body. I never thought I would play tennis again." One of my other students asked her what kind of cancer she had. She said, "I had Stage Three ovarian cancer. Only about ten percent of women who have my kind of cancer survive. So, I am extremely grateful to be here today. I am one of the survivors."

Well, needless to say, the entire tennis drill class now had a totally different, upbeat, fun, "Glad to be out here" attitude. That day Chris made everyone so grateful for our health, something that many times we take for granted. That day, it didn't really matter whether you made every ball over the net. It didn't matter whether you went to hit that winning overhead and you missed the shot into the net. Chris put everything into perspective for us that day. Missing a tennis ball was not the end of the world, (but sometimes, you'd think it was, considering how mad some people get while playing tennis and missing a simple shot like that). Chris Bledy did have a certain aura about her that day; it was hard to explain. She was so absolutely thrilled to be alive and playing the game she has loved for so many years—tennis, the sport of a lifetime.

Since that day, Chris and I see each other and talk regularly. We have talked about her ordeal over the last few years. She is such an inspiring woman with an incredible story. She talks about how many changes she had to make to fight this ovarian cancer with everything she possibly had. She changed to a healthier lifestyle, and she changed to healthier eating habits. She started eating organically. She meditated, she prayed, she talked to other cancer survivors. She had it immersed in her head that she was going to beat her illness.

It took everything Chris Bledy had to beat her cancer. She never gave up hope, and has even just published a book about her survival. It is a truly inspirational story. You will be inspired just as I was when you read her book, titled *Beating Ovarian Cancer: How to Overcome the Odds and Reclaim Your Life.* You can also go to www.BeatingOvarianCancer.com or www.ChrisBledy.com for more information.

An interesting event occurred last February when Chris went to the 8:30 Thursday tennis drill class. That particular morning, when she woke up, she remembered she had a dream about me the night before.

In her dream, she was directed to bring me a present the next morning at the tennis class. She went to her closet and found the gift from her dream and brought it to class for me.

When Chris arrived, she learned a substitute tennis pro had taken my place for the day. The class asked where I was, and the assistant pro said I was in the hospital with a blood clot in my leg and four pulmonary embolisms in my lung that had occurred three days ago.

After class, Chris called me in the hospital and asked whether I was up to receiving visitors. I said yes absolutely, especially given the fact that I felt fine, even though I had all of these clots in my chest. She said she would bring lunch and be right over. She arrived with lunch, which was very exciting, since hospital cuisine is not particularly tasty. She proceeded to tell me the story about her dream. This dream was so detailed it was incredible. She retold the story about an earthquake (it is California, of course), and she was trying to get away, but she had to have her tennis racquet with her so she could come to her Thursday drill class.

Her car was going over the cliff, but she had to make sure she didn't lose her tennis racquet. Chris could not believe how detailed this entire dream was. Then at the end of the dream came a message that she was supposed to bring me a gift inside her closet in her home office. So when she woke up the next morning, she went to her closet, not sure what she was going to get. Then she saw the perfect gift for me. She gave me a little package to open while I was there in my hospital bed.

I opened the package, after reading the card, which made me cry. It was about fighting to get healthy—just very inspirational. Inside the package was a beautiful green box. In the box was a little card which said, "Archangel Raphael...I am helping you heal physical challenges in yourself and others. You are a healer, like me." It was a beautiful deep green emerald Archangel crystal healing stone. The card came with the healing stone. Again, tears welled up in my eyes. What an incredible story!

That's why Chris had to come that day to give me the present. And on that particular day—when I was in the hospital and needed to heal. It just gave me the chills. She'd had no way of knowing I was in the hospital. And what had occurred to her had happened in a dream! That's why I believe people are put into our lives for a reason, a season or a lifetime. I continue to hold and rub that healing stone daily.

"Every day brings a chance for you to draw in a breath,
kick off your shoes and dance."
— Oprah Winfrey

Another really good friend of mine, who was on vacation, in Santa Fe, New Mexico, got up out of bed with severe back pain. She waited for the pain to subside, but instead it got worse. So she went to the local hospital and the emergency room physician ran every test there was until he found the source of her pain. He came back into her room hours later and told her they'd found a tumor in her kidney. It was probably kidney cancer. She told him he must have the wrong chart and to please go check again.

To make a long story short, Ilene did have kidney cancer. She had to wait for the pain to subside for a few days before she was able to fly home to Los Angeles. She went directly to UCLA and had surgery, where the surgeon took out the kidney with the tumor in it.

Ilene is doing quite well now. She has been cancer free for five years. That is a big benchmark to get past. She shared with me some things she has learned after having cancer:

1) **Get rid of the people who are negative in your life**, people who bring you down or do not add anything to your life. Stick with positive people and surround yourself with them.

2) **Do not waste any time...it is precious.** Hug your children every day and tell them you love them. Spend time with your children instead of being on the phone with your friends all the time. If you want to do something, then do it. Live for today because there might not be a tomorrow.

3) **_Eliminate stress._** Instead of engaging with people who want to get a reaction from you, walk away. If you do not want to play ball with them, do not throw the ball back. At work, do not get angry about the small things over which you have absolutely no control. If a co-worker complains about something, point out, "We're not curing cancer here; the delivery is just late." If your plane is late for a business meeting, read the paper or read a book because there's nothing you can do about it.

Ilene learned stress had a lot to do with her cancer. She has cut out those stresses, or at least now has them at a manageable level. She decided to cut out drinking, even though she had a beautiful wine cellar. It was not doctor's orders—it was her decision. She also has a very clean, well-balanced diet, and she gets plenty of exercise.

She said her cancer was her "wake-up" call to change things that were happening in her life. She is happier now than ever before.

> *"The indispensable first step to getting the things you want*
> *out of life is this: decide what you want."*
> — Ben Stein

After battling cancer, or just trying to lead a healthier lifestyle, follow these next steps to improve your overall well-being, reduce your weight and gain more energy in the process:

1) Go to bed early and wake up early.
2) Go to sleep and wake up consistently at the same time.
3) Get eight hours of sleep nightly.
4) Eat at least five to six small meals daily.
5) Drink a glass of water before every meal.
6) Eat breakfast daily.
7) Eat a balanced, healthy diet.
8) Eat lots of fruits and vegetables.
9) Avoid alcohol, tobacco, and drugs.
10) Minimize simple sugars.
11) Eat whole natural almonds as snacks.

12) Eat a high-fiber diet or take fiber supplements.

13) Supplement your diet with vitamins and calcium.

14) Drink 48-64 ounces of water daily.

15) Take breaks every ninety minutes during working hours.

16) Get some physical activity daily.

17) Do at least two cardiovascular interval workouts and two strength-training workouts per week.

18) Get plenty of sunshine and fresh air.

CHAPTER 3:
EXERCISING AND STAYING FIT

A dream is just a dream.
A goal is a dream with a plan and a deadline.
— Harvey Mackay

Do you want to feel better in your body? Do you want to feel better overall? Do you want to have more energy? Do you want to feel alive again? Do you want to, perhaps, even live longer? I know, I know, you want the magic formula. The quick fix, the magic potion, or the pill to fix it yesterday. That is our society these days. Everything is in fast motion. Things are going by in fast forward. One day it is New Year's Eve; in the next blink of an eye, it is the holiday season again.

When it comes to exceptional athletes, there are usually three physical attributes that stand out in any sport.

- Strength
- Speed
- Endurance

In tennis, we need to get to the ball as quickly as possible, so that we can set up and deliver that crushing shot! The faster you get to the ball, the more time you have to hit a great shot. Yes, that is exactly what we want to accomplish. The only way to excel in tennis is by getting in great physical condition.

Have you watched a professional tennis match on television lately? It is amazing to watch how fast both the men and the women are covering the court from side to side. They are really some of the best profession-al athletes in any sport. Their fitness level is superior. What is amazing to watch is when a player starts playing better, and his or her ranking starts climbing upward, the one common factor that is talked about is that they have gotten in better shape. That is always the one constant factor of why all of a sudden they have been improving. No commentator talks about how they have changed their swing on their forehand or backhand; all you hear time and time again is that the tennis player has gotten in better shape. If you get in better shape, your tennis game will improve, guaranteed. When that effort is put forth, magic happens.

So, do you want to improve your tennis game? Then the answer is simple...get in better shape! Get more fit! We have all read the fitness books, the weight loss books, and watched the DVD's (or at least we bought them). When you put all the work into getting more fit, you automatically eat healthier. There is no use in doing all of the work to get in shape, if you then go and order some super-size french fries. Your body will crave more healthy choices.

Here's the good news...you do not have to be skinny to play tennis. You do not have to be in great shape to play tennis. You do not have to be a great athlete to play tennis. You can learn to play tennis even if you did not learn as a young child. You do not have to have great hand-eye coordination to play tennis. You do not have to join a big fancy tennis club to play tennis. Tennis is the sport of a lifetime. It is one of the greatest sports that I have ever played. You can play when you are four, and you can play until you are ninety-four. I still have not met anyone in my thirty years of teaching tennis that could not learn this great game at any age. You can still improve everyday on the tennis court, something about yourself, your game, or your fitness.

About twenty years ago, I received a call from a world-famous tennis player, and he wanted me to coach his son. He knew it was not a good idea to try to coach his son himself. So, at our first lesson, I said to his seven-year-old son, "Do you want to be a professional tennis player like your dad?" Stephen replied, "Yes, I really do. I play with him everyday and I can almost beat him." I said, "That is great, Stephen. Let's hit a few tennis balls so you can show me how good you are." The very first ball that I hit to Stephen, he hit a forehand and immediately did a face plant and fell smack onto the ground. I immediately ran across the net and checked to see how he was. By the time I got to his side of the court, he got up from the ground, and said that he was just fine, and wanted to hit some more tennis balls.

I did not even make him run on that very first shot. That must have been a fluke fall. So, I showed him how to run to the ball, be on balance, and then shuffle back to the middle of the court. He followed me, imitating my footwork. Then it was his turn to run a few steps to the ball. By the third ball, when Stephen was shuffling back to the middle of the court, he once again fell flat on his butt on the court. He laughed, dusted off his shorts, and continued hitting balls with me. I had never had anyone fall that many times on a tennis court, never mind in one half-hour lesson.

Stephen had to have been on the ground more than he was on his feet. I was especially shocked because he told me that he played with his father, and his father was a world-class tennis player. I assumed that he had inherited some of his father's coordination.

Stephen took a few lessons a week, and fell just about every lesson. I wish I had a nickel for every time that he fell on the court; I could have retired from teaching tennis a long time ago. He was such a nice kid too. It is a good thing that he never seemed to mind falling. His feet just didn't get underneath him as quickly as his brain was reacting to the different tennis shots.

The moral to my story is that if Stephen could fall most of his young life while playing tennis, then anyone can learn to play tennis, even if you do not think that you are a good athlete. Stephen is still playing on the men's ATP tour, and currently has a world ranking. So, there is no excuse...anyone can learn to play tennis, and excel at the game.

You can have any body type and still be good at tennis. There is no one perfect body type. So, if you are thinking of using that as an excuse of why you don't play anymore, it will not work. Dust off your cover and go and hit the courts!

We all come in different shapes and sizes. Everyone has a good body weight that they are comfortable at, so be thankful you are at that body weight, and start your tennis and fitness program today. There are many different body types and sizes. Work with what you have. That is always the best place to begin. Even if you have a small body frame, you can still be successful. Just look at Justine Henin; she is only 5'3, maybe, and she was dominating as the number one ranking woman for how many years? She worked very hard on her fitness and conditioning, and that paid dividends for her in many, many of her matches. If you are tall, you do not just have to play basketball; you can still be a great tennis player. Look, for example, at our young Americans coming up in the rankings, such as Sam Querry, 6'6 and John Isner, 6'9. They can actually hit down on their serve. Their wing-span covering shots at the net is like that of a hawk. What a great advantage. So, even if you are tall, tennis is a great sport for you.

Lastly, if you have a muscular body frame, tennis could be your future. Look at Serena Williams for example. She is a great athlete, with daunting power—one of the most powerful women tennis players ever to play the game. She even said that in this year's Australian Open, she came into the tournament not in shape at all, and she worked her way into shape during the two-week tournament. She ended up winning the tournament too. So, all of these examples prove that you can be any size or shape to play this awesome game that has more rewards and benefits than you can even list. Time to get in the game. If you are already in the game, get in better shape to get your game that much better. You will be amazed at the results. Trust me, all your hard work, will pay off!

What do you use that treadmill for in your house? Can you even see that it is a treadmill under all of those clothes? If you are trying to find that perfect outfit, look on the machine, it is probably there. Watch your favorite thirty minute show, and jog on your treadmill. If you are not in that kind of condition yet, then walk or jog during the commercials. The new trend now is to have your dog walk on the treadmill.

Are you going to let your dog get in better shape than you? I watched a television show about how dogs are now walking or running on the treadmill. That is the "New Beverly Hills workout." Jog in place alongside your dog on the treadmill, or jog on the treadmill for ten minutes, then your dog jogs for ten minutes, and keep alternating. Make exercise fun!

A fun game to play on the tennis court is to get a six-pound bouncy medicine ball, and take a friend on the court to challenge them to a set or a mini-set of medicine ball. Keep score like a real tennis match. You may only land the medicine ball inside either service boxes. The ball must always bounce only once, and after you catch the medicine ball, you are only allowed one step before you must throw it over to the other side of the net. It is an unbelievable workout; you use your tennis strategy to run your opponent, and you work your core to get the best six-pack abs that you have ever seen! What could be better?

Whether your goal is to be a professional tennis player or simply to improve your social game, fitness is the key. There are so many benefits to regular exercise besides just improving your game. A regular exercise routine can result in:

- Improved overall health
- Increased muscle and bone strength
- Mood elevation
- Better sleep
- Stimulated formation of new brain cells
- Strengthened heart and lungs
- Prevention of chronic conditions
- Enhanced self-esteem
- Boosted self-confidence

I could go on and on, but I think you get the picture here. Exercise is amazing. Not only can you turn your game around but also it can turn your entire life around! Look at the stories in the previous chapter—people who were knocking on death's door who started exercising and getting back in shape. Now, their life will always include exercise and healthy living. Even if you've already had a serious or life-threatening disease, exercise can bring you back and take you farther than you've ever dreamed. Believe me I know. I've had students come back from heart attacks, heart surgeries, hip replacements, knee replacements, cancer and many more. I'm always impressed with the results a little consistent exercise can produce. Now it is your turn to put some fun kind of exercise back in your life. Live life to its fullest. You will never regret one day of it!

Improve your life.

When was the last time you were on a swing? When was the last time you were on a bicycle? When was the last time you looked for an excuse to go up the stairs one more time? When was the last time you found yourself taking the stairs two at a time? Do you time yourself on how long it takes you to go up the stairs and down the stairs. (No, not that obsessive, eh?)

Exercise.

List three physical activities you had fun doing as a child—either alone or with friends or family:

1._____

2._____

3._____

How do you feel after you've exercised?

Do you engage in moderate physical activity at least three or four times a week?

☐ Yes ☐ No

If you answered no, why?
What are some ideas you have for changing that?

_____

_____

_____

We can't become what we need to be by remaining what we are.
— Oprah Winfrey

It's not easy being grateful all the time.
But it's when you feel least thankful that you are most in need of what gratitude can give you.
— Oprah Winfrey

Stories about staying physically fit

Martina Navratilova came out of retirement, to get back in the game, not for the records, but because of her weight. Therefore, she started training to get back in shape. She really likes how she feels when she is working and training for something specific. She returned to competition in 2000. In January 2003, she won the Australian Open with Leander Paes. At forty-six years old, she was the oldest player, male or female, to win a Grand Slam title. She started her comeback at the age of forty-three. She also played in the 2004 Olympics.

Navratilova would have missed winning two more Grand Slam titles if she had listened to critics. But, she didn't listen to them; she listened to her heart instead. She wanted to get back in shape again. Just being physically fit allowed Martina Navratilova to open doors and go past her wildest dreams. Many great things can happen when you are confident as a result of being fit.

At the British Open in July 2008, Greg Norman, who was fifty-three years old, had not played a "Major" in over three years. He said that by being and keeping yourself physically fit, you could set yourself up for being in contention to win a golfing major championship, mentally and physically at any age. The key is keeping yourself physically fit at all times, in case this type of situation arises.

Every Little Bit Helps

How much exercise do you think you should do per week? Do you have to hire a personal trainer to get a good workout? How much money do you need to join a gym? How can you find time to work out when you have a job, husband and kids? Is there a solution?

According to the President's Council on Physical Fitness and Sports:

Walk for two miles in thirty minutes. Or, you can also try your two-mile walk, after the first ten minutes, spend the next ten minutes pumping your arms more, and increase your speed as much as you can. After completing ten minutes of a vigorous walk, complete the last ten minutes back at your regular pace.

By the way, basketball is one of the best cross-training sports for tennis that you can do. It encompasses all of the movements in tennis...shuffling, running, side stepping, quickly changing direction, balance. Remember to bring water and a towel. Martina Navratilova said doing this cross-training, playing basketball, was the best sport to keep her in shape for tennis.

I do a lot of my strength training and some cardio training in the house. Besides keeping myself healthy, it sets an example for my child. Children learn by example. When they're young, they are just like little sponges. They try to imitate anything you do, even if they are not good at it.

I'll give you an example. I was working out with a jump rope in the house and watching TV (probably "Sponge Bob Square Pants") with my step-daughter, Remi. Remi was engrossed in the TV show, as all children are—in the TV trance. Anyway, the longer I worked out, the more I huffed and puffed. My step-daughter came out of her TV trance and asked, "Why are you jumping rope?"

"I'm trying to stay in shape," I replied, not being able to have a long conversation with her, as sweat was dripping down my face.

She continued to watch her television show, and I continued with my workout. When I was finished, she went into her room and came back with *her* jump rope, one she'd had for quite some time, but had never used. She asked me to teach her how to jump rope. She told me she wasn't very good at it, so she did not like it very much.

I was glad to teach her how slowly to turn the rope over, let it lay on the ground, jump over it, when it really wasn't moving and then twirl it over her head to do again. Every jump was a great success. And, of course, I told her that it's important to keep track of how many she did—even if it's only three at the beginning. The moral of the story (other than we all set an example for our children) is that kids don't enjoy doing activities they are not good at. We must take the time to help them become good at an activity so they will enjoy it, have fun with it and do it again.

I then progressed to planks (where you go onto both of your elbows, toes on the ground, and you hold your core off the ground for one minute). All of a sudden, Remi was next to me, asking me the proper way to do it. So, I helped her get into plank position and hold it. We both alternated counting to ten. Then she wanted to do push-ups with me, and then we moved on to different types of sit-ups. Her favorite sit-ups were bicycle crunches, as if she were riding her bike. We also did stretching after our workout was over. We talked about how important it is to stretch a little before your workout, but more importantly to stretch after.

A few days later, I came home from teaching tennis, and Remi ran up to me and said, "Come into the living room right now! I have to show you something." I went into the living room, just barely having time to put my bags down. She said, "Watch—I've been practicing." Then she grabbed her jump rope and jumped without stopping for eleven jumps. She was jumping up and down with excitement. I gave her high-fives, hugs, and praises upon praises for her accomplishment. She could not have been more proud of herself. That was worth everything!

Now, just about everyday, while Remi watches TV, she does exercises with me and tells me that she has to exercise today. Even if we just do a few things, it is instilled in her mind that exercise is fun and to try to do a little everyday. Remember, your children imitate what they see. If they always see you with a cocktail or eating junk food in front of the TV, that is what they may imitate later in life. Children learn by watching, so try to set a good example by having them watch you performing good habits. Have them learn at a young age. They will be much happier when they get older.

Exercise

What exercises can you do daily?

_____

_____

_____

_____

In what ways have you set a good example for your children when it comes to physical activity and exercise?

_____

_____

_____

_____

Cross Train in Different Sports

Cross training is becoming more and more popular to help your tennis ability get better. Here are some good ideas for cross training:

- Playing basketball will help you with balance, change of direction, quickness, agility and stamina.
- Pilates will work on your core strength.
- Yoga will work on your balance and calmness.
- Soccer will help your footwork.
- Bicycle riding on a trainer or at a spin class will help your ability to sprint to the ball.
- Jumping rope will help your stamina, footwork, endurance and coordination.
- Swimming will help your overall fitness and endurance. It will also train and strengthen the non-dominant side of your body, which will help your back and symmetry.
- Jogging helps in developing speed and power as well as endurance. For specific tennis training, do not run more than a couple of miles; rather, spend your time doing interval sprints. Short distance sprinting and recovering is a perfect fit for improving your quickness on the tennis court.

It's Not Rocket Science

To lose one pound, you need to burn roughly 3,500 calories more than you already do—either through what you eat or exercise. You should not try to lose more than one or two pounds in one week. Rapid weight loss is almost NEVER successful in long term. The best method is slow and consistent.

Working Out Takes Patience

So many people decide they are going to start working out, especially on January 1. They work out like maniacs for a few weeks but do not see enough results, so they get discouraged, then they are depressed, then they eat more since the working out didn't work. Then, the vicious cycle returns by the next January 1, and they have gained more weight than the previous year. Therefore, the hill begins to look steeper and steeper.

How high do you have to climb to get to the top, to accomplish the weight loss goals that you have set for yourself? The key to reaching your goals is that you want to think of this as a lifestyle change, not a "diet." So, when you are planning your workout, make sure it is an activity you will have fun doing. Changing up the activity always helps to keep it fresh and enjoyable.

How Can You Really Lose Weight?

How can people actually lose weight and keep it off? Have you been on a perpetual diet for most of your life? As you get older, do you find it harder to lose weight? How many calories do you need to burn to lose weight?

Here's an idea of how many minutes you need to spend at some popular activities to lose ONE pound:

Playing Tennis — Singles:
>140 lb. woman, it takes 543 mins. to lose ONE pound,
>>OR   9 hours and 3 mins.
>160 lb. woman, it takes 475 mins. to lose ONE pound,
>>OR   7 hours and 55 mins.
>180 lb. woman, it takes 422 mins. to lose ONE pound,
>>OR   7 hours and 2 mins.
>200 lb. woman, it takes 380 mins. to lose ONE pound,
>>OR   6 hours and 20 mins.

Playing Tennis — Doubles:
>140 lb. woman, it takes 781 mins. to lose ONE pound,
>>OR   13 hours and 1 min.
>160 lb. woman, it takes 683 mins. to lose ONE pound,
>>OR   11 hours and 23 mins.
>180 lb. woman, it takes 607 mins. to lose ONE pound,
>>OR   10 hours and 7 mins.
>200 lb. woman, it takes 546 mins. to lose ONE pound,
>>OR   9 hours and 6 mins.

Playing Tennis — Lesson:
>140 lb. woman, it takes 350 mins. to lose ONE pound,
>>OR   5 hours and 50 mins.

Having sex — Intercourse:
>140 lb. woman, it takes 781 mins. to lose ONE pound,
>>OR   13 hours and 1 min.

Having sex — Foreplay:
>140 lb. woman, it takes 2,272 mins. to lose ONE pound,
>>OR   37 hours and 52 mins. (fun, eh?)

Bicycling — Leisure:
>140 lb. woman, it takes 833 mins. to lose ONE pound,
>>OR   13 hours and 53 mins.

Bicycling — Mountain:
>140 lb. woman, it takes 390 mins. to lose ONE pound,
>>OR   6 hours and 30 mins.

Bicycling — 12-14 mph:
>140 lb. woman, it takes 378 mins. to lose ONE pound,
>>OR   6 hours and 18 mins.

Bicycling — 14-16 mph:
>140 lb. woman, it takes 312 mins. to lose ONE pound,
>>OR   5 hours and 12 mins.

Elliptical Trainer:
> 140 lb. woman, it takes 290 mins. to lose ONE pound,
>> OR   4 hours and 50 mins.

Stationary Bike — Moderate:
> 140 lb. woman, it takes 429 mins. to lose ONE pound,
>> OR   7 hours and 9 mins.

Stationary Bike — Vigorous:
> 140 lb. woman, it takes 290 mins. to lose ONE pound,
>> OR   4 hours and 50 mins.

Weight lifting — General:
> 140 lb. woman, it takes 961 mins. to lose ONE pound,
>> OR   16 hours and 1 min.

Weight lifting — Vigorous:
> 140 lb. woman, it takes 543 mins. to lose ONE pound,
>> OR   9 hours and 3 mins.

Golf — With a cart:
> 140 lb. woman, it takes 961 mins. to lose ONE pound,
>> OR   16 hours and 1 min.

Golf — Carrying clubs:
> 140 lb. woman, it takes 543 mins. to lose ONE pound,
>> OR   9 hours and 3 mins.

Jumping Rope:
> 140 lb. woman, it takes 328 mins. to lose ONE pound,
>> OR   5 hours and 28 mins.

Swimming — Moderate:
> 140 lb. woman, it takes 543 min. to lose ONE pound,
>> OR   9 hours and 3 mins.

Swimming — Vigorous:
> 140 lb. woman, it takes 337 mins. to lose ONE pound,
>> OR   5 hours and 37 mins.

Hiking:
> 140 lb. woman, it takes 337 mins. to lose ONE pound,
>> OR   5 hours and 37 mins.

Jogging:
> 140 lb. woman, it takes 471 mins. to lose ONE pound,
>> OR   7 hours and 51 mins.

Running — 5 mph:
> 140 lb. woman, it takes 390 mins. to lose ONE pound,
>> OR   6 hours and 30 mins.

Running — 7 mph:

    140 lb. woman, it takes 287 mins. to lose ONE pound,

        OR   4 hours and 47 mins.

Running — 10 mph:

    140 lb. woman, it takes 183 mins. to lose ONE pound,

        OR   3 hours and 3 mins.

Running — 12 mph:

    140 lb. woman, it takes 147 mins. to lose ONE pound,

        OR   2 hours and 27 mins.

Walking — 2 mph:

    140 lb. woman, it takes 1,190 mins. to lose ONE pound,

        OR   19 hours and 30 mins.

Walking — 3 mph:

    140 lb. woman, it takes 757 mins. to lose ONE pound,

        OR   12 hours and 37 mins.

Walking — 4 mph:

    140 lb. woman, it takes 641 mins. to lose ONE pound,

        OR   10 hours and 41 mins.

Men burn more calories, given their greater muscle mass. Woman can approximate from their weight, how many calories different exercises would require in order to lose ONE pound. As you can see, it does take a lot of time and patience to lose ONE pound. That is why eating healthy, along with exercise, makes for a perfect "recipe" for weight loss. You cannot just do one without the other and expect the same results.

Cut Out Fast Foods

This is just an example of the calories in fast foods. You also do not know all of the hidden fats that are in fast foods, even though the food may be advertised as a healthy alternative.

Calories in fast food French fries:

    Small — 250 calories

    Medium — 370 calories

    Large — 580 calories

To burn off the calories gained from eating a medium-size order of French fries, it would require thirty minutes of high aerobics. How much would you have to work out if you ordered a #2 special of a Big Mac, large fries (super size, of course), and a Coke with an apple pie turnover? I hate to think how many hours I would have to sweat and struggle, just to break even in my daily calorie count after that. When you look at your calories like that, how can you really put that in your body? Is it really worth it?

Make Small Changes, A Little Bit At A Time

Cut only 250 calories a day (one piece of cake) and exercise enough to burn 250 calories (you burn about 100 calories walking a mile) and you could lose about ONE pound. Bicycling at a leisurely pace for twenty minutes and cutting out one dessert per day would result in losing approximately one pound per week.

You have to burn 3,500 calories to lose ONE pound!

Make Physical Activity a Regular Part of the Day

Choose activities you enjoy and can do regularly. Fitting activity into a daily routine can be easy, such as taking a brisk 10-minute walk to and from the parking lot or bus stop. Or, join an exercise or tennis class! Keep it interesting by trying something different on alternate days.

What's important is to be active most days of the week and make it part of your daily routine. For example, to reach a thirty-minute goal for the day, walk the dog for ten minutes before and after work and add a ten minute walk at lunchtime. Or, take a drill class three times a week and take a yoga class on the other days. Make sure to get at least ten minutes of activity at a time, because shorter bursts of activity don't give you the same health benefits. To be ready at all times, keep some comfortable clothes and a pair of tennis shoes in your car and at work.

Easy ways to Increase Physical Activity

At home:

- Join a walking group in the neighborhood or at the mall. Recruit a partner for support and encouragement.
- Push the baby in a stroller.
- Get the whole family involved. Enjoy an afternoon bike ride with your kids.
- Walk up and down the soccer or softball field sidelines while watching your kids play.
- Walk the dog; don't just watch the dog walk!
- Clean the house or wash the car.
- Walk, skate or cycle more and drive less.
- Do stretches, exercises or pedal a stationary bike while watching television.
- Mow the lawn with a push mower.
- Plant and care for a vegetable or flower garden.
- Play with the kids. Tumble in the leaves, splash in a puddle or dance to favorite music together.

At work:

- Get off the bus or subway one stop early and walk or skate the rest of the way.
- Replace a coffee break with a brisk 10-minute walk. Ask a friend to go with you.
- Take part in an exercise program at work or a nearby gym.
- Join the office softball or bowling team. Or start an office tennis team!

At play:

- Walk, jog, skate, or cycle.
- Swim or do water aerobics.
- Take a class in martial arts, dance or yoga.
- Step it up to the next level in whatever sport you enjoy.

- Golf (pull cart or carry clubs).
- Canoe, row or kayak.
- Ski cross-country or downhill.
- Play basketball, softball, or soccer.
- Take a nature walk.

Most important—have fun while being active!

Choose activities that work all the different parts of the body—your legs, hips, back, chest, stomach, shoulders, and arms. Exercises for each muscle group should be repeated eight to twelve times per session.

Try some of these activities two or three days each week:

- Heavy gardening (digging, shoveling)
- Lifting weights
- Push-ups on the floor or against the wall
- Sit-ups
- Working with resistance bands (long, wide rubber strips that stretch)

Some people like resistance bands because they find them easy to use and put away when they are done. Others people prefer weights. You can use common grocery items, such as bags of rice, vegetable or soup cans or bottled water.

For best success, team up with a friend. It will keep you motivated and be more fun. Track your time and progress to help you stay on course. Add in more strength-building activities over time. For example, you can do sit-ups or push-ups. If you haven't been active in the past, take it easy—one step at a time—and work up to a pace that feels right for you. Then increase your time and before you know it, you'll be able to do at least two hours of activities at a moderate level each week!

SECTION TWO:

THE GAME OF TENNIS

CHAPTER 4:
PLAYING TENNIS IS AS EASY AS 1, 2, 3

Practice builds skill. I've heard tennis players and golfers say,
"The harder I practice, the luckier my game gets."
— Marsha Sinetar

Introduction

There are many ways to teach tennis. You could take a lesson with twelve different tennis pros, all about how to hit a forehand, and you would get twelve different opinions of how to hit a forehand! There is no right way or wrong way to teach the game of tennis. The best method seems to be the simpler, the better. The less the student has to think about, the better.

Think of the best day of tennis you ever had. What did you think about? Did you think about how to hit your shots? Did you get your racquet back in time? Were you in the right position? Did the ball look as big as a grapefruit, or as small as a lemon? Did the ball seem to move slow or fast? Did you think about how to move your feet?

When you talk to people about their best day of tennis, they can usually remember it like it was yesterday. Why can't we play like that all the time? What did we do right on that day of magic? When most people try to recall what happened on that day, they aren't quite sure why it happened. They would like it to happen again, though! The magic on that day was that the ball looked as big as a grapefruit and seemed to slow down as it came toward them, where their feet were always in the correct spot to hit the right shot.

The reality of it is, *they did not think*. Their minds were clear of clutter. Clutter screws up our game. I call it, "the committee." The committee in our head starts talking, starts conversing. One person on the committee tells us to do one thing, while another person on the committee tells us another. So, we have four conversations going on in our head before we ever hit the ball. When we are not thinking, when we are just playing or reacting, we stop thinking and just let it all flow. Play freely. Wouldn't that be nice to do all the time? It takes a lot of practice. You must practice clearing your mind to let it flow, the same way that you practice forehands and backhands. It won't just come naturally because you now understand it.

I think there are three components to tennis:

1) Drilling or practicing: This is where you work on how to hit certain shots. You work on your stroke to fine-tune all the different parts involved in each stroke. At certain times, you concentrate on where the racquet is in relationship to the ball coming at you. Other times, you practice where you want to feel your contact point. Another time during a drill, you may work on bending more with your legs to hit an open stance forehand. When you drill, you should not worry about the ball going in or out. If you always worry about the results, then you won't be able to make changes to your stroke. The conclusion of this is do not practice different shots when you are playing a match unless you just want to get frustrated.

2) Playing or competing: This is where you work on freely playing. Your focus changes to:

1)   Knowing where you are aiming; knowing where your target is;
2)   Focusing on watching the bounce of the ball; and
3)   Seeing the ball from the bounce to your racquet.

Players get too caught up in how to hit the ball when they're in the middle of a match. Work only on fixing your strokes when you are drilling or practicing—not when you're playing, where it's important!

This chapter will cover drilling and practicing and how to hit the different tennis shots with proper form. When you work enough on proper form in practice, it will translate to playing that way in a match. That is, if you trust your practice, then you will trust your shot.

I like to start close to the net and work my way back to the baseline. That way, students are successful right away getting the ball over the net. They are not frustrated by trying to hit balls over from the baseline first. Most people miss more than they make if they start from the baseline. They do not have as much control from back there, especially at the beginning of the practice.

If you watch doubles teams, for example, warm up at any club, they usually use the first ten minutes (if you are lucky, it's only ten minutes) to warm up their mouths. They chat about what their kids are doing, or what movie they saw last night, or their last great tennis match, or what they are having for dinner that night.

Then watch any tennis pro. No one warms up from the baseline first. They always start close to the net and work their way back to the baseline. You can focus on the ball better; it is easier to see the spin sooner and your feet start moving better up close. You get a better feel and your body warms up properly so that you don't get injured. The older we get, the more important avoiding injury seems to become to us.

My method for teaching most strokes is three simple steps (I can't count higher than three, so that works out well!) The following examples are all for right-handed players. If you're left-handed, the steps are the same, but step with the opposite foot and the racquet hand is obviously your left hand.

3) Learning the secret to great tennis: "The Bounce"

Start playing tennis by simply having a partner. Bounce and catch the ball to each other over the net. Really notice the bounce of the ball. How many rotations does the ball have before it bounces? How many times does the ball rotate after the bounce? Does the ball seem to speed up after the bounce, or does it slow down? Can you actually see the seams of the ball as it spins through the air? There are many things to notice with this exercise. This is simply practicing how to **watch the** *ball* that you hear about in any ball sport. The important thing is how to watch the ball by having your eyes focus on it.

Without a Racquet

1) While doing this exercise, you and your partner should each stand no more than three feet away from the net. Really notice how the ball comes off the ground, and watch the ball into your hand. You can call it, find the ball with your hand or feel the ball with your hand. To master this little drill, say aloud, "Bounce" exactly when the ball bounces and then catch the ball with your hand. Say "Bounce" and "catch."

"BOUNCE"
AND "CATCH"

The reason for saying this aloud is to get your mind really seeing the ball. You want to say that word, exactly when the action is happening, not before and not after the bounce. The key is to master the action exactly when it happens. Be sure to toss the ball on both sides of your body. If the ball is hit toward the right side of your body, catch the ball with your right hand. If it is hit toward the left side of your body, then catch the ball with your left hand.

2) The next step is to say, ***"Bounce and hit"*** and "hit" the ball over the net with the palm of your hand. Not hard, not fast, just very easy. Again, try to master the calling aloud with the action of the *bounce* and the *hit*.

3) The third step is to say, *"Bounce, hit and finish."* The *finish* is the action of hitting the ball over the net with the palm of your hand, and then the back of your hand goes up and almost touches your opposite ear. If you are right-handed, hit the ball with your right palm and follow-through across your body until the back of your right hand touches your left ear. Vice-versa for lefties.

Your success rate should be extremely high if you really watch the actual bounce and see the ball into your hand. Then softly hit it over the net with your palm and the back of your hand goes to the opposite ear. Be sure to hit with both hands on this exercise. It is extremely important to do both sides. Then both sides of your brain are working, and tracking the ball all the way into your palm of your hand.

With a Racquet

To grip your racquet, hold it in the palm of your right hand (even if you're left-handed), so that you are gripping the throat of the racquet. Your index finger should be inside the throat of the racquet. You are playing with the racquet in what is called the short grip. Your hand is on the top of where the grip tape starts.

Repeat the three steps above. First, say *"Bounce,"* then *"Hit,"* and then *"Finish."* Try not to swing hard at all. The entire goal of this drill is to feel the ball over the net, not to hit at it. Make sure to finish with the back of your hand ending all the way up to your ear. Keep saying those three words...*"Bounce, Hit and Finish..."*

Now, switch the racquet into your left hand. Everything is the same. The grip is short; your index finger goes inside the throat of the racquet. You are still mastering practicing saying *"Bounce, Hit and Finish."* Make sure you are running to the ball from side to side. Continue to feel the ball easily on your racquet.

BOUNCE   HIT   FINISH

Graduation to the Service Line

This next step is the most important lesson of all. Have one person stand on the service line. The other person remains standing on the other side of the net and tosses the ball to the person at the service line. Toss to forehand side first. Tell the student at the service line to stand with her back to the net—standing backwards. The tosser tosses the ball and says, "Turn." The student then turns toward her forehand side, and tries to hit the ball over the net. She tries this three times. After the third attempt, she is now going to "Look for the bounce" as she turns from backwards to forwards, and then hit the ball. This will make an unbelievable difference, because when a person looks for the bounce, the mind slows down and is calm, and therefore does not panic about not being able to hit the ball. Do this three times. By the last time, the student should be able to look and find the ball pretty easily, and success is inevitable! Do the same drill on the backhand side. You should see the same results.

What this last drill teaches: Without the student seeing the ball being hit, or coming over the net, if she **looks and finds the bounce,** even at the last second, she can still hit the ball over the net. Therefore, the most important part of tennis is **seeing the bounce.** When you do that, you are really watching the ball, which you have told yourself so many times, but never really known how to do. Now you have the SECRET!

The next portion of this book will talk about all 12 different parts of the tennis strokes. If you have trouble with one certain shot, you can go to that one section and it will give you all of the ingredients to make that stroke improve immediately.

I. The Grip

In the "olden days," it was easy to teach the grip by saying. "Shake hands with your racquet, and there is your universal grip. Use it for all your strokes." That grip is now called the continental grip. It was like a universal remote control, one grip for everything. Several grips are used in today's game, which has changed dramatically. With these newer grips, there is so much more speed, power and spin on the shots in today's game. Grips may vary based on the type of shot you are trying to hit. For example, the serve, volley and overhead are appropriately hit using the continental grip. For the forehand and backhand, use a grip anywhere from an eastern grip to a full western grip.

Your grip is always the number one thing to notice before you hit any balls at all. The grip of the racquet is the foundation of all tennis shots. How you hold the racquet influences the angle of the racquet face, where you meet the ball in relationship to your body and especially what happens when the impact between the ball and racquet occurs.

One thing I know from my thirty years of teaching is that if your grip isn't correct, your stroke production will break down, especially in an important match. The other common flaw that occurs when people use incorrect grips over time is that they get an injury due to using this wrong grip for so many years.

Tennis elbow is the main problem I see that is the result of incorrect grips. Shoulder injuries also can occur from using the wrong grip. Using the correct grip is just a matter of changing habits. If you have been doing the same bad habit for years, then yes, it will take some time to change your grip to the correct one. Grip selection may be awkward or uncomfortable initially, but with practice and work, the desired result will be achieved and the grip will feel more natural. It all depends on what your goal is for your own personal tennis game.

There are three main, basic grips in tennis. We will talk about all three and also give you illustrations of each of them. There are three other more advanced grips that you can experiment with also. In the illustrations below, notice that I talk about the heel of the hand, and the base knuckle of the index finger. These two parts of the hand will be referred to later in the chapter. An example is if I say that your hand should be in the eastern forehand grip; that means that you should place the heel of your hand on panel #3 (refer to the illustration) and you place your base knuckle of the index finger on panel #3 also. Therefore, later in the chapter I may just simply talk about the eastern forehand grip as #3-3, which indicates on which panel the heel of your hand must be placed, which is always the first number, and the second number refers to where the base knuckle should be placed on the handle of the racquet.

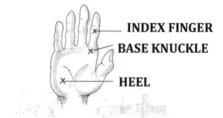

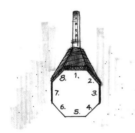

HEEL OF HAND

BASE KNUCKLE OF THE INDEX FINGER

1) **The Eastern Forehand Grip:** This grip is used for your basic forehand groundstroke.

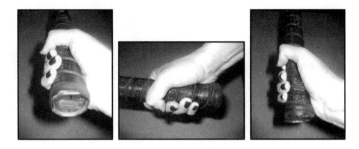

EASTERN FOREHAND

Heel of the hand goes on panel #3; Base knuckle of the index finger goes on panel #3.

2) **The Eastern Backhand Grip:** This grip is used for your basic backhand groundstroke.

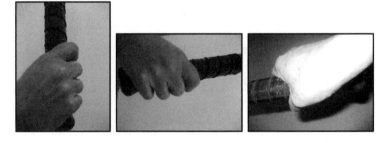

EASTERN BACKHAND

Heel of the hand goes on panel #1; Base knuckle of the index finger goes on panel #1.

OR

The Two-Handed Backhand: This grip is used for your basic backhand groundstroke, especially for students just starting to play the game. It is a little easier when you are learning.

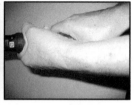

TWO-HANDED BACKHAND

Heel of the right hand goes on panel #2; Base knuckle of the index finger of the right hand goes on panel #2. Heel of the left hand goes on panel #7; Base knuckle of the index finger goes on panel #7.

3) **The Continental Grip:** This grip is used for your vollies, overhead and the serve.

CONTINENTAL

Heel of the hand goes on panel #2 and the base knuckle of the index finger goes on panel #2.

The Basic Forehand Grip (Eastern Forehand Grip)

For me, the easiest way to teach a new player the "new correct grip" for the forehand is to lay a tennis racquet flat on the ground and just have the student pick it up. When you tell a player simply to pick the racquet up, the grip is in the correct place for a good beginner level. This is the eastern forehand grip. That is where the heel of the hand is on panel #3, and the base knuckle of the index finger is on panel #3. If students forget where the grip should be, I just tell them to place the racquet on the ground, pick it up and presto!—there's the perfect "new grip" for your forehand.

The most common flaw with people's forehands is that the heel of the hand is not enough on panel #3; it is too much on top of the racquet, or on panel #2. This is usually because people learned to play tennis years ago, and they learned the continental grip. By making this slight change of the hand on the grip, the forehand groundstroke improves almost instantly. Be sure to aim higher over the net, as you will get more topspin on the ball with the proper forehand grip. You'll see dramatic results after working on it for just an hour—guaranteed!

I will refer to this grip as your "new ready position" grip. When you are at the baseline, you always want to wait in this "new ready position grip," which is your eastern forehand grip. To make this feel easier on your forearm and wrist, tilt your racquet toward the ground, with the strings pointing to the ground. Don't point the edge of your racquet to the sky; it should point at a 45-degree angle toward the ground. This way, you are already in the eastern forehand grip and your hand will stay more relaxed.

The Basic One-Handed Backhand Grip (Eastern Backhand Grip) or the Two-Handed Backhand Grip

One-Handed Backhand Grip for Topspin

If you wait in your "new ready position" that we discussed in the forehand section, your right hand is panel #3-3 and your left hand is cradling the racquet at the base of the strings. I like to make a tripod with my thumb on one edge of the racquet, with my left index finger on the base of the throat of the racquet where the strings attach, and the other three fingers resting on the opposite edge of the racquet. That way, I have great control of the racquet, just with my left hand.

Your left hand is still the key to the preparation phase of the swing. As your left hand pulls the racquet back while your shoulder is turning, your right hand is relaxed and not gripping too tightly, so your grip can change. At the same time, your left hand brings your racquet back, as your right hand grip changes over so your right hand is resting on panel #1-1. So when the racquet is in the "set-up" position, your grip has already changed. When this grip change occurs, your racquet angle will be a vertical racquet face on contact with the ball. When you first make this grip change, you must really swing up on the ball because your racquet face will be so straight. If you do not swing up on the ball and aim high over the net, the ball will go into the net almost all the time. When your grip change is correct, your right wrist doesn't move when you make contact with the ball, and your elbow will remain straight throughout the swing and follow-through.

Two-Handed Backhand: Basic Backhand Grip

If you wait in your "new ready position" we discussed in the forehand section, your right hand is panel #3-3 and the left-hand is resting on panel #7-7. When you are in the forehand ready position and the ball comes to your backhand, your left hand pulls the racquet back. That grip, where your left hand is, does not change, and at the same time, your right hand will move over the left, and that hand will now be on panel #2-2. That is why I emphasize that the left hand is the "driver" of the racquet, and the right hand is the "rider" of the racquet (Just like being in a taxicab in New York, the left hand is the "driver," and the right hand is the "rider"). You still use your right hand while you are hitting, but not as much as the left. The easiest way to learn and to get the feel of a two-handed backhand is to hit tennis balls just with your left hand on the racquet. Your left hand can be up higher on the grip, where it would be if you had both hands on the racquet. When you hit left-handed forehands, your body and brain now can "feel" what the motion is and duplicate it.

In my junior playing days, I went back and forth between a one-handed backhand and a two-handed backhand. I don't recommend it; trust me on this. As a result, my brain never knew which shot I should use at certain times. Consequently, neither backhand improved very much.

When I was in college, I had elbow surgery and I had my right arm in a sling, because I was trying to rehab it back to playing after resting for a few weeks. I was going a little crazy not playing, so I decided to mess around and hit some tennis balls left-handed. That's when I finally realized how to hit the proper two-handed backhand. After my elbow surgery, when I went back to playing, I finally switched permanently to a two-handed backhand when I played from the baseline—unless I was hitting a slice backhand; then I used one hand. My backhand immediately improved for two major reasons. First, I made the decision to hit a two-handed backhand, so I worked on it more and did not resort to one-hand if I were out of position. Second, I used my left hand the most when I hit a backhand shot. It was much stronger, since I had been playing with my left hand.

If you want to improve your two-handed backhand, go hit tennis balls against a wall with your left hand. Your backhand will immediately improve. Remember which hand is the "driver" and which hand is the "rider."

The Continental Grip

This grip is used for the forehand and backhand volley, the overhead, and the serve. When beginners first use this grip, they do not feel like they have very much strength in their grip. That will change quickly, the more you practice the correct grip. This grip is hit with the right hand on panel #2-2. At first, you may find that your grip slips back to your eastern forehand grip, which is on the #3-3. However, just keep noticing where it is as you are volleying.

With this grip, you will be able to handle low volleys much better, because your racquet face is already slightly in the open position. Therefore, it will be easier to hold the racquet still, and let the ball bounce off the strings, as the racquet is already slightly tilted upward.

The continental grip on the overheads and the serve is also essential as you progress your game to the next level. With this grip on the serve, you now will be able to have four different varieties of serves. They will include the flat, slice, topspin, and the kick serve.

Be sure that after your serve, if you stay back at the baseline, that you now change your grip back to your "new ready position grip" waiting for the shot to come back toward you.

Also, remember that if you are coming to the net from the baseline, and you hit an approach shot, that after the approach shot, you quickly change your grip to the continental grip.

The next three grips are more advanced grips that are also used in this modern game of tennis.

1) **The Semi-Western Grip:** This grip is used for a more advanced forehand groundstroke.

SEMI-WESTERN FOREHAND

Heel of the hand goes on panel #4; Base knuckle of the index finger goes on panel #4 also.

2) **The Full Western Grip:** This grip is a very extreme forehand groundstroke grip.

FULL-WESTERN FOREHAND

Heel of the hand goes on panel #5; Base knuckle of the index finger goes on panel #5.

3) **The Basic One-handed Backhand for the Slice:** This grip is used when the ball is well above your waist, when the ball is really low or a little bit out of your reach. Heel of the hand goes on panel #2 or #1; Base knuckle of the index finger goes on panel #2. Depends how much time you have to make the change.

The Semi-Western Forehand Grip

This is the grip most of today's competitive players use for a number of reasons: More topspin, easier to hit high balls, better for disguising shots, passing shots and you get more power with this shot. The grip is with the heel of the hand on panel #4 and the base knuckle on panel #4.

The Full Western Grip

This grip is used more often on clay courts and in European countries. The grip change is much more exaggerated. If you use this grip for your forehand, you have a long way to go to change your grip over for the backhand. It is also a big change to switch to continental if you come toward the net. Players who use this grip are mostly baseline players and do not come to the net very often. The grip is with the heel of the hand on panel#5 and the base knuckle on panel #5. Most recreational players find this grip very uncomfortable and find it hard to control the ball.

The Basic One-Handed Backhand Grip for Slice

If you wait in your "new" ready position that we discussed in the forehand section, your right hand is #3-3, and your left hand is cradling the racquet at the base of the strings. See my recommendation about making a "tripod" outlined above.

Your left hand is still the key to the preparation phase of the swing. As your left hand pulls your racquet back, while your shoulder is turning, your right hand is relaxed and not gripping too tightly, so that the grip can change. At the same time, your racquet is being pulled back. When your left hand brings the racquet back, your right hand grip changes over so your right hand is resting on panel #2-2, the continental grip, or on panel #1-2—the same as the backhand continental volley grip.

Therefore, when the racquet is in the "set-up" position, your grip has already changed. When this grip change occurs, your racquet angle will be slightly tilted in an open position, toward the sky. When your grip change is correct, your right wrist does not move when you make contact with the ball, and your elbow remains straight throughout the swing and follow-through.

Continental Forehand—Flaws

These are some of the reasons why you do not want to use a continental grip on your forehand groundstroke. Use either an eastern forehand, a semi-western, or a western grip. Use the continental grip only for your volleys, overheads, and serves:

- You must hit the ball later at contact point in order for your strings to be straight.
- If you hit the ball in front of your body, as you are supposed to, the ball will go long, because the racquet face is open and the strings are tilted up.
- People have to use their wrists to get the racquet angle in the correct position.
- It is very hard to hit high balls well.

- People develop tennis elbow from hitting the ball so late with this grip.
- Tennis elbow is also a problem with this grip because you try to get topspin by rolling your wrist over the top of the ball, which causes tension on the tendon, which is attached at the elbow joint.

A good friend and client had been playing tennis for twenty years. She was a good player and played in all the tournaments at our club against other local clubs. She decided she wanted to take her game to a new level, so she wanted to take some lessons from me. She had been self-taught from years ago.

At her first lesson, she warmed up with me, and I noticed that she hit her forehand and backhand with the same side of the racquet face. I knew she had been doing this for years, but we had never talked about it before. She then warmed up her volleys, and she did the exact same thing. She never changed her grip to go from a forehand to a backhand, with either her groundstrokes or her volley. She was very proficient and very fast, so fast that most people never even noticed that she did it. She wanted to work on her backhand groundstroke and her back-hand volley.

We talked about her overall game. I said, "Marilyn, you know that you do not change your grip on either your forehand or your backhand, right?" She said, "I heard that you could use just one grip for all of your shots. So that's what I did." What Marilyn didn't know is that they were talking about the "one grip," being the continental grip, years ago. She had an extreme western forehand grip on her forehand groundstroke, and then when it came to her backhand, she used the same side of the racquet to hit a backhand and basically just flipped it over.

It looked like she was washing a window, a really big one! Wow, she was fast when she did it. She had no idea she did it at all. When I told her what she did, she disagreed with me and thought I was seeing things. I had to bring out the video camera to show her. She really didn't believe me.

She washed the same window when she hit her volleys. Low backhand volleys were almost impossible for her to get. She had to bend so low because of needed racquet angle to make contact with the ball; I thought her knees would have permanent scrape marks on them from the court. I was still impressed at how well she hit the ball, despite using the same side of the racquet.

We tried to switch her grip, using two hands, etc., but it was really hard for her, because she had been playing that way for so many years. She decided she did not want to spend time to work on changing it, so we worked with what she had, and she still got much better. She still plays a good 4.5 women's game, and most people still don't notice how she is universal in her own way with her grips. They just know that she comes to the court, hasn't played in weeks and beats the pants off of her opponents.

II. How to Hit Forehand and Backhand Vollies

Now, when you are at the net, your "new ready position grip" is different than at the baseline. At the baseline, you wait with the head of the racquet, slightly tilted downward, with your right hand waiting on panel #3-3, while your left hand waits on panel #7-7. Ready position now changes when you are waiting at the net, to the continental grip #2-2.

Start by standing halfway between the net and the service line, so you are in the middle of the service box. Stand with your feet comfortably shoulder-width apart and your racquet in ready position. To get in proper ready position, hold the racquet in your hitting hand, and then put your arms as straight out in front of you as you can; that is one exaggeration. Then, bend your elbows into your body as much as you can; that is the other exaggeration. Now put your arms halfway between those two positions that is your proper ready position. Use this progression, of first not moving your feet, and then moving your feet on both the forehand and the backhand volley to understand how these shots are executed.

DO NOT MOVE YOUR FEET:

1) Set your hand with the racquet in it.

2) Straighten your elbow with your strings pointing to your target.

3) Go back to ready position.

Hold each step for 1-2 seconds, exaggerating the separation between all of the steps. When people swing at their volleys, it is because they put all three steps together. Then they lose control over where they are hitting the shot.

NOW, MOVE YOUR FEET:

The next three steps are the progression using the correct footwork for the volley.

Now, you will do the same three steps as talked about above, but you will now move your feet as you are hitting the volley. This applies to both the forehand and the backhand volley.

Step #1: Set the racquet.

This occurs as soon as you see your opponent hitting the shot, and you decide it is a forehand. That is when you set your hand, or the racquet. You cannot set the racquet too early. Start straightening your elbow when the ball is crossing the net, so that your elbow is straight as you make contact with the ball. The elbow straightening motion is known as the "punch."

On the backhand volley, set the racquet with your left wrist or hand. This is also when you change your grip to the continental backhand, which is panel #1-2.

After you hold that position for one second, go back to ready position, with the racquet right in front of your body. *Squeeze and freeze* the racquet at the moment of contact point. In ready position, hold the racquet lightly, and then squeeze the racquet the second before contact, and freeze the racquet for one second. That will create more power coming off the racquet, with much less effort.

Step #2: Now add a step with the left foot for the forehand volley, or the right foot for the backhand volley.

- Set your hand with the racquet.
- Step with your left foot for the forehand or right foot for the backhand forward at the *same time* that you hit the ball (or straighten your elbow). You should hear the sound of your foot hitting the ground, and the ball being hit at *exactly* the same time. Straighten out your right elbow for the one-handed backhand volley. Straighten out your left elbow for the two-handed backhand volley.
- Go back to ready position.

Step #3: Now add a shuffle to the side, then step.

- Set your hand with the racquet.
- Shuffle over to get your feet behind the ball, sideways, and then step forward at the same time that you hit the ball.
- Go back to ready position with your foot and racquet as you shuffle back toward the middle of the court.

These are the basic steps for the forehand and the backhand volley. Now, here is more detail for both of these shots.

1) How to Hit a Forehand Volley

You want to start in a continental grip which is on panel #2-2. (See grip illustration) There are many people who are afraid to come to the net. The main reason is because they are worried about a lob going over their head, or that they simply do not want to get hit by the ball. If you improve your volley, you will not get hit at the net, and if you place the volley in the proper spot on the court, you will not get lobbed very much.

Another factor in being scared playing the net is because most people do not stand in the proper location. Remember, the correct stance is halfway between the net and the service line. Therefore, you are not too close to the net, and you are not too far away from the net, where it is easier for your opponent to hit the ball down at your feet.

2) How to Hit a One-Handed Backhand Volley

When you set your racquet using a "one-hand," you set your racquet with the left wrist. The key with the backhand is the opposite hitting hand. The left hand does all the work, setting the racquet in the proper position.

Some people teach that you do not change your grip on the volley. If you do not have time to change your grip, that is one scenario, but if you do have a little bit of time, you get a much better volley if you move the heel of your right hand one slight turn to the left. Your right hand of the heel of the hand is in position panel #1 on the grip, and the base knuckle of the index finger is on panel #2. This can now be called, #1-2. I call this the continental backhand grip. It is a much stronger volley. (This grip is a little more advanced, and was not discussed in the grip section. This grip is only used for the one-handed backhand volley). If you use your left hand properly, you usually have time to change the grip. The top part of your hand basically stays the same, but the heel of your hand will change slightly. Remember, the right hand is just holding the racquet lightly, and when the left wrist sets the racquet, it gives the right hand time to switch the grip to backhand continental. Do not let go of the racquet until you go forward to get the volley. The left hand does not move very much after the volley is hit. (It looks like you are holding a plate of desserts with your left hand).

3) How to Hit a Two-Handed Backhand Volley

You should have your right hand in the continental grip, panel #2-2 and your left hand should be on panel #7-7. It is easier for beginners or children to start with a two-handed backhand volley. You do not have to change your grip and you have more control of the ball right away. It is also easier to start with a two-handed backhand volley, and later release the left hand as you go to hit the ball. Then you can eventually move to a true one-handed backhand volley.

Hitting this shot is exactly the same technique as the one-handed backhand volley, except that the left hand is the hand doing most of the work punching and straightening of the elbow. Both arms work as one unit. Therefore, no wrist is involved in this volley.

Forehand or Backhand Volley 1, 2, 3...

- Set the Racquet
- Straighten the Elbow
- Ready Position!

III. How to Hit Forehand and Backhand Groundstrokes

There are many ways to hit a forehand or a backhand, depending on your level of play. You could be a raw beginner. You could be the player who played a little in high school, twenty-five years ago. You could be a working woman or a mom who has raised her children and now that they're in school, you want to play tennis again. Or you could be an advanced–level player, which means hitting the ball as hard as you can with no idea where it is going. Finally, you could be a tournament-level junior or adult player.

The Forehand and Backhand Swing

There are three basic parts of the swing: 1. Turn 2. Drop 3. Swing. This basic swing is the exact same on both sides of your body, meaning, the forehand and the backhand swings are the same. The reason that I grouped these two together is because there are so many similarities between the two swings. When the swings are the same, you can then develop your consistency and your brain does not have to remember anything different between a forehand and a backhand.

1) Turn. The first thing to do, once you've decided whether it's going to be a forehand or a backhand, is *turn*. This involves turning your shoulders, not just your arm, which gets the racquet into the proper position. Instructors used to say, "Get your racquet back." People got their racquets back, but their shoulders never turned, so they never generated any power or torque from their bodies. From your ready position, if you turn your shoulders, your racquet should go behind your body, with the racquet face slightly pointing to the ground. Your right arm stays close to your body on the forehand, and both arms stay close to your body on the backhand, as your shoulders make the turn. To practice this, place a tennis ball under your right armpit for a forehand, and put the ball under your left armpit for the backhand. When you make the shoulder turn, the ball should stay under your armpit until after you hit the tennis ball. I call it the "A.T.A. = Air The Armpit," when students put their arms up way too high in the back-swing. It would make a good deodorant commercial!

Now that you are doing groundstrokes, go to your "new ready position" grip, which is the Eastern Forehand grip. From your "new ready position," tilt your racquet head slightly down in front of you, almost parallel with your head. By doing this, you are already in the forehand grip, which is panel #3-3. When you make your initial *turn*, your racquet head should be level with your own head, and not much higher in the backswing.

From your ready position, when getting ready to hit a backhand, you use your left hand to pull the racquet back, as it turns your shoulders. That is when the grip change will occur. Your left hand is bringing the racquet back, which will allow the right hand grip to change to panel #1-1 for the one-handed backhand, or to panel #2-2 (with the right-hand) and panel #7-7 (with the left-hand) on the two-handed backhand.

We will call this the "set-up" position. Your racquet head is slightly higher than your hand in the backswing; it is not pointing to the ground, which is how it was once taught. Grip tension should be relaxed; no death grip, please. You do not need to squeeze the racquet until you are almost ready to make contact with the ball, and then squeeze a little bit. Think of squeezing the racquet like a heart beating, just a little squeeze right before you hit the ball. Do not squeeze it tightly the entire time. This is another way to get tennis elbow. Your muscles cannot stay contracted for a long time, so if you do hold your racquet really tight, when the ball finally comes, the grip slips in your hand anyway. So, hold the racquet tension as though you were picking up a hurt bird. Don't pick up the bird and squeeze it to death, but hold it firmly enough so it does not try to fly away. That is your perfect grip tension.

2) Drop. *For the forehand, the one-handed or two-handed topspin backhand*, the racquet starts slightly higher than your hand in the backswing. The top of the backswing is at the completion of your turn. Think of your racquet imitating a small "C" with a long tail that then travels upwards. Then when your racquet is at the top of the backswing, think of it like a roller coaster. At the top of the roller coaster, there's always a very slight pause before the coaster flies down the tracks. Your racquet imitates that same pattern. It pauses very slightly at the top of the swing and then travels downward, with no tension in your hand or your arm. This allows you to create maximum racquet speed.

For the one-handed slice backhand, the racquet head starts slightly higher than your hand in the backswing, the same as the topspin backhand. As you start your forward motion, the racquet goes in a more high-to-low swing pattern, rather than low-to-high. The racquet actually goes from high, slightly lower and back up to a high position at the finish. The racquet head does not drop below your waist level.

3) Swing. The last part of the swing is striking the ball. The most important part of this phase is to try to see the blur of your racquet hitting the ball. People often hear the phrase, "Watch the ball to contact." In reality, the naked eye cannot see that, because the ball usually travels too fast. Nevertheless, you will see the blur of your racquet going past your eyes. That's where you want to keep your head—right there, at contact, until you hear the sound of the ball hitting your racquet. Then feel free to look up to see where you hit the ball. The word "swing" means free-flowing movement. Don't try to hit the ball hard. Just let the momentum from your racquet, starting slightly high, drop down to low and then the finish will be somewhere over your shoulder.

The swing on the one-handed backhand, topspin or slice comes from the shoulder. The wrist and elbow stay very firm from the beginning of the backswing, or the turn, to the contact point, to the finish. The wrist and elbow do not move during the swing.

One-Handed or Two-Handed Backhand Groundstroke

Once again, there are many different ways to hit a backhand, depending on your level of play. Years ago, they only taught a one-handed backhand. Then, in the days of Jimmy Connors and Chris Evert, it became "cool" to try a two-handed backhand. Both Connors and Evert were great at this shot. They seemed to make the backhand much more consistent with two hands on the backhand side. A few years ago, there was more of a mix between one-handed backhands and two-handed backhands. Recently, you see more two-handed backhands. It is easier for kids who are just learning tennis to hit the ball with two hands and get it over the net. With adults, the grip change is not so drastic, and people feel they have more control and power with the two-handed backhand. Remember, the key in any groundstroke is to see where the ball has bounced in order to get into the right position to hit the ball back properly.

In order to make a good decision about which backhand to hit, either topspin or slice, the key is to make the decision before the ball bounces and then stick with your decision. Try not to change your mind in the middle of the swing.

A rule of thumb is:

- If the ball is below your waist level at contact, hit a topspin backhand.
- If the ball is above your waist level at contact, hit a slice backhand.

If you have decided to hit a slice backhand and the ball contact is going to be lower than your waist, stick with your decision, but realize you must bend your knees more, and then hit the slice in the same manner as a regular slice backhand. You just have to bend your knees much more.

Forehand or Backhand Swing 1, 2, 3...

- Turn
- Drop
- Swing!

IV. Stances with your Feet

The Forehand and Backhand Stance

There are three different stances in the forehand or backhand groundstroke:

1) The open stance
2) The square stance
3) The closed stance

1) The Open Stance: This is the most common in the new era of power tennis. The open stance gives players the ability to hit the ball much harder and with more spin on the ball than was possible in years past. The open stance gives players the ability to hit the ball if they run out of time to step forward into the shot. It is used much more in the return of serve, especially with the speed of the serves.

The simplest way to learn the open stance forehand or backhand is to stand on the baseline in your "new ready position." Then turn your shoulders and start walking parallel to the baseline toward the singles sideline. Stop walking with the last step being on your right foot for forehand and the left foot for the backhand. Notice that your right foot or left foot is slightly behind your front foot, in the "open" position, and that your back foot is parallel to the baseline. From this position, your weight should be on your right foot for the forehand, or on your left foot for the backhand.

- **Turn your shoulders**
- **Bend from your knees**
- **Explode upward**, so that your weight shifts from your back foot to your front foot which will also turn your entire core, or belly button, toward your target. This is also known as coiling.

Once you feel this movement, you can then run to the ball instead of walking, and you will still have your last step with the right foot on the forehand, or your left foot on the backhand. Your upper body starts in the sideways position to the net, and after hitting the ball, your belly button faces your target, and your shoulders face the entire opposite direction. So your shoulders have turned in a 180-degree turn.

The faster you do this movement, the more you will automatically jump off the ground right before you hit the ball, because of your coiling and exploding, using the ground as your take-off pad.

The easy way to know when to bend is to remember, "**B & B = BEND on the BOUNCE**." Then your timing will always be correct. No matter if the ball is high or low, "B & B."

The open stance is also used much more now because you have to take fewer steps to a ball that is wide, and you have to take fewer steps back toward the middle of the court. So, for every forehand or backhand that is wide, you have to take two less steps for every one of those shots in the rally. Therefore, if your opponent hits to your forehand five times in a row, you have to take ten more steps, just in that one point. Using the open stance, you have to take fewer steps to every forehand or backhand, so you run less and your opponent runs more. I think that's one of the objects of playing a fun game of tennis, isn't it?

Forehand or Backhand Open Stance 1, 2, 3...

- Turn
- Bend
- Explode!

I loved watching Steffi Graf play tennis. She was a true athlete. I'd watched her play, and then run out to the tennis courts to try to imitate how she played. I tried to jump and hit a forehand in the air as she did, but I was not successful. I asked other tennis pros way back in the day how she did that. They all said the same thing, which was that she was a very gifted athlete and you cannot teach people how to hit a forehand like that. At the time she played, she was one of the only women who hit with an open stance, and she came off the ground every time she hit the ball. She was ahead of her time doing that kind of forehand, because no one knew how to teach that at the time. If only I'd known...

2) The Square Stance: You set up running to the ball by planting your right foot first for a forehand, or planting your left foot first on a backhand. Then shift your weight forward, and step onto your front foot, which makes you step toward the net. The left foot is stepping forward toward the net on the forehand side and the right foot is stepping forward toward the net on the backhand side. Make sure that the step is not sideways or parallel with the baseline. The square stance is used more when the ball is hit short and in front of you, rather than wide and to the side of you at the baseline. You still want to bend on the bounce, and turn your core, or your belly button, toward your target. You will feel that it is easier to turn your whole core with the open stance. You can do it with the square stance, but you do not rotate as much.

With a two-handed backhand, you will feel the rotation of your body because your left hand helps coil your body around, as if you were doing the open stance footwork for the backhand.

Forehand or Backhand Square Stance 1, 2, 3...

- Turn
- Step
- Hit!

3) The Closed Stance: This is the "old way" that they used to teach hitting forehands. When you "got your racquet back," your front foot moved sideways, parallel to the baseline at the same time. If you try this method now, you will feel all jammed up, almost like your body is in the way of hitting the ball. We don't teach this stance anymore. If you use this stance, look at the other two options of open stance or square stance.

The reason this stance was used so much in the past was because most people didn't know about the concept of getting your back foot more behind where the ball was bouncing. In my experience, the back foot plants too far away from where the ball is bouncing, and then the only way to hit the forehand or backhand is by stepping sideways or parallel to the baseline. All of your energy is sideways and you cannot shift your weight properly to get it going back forward toward your target to hit the groundstrokes well.

Forehand or Backhand Closed Stance 1, 2, 3...

- Avoid this stance
- Outdated
- No longer used

V. Left Hand or Non-Dominant Hand Functions

The left hand or your non-dominant hand has many very important functions in both the forehand and backhand ground strokes and approach shots. The three strokes where it is imperative to use your left hand are 1. On your forehand shots 2. On the two-handed backhand shots 3. On the one-handed backhand shots.

1) Forehand Groundstroke and Approach Shot:

The left hand is important in the forehand stroke, even though it is your non-hitting hand. The left hand gives you balance, power and helps as a visual aid of where to strike the ball in relationship to your body. When you do your shoulder turn as stated in Step #1 of the Forehand and Backhand Groundstroke section, the left hand helps turn the shoulders. Therefore, when your racquet is behind you in the proper "set-up" position, your left hand should be parallel to the baseline. Think of it as parallel to the net. The left hand serves three main functions:

- Having your left hand parallel to the baseline ensures that your shoulders have completed their turn. Many people turn their shoulders, and leave their left hands directly in front of them, which makes it only half of a shoulder turn.
- Your left hand is your visual aid as to how far you want the ball to be away from your body, which will give you much more room to turn and coil. Most people have heard the saying, "Point to the ball." If you point directly to the ball after it bounces, you will always be lined up too close to the ball and will feel extremely crunched up as you try to make contact. You should use your hand as a landmark, and feel that the ball is a racquet length away from your left fingertip. Then you will have plenty of room to swing freely.
- Your left hand moves across your body, clearing out your hips to swing, and since it is out there in front of you, use it to catch the racquet after hitting the ball. That helps ensure a good fol-low-through.

Forehand Non-Dominant Hand 1, 2, 3...

- Shoulder Turn
- Visual Aid
- Catch the Racquet!

2) Two-Handed Backhand Groundstroke:

The left hand is important in the backhand stroke, as we discussed before. The left hand gives you balance and power and helps control the ball in the proper direction that you would like it to go. When you do your shoulder turn as stated in Step #1, the left hand should be pulling the racquet back, as your grip changes on the right hand toward the left. When your racquet is back behind you in the proper "set-up" position, your left hand and your right hand fit into each other like perfect puzzle pieces on the grip. This way, you can feel whether the grip is right, instead of having to look at it. The left hand serves three main functions:

- The left hand pulls your racquet back, which ensures that the shoulders have completed their turn. Many people turn their shoulder, but use the right hand to do that, which makes it only half a shoulder turn.
- The left hand is your dominant arm, starting your drop in the swing. Think of the swing as a left-handed forehand. It pushes your racquet in a forward motion.
- The left hand brings your racquet across your body and finishes up and over your shoulder.

Two-Handed Backhand Non-Dominant Hand 1, 2, 3...

- Shoulder Turn
- Does the Work
- Finishes Over the Shoulder

3) One-Handed Backhanded Groundstroke:

The left hand is important in the backhand stroke. With a one-handed backhand, the left hand gives you balance. When you turn your shoulder as stated in Step #1, the left hand should be pulling the racquet back, as your grip changes on the right hand to panel #1-1. The right hand moves on the grip, depending on whether you plan to hit a topspin backhand or a slice backhand.

As you hit the one-handed backhand, your left hand stays on the racquet, until your right arm starts the motion forward toward your target. A bad habit people have in the one-handed backhand is that they bring the racquet back with the left hand, and then let go of the racquet way too early. Therefore, they lose control of the racquet and are not sure where the racquet is behind them. After the ball is struck, the left hand should point to the back fence behind you. If you point your left hand to the fence behind you, then you will always have the correct finish at the end of your swing. The left arm pointing behind you keeps your body sideways longer to the net.

One-Handed Backhand Non-Dominant Hand 1, 2, 3...

- Shoulder Turn
- Left Hand Points to Back Fence
- Finish Straight Ahead

VI. Contact Point

Contact point is absolutely essential when trying to hit the ball the same way as consistently as possible. We will talk about the footwork as it relates to the contact point of where you are actually hitting the ball. Remember, you should be watching the bounce, and the hit, which is your contact point.

The front foot is always the closest foot to the net, regardless of which stance you use, open stance, square stance, or closed stance (hopefully you do not use this last stance). We will focus on:

1) **Contact point #1 =** in front of the front foot.
2) **Contact point #2 =** next to the front foot.
3) **Contact point #3 =** behind the front foot.

The Forehand and Backhand Contact Point

If we could all make the exact same contact point every time we hit the ball, we'd all be on the professional tennis circuit. We're not there, yet, but it's the goal of every tennis player. The better you are, the closer you are to mastering this concept.

There is a two-foot space where you can hit the ball and still get it over the net. In that two-foot, or 24-inch, space, there are more optimal ways where contact point should be. The most optimal place is at contact point #1. The second best place is at contact point #2 and the hardest contact point to hit a good shot from is contact point #3.

Contact point #1 is in front of the front foot; contact point #2 is parallel or next to the front foot; and contact point #3 is behind the front foot. We can hit the tennis ball over the net from all three of these positions, but the more we hit the ball at contact point #1, the better we hit the ball. You do not want to hit the ball later to go down the line, or hit the ball earlier to go cross-court. You want to try to hit the ball in the same contact point as much as possible. Hitting the ball later or earlier is the "old way" that the stroke used to be taught.

A great way to practice this is to have someone hit tennis balls to your forehand side. Your entire job is simply to call aloud the number one, two or three after you have hit the tennis ball. You are just reporting what you saw at contact, or what you felt. There is no right or wrong answer. Pretend you are on the sideline reporting to an audience what number the player hit the tennis ball from, according to his front foot. The drill is simply designed to make you start noticing where you actually hit the ball.

A student of mine named Janice did this for the first time. At first, she could not even figure out what number to call out because she never watched the contact point that closely. She couldn't stay aware of where the ball really was according to her foot or body. We had to review again. # 1 is in front of the left foot; #2 is parallel or next to the left foot; and #3 is behind the left foot. For the first ten balls, she was so cluttered with trying to say the "correct" number that she was "tangled up in her underwear." Too much clutter. When I reminded her again that there was no prize for calling out the number correctly, she relaxed a little bit. Then, when she still was trying to be perfect with knowing what number she was hitting the ball at, I reminded her that there was no Starbucks gift card waiting if she were right. Now, the pressure was off her altogether.

Eventually, she became very proficient at this drill. After the drill, Janice said, "When you made me call the number aloud where I made contact, I never realized how I really didn't see the ball at contact point. I was always looking over to the other side of the net to see whether I made it over. I also did not panic even if I said #3 because I still could hit the ball over the net. Your drill taught me to stop beating myself up even as I was getting ready to hit the ball if I did not hit it out in front of me. That was the first time I really saw the ball at contact point. The ball started looking bigger to me. I even noticed that it was yellow. Hah-hah."

Forehand and Backhand Contact Point 1, 2, 3...

- **Contact Point #1** = In Front of Foot or Body
- **Contact Point #2** = Next to Foot or Body
- **Contact Point # 3** = Behind Foot or Body

VII. Finish or Follow-Through

The finish or the follow-through is the part of the swing that helps give the ball speed and power. The finish of the stroke is determined by where the contact point is according to your front foot or your body. Sometimes by just simply finishing the stroke, even if you do not feel as if you hit the ball well, the finish will still help get the ball over the net. It does not always have to be the perfect striking of the ball to get the ball over the net. The follow-through many times helps flaws that may happen during the stroke. There are three shots that we will examine in this section: 1. The forehand follow-through. 2. The two-handed backhand follow-through. 3. The one-handed backhand follow-through.

1) The Forehand Finish or Follow-Through

The follow-through is a result of you turning your core through the forehand swing. If your core completes the turn and the coiling and uncoiling, then your follow-through will usually be good. If your arm does all the work of swinging the racquet, then your follow through will tend to stop right after contact, for fear of the ball going out. The more you use your core, the more you will automatically follow through.

Remember that the most common finish is with the back of your hand swinging all the way up to almost touching your ear. Where your contact point is usually determines where the finish is going to be.

- If your contact point is #1, then the finish should be with the back of your hitting hand almost touching your left ear.
- If your contact point is #2, then the finish should be with the back of your hitting hand almost touching your left shoulder.
- If your contact point is #3, then the finish will be with the palm of your hand facing your right ear. Your swing plane is almost vertically upward from the contact point, which is behind your body. Some people also refer to this as "the buggy whip."

Remember, the key to the follow-through is to turn your core or your belly button to your target. The follow-through will go where it is supposed to go without you having to think about where it is very much.

Forehand Follow-Through 1, 2, 3...

- **Contact Point # 1** = Back of Hand to Ear
- **Contact Point #2** = Back of Hand to Shoulder
- **Contact Point #3** = Vertical

2) The Two-Handed Backhand Finish or Follow-Through

The follow-through is a result of you turning your core through the backhand swing. If your core completes the turn and the coiling and uncoiling, then your follow-through will usually be good. If your right arm does all of the work swinging the racquet, then your follow through will tend to stop right after contact, as you will probably be worried that the ball will go out. The more you use your core, the more you will automatically follow through.

Remember the most common finish is with the back of your *left* hand swinging all the way up to almost touching your right ear.

Your finish is different depending on whether you hit an open stance backhand or a square stance backhand.

The Open Stance: With this finish, your racquet and arm always go up and over your shoulder. When hitting the open stance, after you make contact, you are already in the "recovery step" position with your footwork. So all you have to do is recover back toward the middle of the court.

The Square Stance: With this finish, your racquet and arm always go up and over your shoulder. When running to the ball, you plant your left foot first and then step forward toward the net. Then after you make contact, your left foot comes forward until it is parallel with your right foot. This is called the "recovery step." It is part of the follow-through on a square stance backhand.

Two-Handed Backhand Follow-through 1, 2, 3...

- Finish Over Your Shoulder
- Recovery Step
- Ready Position

3) The One-Handed Backhand Finish or Follow-Through

The follow-through is a result of you swinging from your shoulder. Your core turns slightly when you step toward your target. Your hips turn slightly, starting your core rotating, and then the finish is:

On a topspin backhand, with the shoulder swinging, so that the racquet head ends up above your head. The swing is a low-to-high motion, so that the finish is with the wrist and elbow straight, above the level of your head. The edge of the racquet ends up pointing up toward the sky.

For a regular slice, with the shoulder swinging, so that the racquet head ends up in front of you, about level with your head. The swing is a high-to-low motion, so that the finish is with the wrist and elbow straight, parallel to the level of your head. The follow-through is much shorter than the follow-through on the topspin. The edge of the racquet ends up pointing toward your target.

For a slice on a low shot, the follow-through is the same as the regular slice. The minor adjustment is that you do bring the racquet up a little more on the follow-through. Therefore, the swing pattern is high to low back to high.

One-Handed Backhand Follow-Through 1, 2, 3...

- For Topspin, the edge of the racquet points to the sky.
- For Slice, the edge of the racquet points to the target.
- For Low Slice, the edge of the racquet points to the target, with your knees bent more.

VIII. How to Hit Forehand and Backhand Approach Shots

There are many different types of approach shots, and many different heights of the approach shots. We will deal with three types: 1. The regular approach shot, which is hit at about waist level. 2. The low approach shot which is hit with a little bit of topspin to help get it up and over the net, and drop into the court quickly. 3. The high approach shot. On the forehand side, the high approach shot is called the "rollover" and on the backhand side, it is called the slice.

The approach shot is used when the ball lands around the service line. You want to hit the ball to one of the corners, and then approach the net, so your next shot will be a volley. All approach shots are hit with either a forehand or backhand grip—whichever you use from the baseline. When you see an approach shot hit from the baseline, the first few steps are the biggest and fastest. As you get closer to the ball, you can make your steps smaller to help you set up properly to get the correct distance from the ball. To make your first few steps explosive, run with your racquet directly in front of you, in ready position, and then turn your shoulders as you get closer to the ball. Your footwork should be such that when you hit the ball, you are slowing down. Do not hit the ball when you are totally stopped. You don't want to hit the ball when you are running full steam ahead; you want to hit the ball when you are slowing down.

1) How to Hit a Forehand Approach Shot

We will address three types of forehand approach shots:

A regular approach shot: This is a short ball, that when you run to it, the ball is below the net level. As we discussed before, as you get closer to the ball, you want to plant your back foot, which will help slow you down as you hit the shot. You want to feel that your body is in control of the shot as you hit it. If you are flying through the air hitting it, you will not know if the ball is going in or flying out. If the ball is below the net, you must bend your knees to get down to the level that the ball is. Contact point is still in front of your body. Roger Federer hits this shot better than anyone I have ever seen.

Forehand Approach Shot 1, 2, 3...

- Run
- Plant
- Hit

Low jumping approach shot: This is a more advanced approach shot. As you run toward the short ball that is low, bend your knees, and step forward with your left foot toward the net. Hit the forehand and jump up in the air, landing on your left foot. Even though the ball is below the net, by bending your knees and jumping up off the ground, it helps your body follow-through, which creates more topspin on the ball, which keeps it from flying long past the baseline. Jumping also keeps you moving through the ball so you can get in a good volley position. Contact point is still in front of your body.

Low Jumping Forehand Approach Shot 1, 2, 3...

- Bend
- Hit
- Jump

High approach shot called the "Rollover": This is a short ball, and when you run to it, it is above the net level. This shot is very effective because you can hit it with more power, more spin and you can usually get better placement on the ball. Hitting the ball when it is above net level also takes time that would allow your opponent to get ready for the next shot. So this shot is particularly good for offensive play.

In order to hit the ball correctly, make sure you have the proper forehand grip—either the eastern forehand or the semi-western grip. You can hit the shot by either using the square stance or the open stance. When the ball is high over the net, most people feel that open stance footwork works best. With open stance footwork, they run up to a short ball quickly, then turn their shoulders, bend and explode up to the level of the ball.

When you run up to the ball quickly, hit it with plenty of topspin, so you can swing very hard, and the ball will stay in the court. In order to do this, your backswing will be slightly different from your regular forehand backswing at the baseline. At the baseline, the swing is turning your shoulders (where the racquet starts parallel with your head). Then drop the racquet and then swing.

In this instance, the beginning of the swing is exactly the same. Turn your shoulders so the racquet is parallel with your head in the back-swing. Do not drop the racquet. Keep the racquet head high, or next to your shoulder. The racquet should swing parallel with your shoulder so you hit the ball between chest and shoulder height. It is crucial to hit the ball in front of your body, at contact point #1. As you hit the ball at chest height, you must get spin on the ball, or it will fly out past the baseline. So as you feel the ball hitting your racquet in the center of the ball, bend your elbow, and "roll over" the top half of the ball. Follow-through is with the palm of your hand pointing to the ground, behind your left shoulder. One of my students calls this shot "Cover the baby with the blanket" because that's what it feels like she is doing with her racquet hand.

Once you've practiced this shot, you will love it when your opponent hits short balls to you, instead of dreading it, and hoping you can just push it into the court. You will win the point outright when you hit the "roll-over" this way, or it will set you up for an easy volley winner!

You can also hit this shot from the baseline. Your technique is exactly the same, except that you aim to hit it to the opposing baseline so you are not hitting "down" on the ball. You must still make contact at chest to shoulder height at the baseline. It is a great strategy to use if you are playing an opponent who hits with a lot of topspin that kicks up high at the baseline.

High Forehand Rollover Approach Shot 1, 2, 3...

- Turn. So that racquet head stays high in backswing
- Rollover the top half of the ball
- Finish with the racquet head facing the ground and elbow bent

2) How to Hit a Backhand Approach Shot

As with the forehand approach shot, the strategy for hitting the backhand approach shot is the same. Refer to the forehand approach shot section. Take your fastest steps at the beginning of the shot, so you have time to slow down and execute the shot properly, with plenty of control. Hit the approach shot when you are slowing down, not totally stopped and not full steam ahead.

We will address two types of backhand approach shots:

Topspin can be hit with a one-handed backhand or a two-handed backhand. The only difference is how many hands you have on the racquet when you make contact with the ball. The footwork is essentially the same and the contact point is exactly the same. The other difference is the follow-through. The follow-through is the same as hitting a backhand from the baseline. The one-handed backhand follow-through goes up above your head, and the two-handed backhand follow-through ends up around your body, to the opposite shoulder.

Again, as with the forehand approach shot, run as quickly as you can to get the short ball early. The higher above the net the ball is when you get to it, the better you will hit the approach shot. Plant your back foot (your left foot) to help slow you down, step forward with your front, right, foot and hit the ball at contact point #1. Let the follow-through happen to get enough spin on the shot. Then, split-step and get ready for a volley.

Backhand Topspin Approach Shot 1, 2, 3…

- Run
- Plant Your Back Foot
- Finish

Slice can be hit on a high-ball approach shot, or a low-ball approach shot. The slice is hit best using a one-handed backhand. Therefore, even if you use a two-handed backhand at the baseline, if you want to hit an effective slice shot, use one-hand as you come forward. The footwork coming forward is the same as the topspin backhand, where you run, and then plant your left foot first, to help you slow down. The difference is in the step after you plant your foot, and then in stepping forward. It needs to be what is called a "carioca" step. This involves stepping backward as you face sideways to the net.

The sequence goes like this: Plant your left foot when you are close to the ball; step forward toward your target with your right foot; hit the ball and then do a carioca step. The carioca step will keep you sideways to the net longer, ensuring the ball stays on your racquet longer, which will get more underspin or slice on your shot. You will get much more acceleration through the shot with this footwork. It also disguises your shot very effectively.

Backhand Slice Approach Shot 1, 2, 3...

- Plant
- Step Forward & Hit
- Carioca Step Behind

If you are missing the forehand or the backhand approach shot, it is usually due to one of these three reasons:

1) If it goes long, the contact point was late.
2) If it goes into the net, you stopped your follow-through.
3) If you hear a mishit sound, you did not see the ball all the way to your racquet; you were probably looking at the spot on the court that you were going to hit the ball.

IX. How to Hit an Overhead

An overhead is one of the greatest shots to hit in tennis. If you're having a bad day, just go out and hit some overheads. But if you're not good at hitting overheads, it can also be one of the most humiliating shots in tennis. Even pros who practice this shot repeatedly miss it badly sometimes. Isn't it terrible how we somehow feel better when we see pros missing this shot? In some way, we don't feel so bad ourselves; we are all human.

There are two types of overheads: A step-in overhead and a scissor-kick overhead. You should hit the overhead with the continental grip. Your grip is the continental grip with the hand on panel #2-2.

Step-In Overhead. The lob for this overhead is not very deep. It usually lands in front of the service line, inside the service boxes. Therefore, it should be treated as a relatively easy overhead, but these are probably the ones we miss the most. It happens because it looks easy; we do not see the contact with the racquet and miss the shot badly. There's a tendency when we see an easy overhead coming toward us not to move our feet enough because it looks so easy.

No matter what, use your left hand to put the racquet up behind your head. This also ensures a good shoulder turn at the beginning of the stroke. Your left hand is also used to site the ball. This means if the ball were to come down, you should be able to catch it with your left hand. Your left hand should always be in front of you, slightly to the right side of your head. Hit the ball a racquet-length above your left hand. Next, you want to get behind the ball as much as you can, then move your feet forward, to step in with your left foot right before you hit the ball.

Step-In Overhead 1, 2, 3...

- Use your left hand to put the racquet behind your head
- Point to the ball with your left hand. Hit the ball a racquet-length above your left hand, which is to the right side of your head
- Step forward into the court with your left foot before you hit the ball

Scissor-Kick Overhead. The lob for this overhead is usually hit past the service line and very deep. You must know how to hit this overhead because the ball usually has to be hit when it is behind your head. Instead of always saying, "Yours," take the overhead yourself! If you have a choice, you should always try to hit the overhead if it is over your head, rather than letting your partner get it. This is because you don't give up court position at the net and when most people have to switch to another side of the court because of a lob, they end up losing the point. Therefore, it is better to take anything over your head, as your overhead.

The key to a good scissor-kick overhead is usually at the beginning. If you have a good start to the ball, your overhead will be much stronger. In the "old days," they used to teach that the best way to go back for an overhead was to shuffle. Shuffling is always better than running backwards (and you feel like you are going to fall backwards on your butt!) The new style is to turn and run back, as if you were running back to catch a fly ball in center field. You never lose sight of the ball;

just turn and run. When you get back where you are almost behind the ball, take off with your right foot, jump backwards up in the air and swing up to the ball to hit the overhead. Yes, you hit this shot as you are in the air. When you land, you land on your left foot, which gets your balance. Then you can come back in to the net again. Your feet make a scissor-like, crossing motion while you are jumping, and that is where the scissor-kick overhead gets its name. You still use your left hand to put the racquet up behind your head. You still site the ball with your left hand and hit the ball a racquet-length above your head. You may not actually see the racquet hitting the ball because the contact point is behind your head.

At contact point, with your continental grip panel #2-2, you want to pronate your forearm. That will get the power on the ball. Some people have heard, "Snap your wrist on your overhead." That's just an expression used to get people to let the head of the racquet come down over the top of the ball. Nevertheless, the forearm pronates, but of course the wrist never actually snaps. The word "pronate" just means that your forearm is moving from an inside position going toward the outside. A simple way to think about it is simply to throw a ball over the net, or to throw a football over the net. That throwing motion is the pronation of the forearm.

Placement of the overhead is critical. You can hit an angle overhead, where the ball lands in the service box, diagonal from where you are standing. On the other hand, you can hit the overhead deep into one of the corners. If your placement on an overhead is good, you do not have to hit the cover off the ball to win the point.

Scissor-Kick Overhead 1, 2, 3...

- Use left hand to put racquet up behind your head, turn, and run
- Turn and run
- Jump and hit

X. How to Hit Serves

The serve is probably the most important stroke in tennis, and it is the only shot you completely control. If this is the case, why don't more people go out and take a bucket of balls and work on their serves? If you "hold your serve," you will win at least fifty percent of the games you play. That means you only have to "break the serve" of your opponent once in a set and you win the set. Sounds simple, doesn't it?

If you are scheduled to play a match at 9:00 a.m., why not get to the court fifteen minutes early and work on your serve? The worst thing ever invented was "first ball in." Who invented that? It's the most awful thing you could think about for your serve. "First ball in" means you'll serve and the first ball to go into the service box counts. Well, that's a no brainer. Of course, the very first ball you serve will go in—there's no pressure on you. In your mind, it doesn't matter, because you're thinking that you can keep going if the ball doesn't go in, so you are calm and relaxed. That is when we are always successful. As soon as it "counts," we freeze up. So, you haven't hit any practice serves, and you walk up to the line and say, "First one in." You haven't had any warm-up from your shoulder, but the serve goes in and now the rest of your serves count, even though you're not warmed up. So, from now on, you should warm-up your serves together. Yes, even in doubles, all four people take practice serves at the same time.

When I was a junior tennis player, my coach told me the only two things I had complete control over in tennis were my serve and my fitness. My coach also told me that my serve should be the best part of my game because I didn't need anyone else to practice it, and I could improve by practicing on my own. I'd hit at least 200 serves a day, five or six days a week.

I didn't even need lights to practice my serve during the winter when it was dark. There was a parking light spotlight next to the college tennis courts, but no regular lights on the tennis courts. But with that parking lot light, I could see just well enough to know whether the ball had gone over the net. So I learned by the feel of the ball whether the serve had gone in. That taught me a lot about how to hit the serve the proper way, and the results spoke for themselves. I could not see the results when I practiced because it was too dark. That was also where I jumped rope three-thousand times in the morning and three-thousand times at night. I was very fit. There weren't many tennis balls I couldn't run down.

When I practiced my serve, I always practiced with targets on the court. I loved the sound of smacking those tennis cans—they were metal back then and it made a great noise when you hit them squarely. I always had a plan, even when I was practicing 200 serves—where I was aiming, what kind of serve I was practicing, things like that. Then, when I got into a match, I just called out a number in my head, where I would aim and hit the serve to that spot. I didn't care where my opponent was standing.

Toss, a.k.a. "Placement"

How to hold the ball in your hand: One of the most important aspects of the serve is the toss. People hear this all the time, but they do not know exactly where the toss should be. First of all, I think the word "toss" is the worst word you could use for this action. But that's exactly what people do; they "toss" the ball up to the sky and then they have no control over where it goes. Think of the "toss" as a *placement*, or putting the ball up on a high bookshelf, or *placing* the ball up toward the sky—as if you're in an egg tossing contest and don't want the egg to splatter all over your face.

In order to do that, place the ball on the first line of your four fingers, just below your fingertips, or on the first part of your finger that bends. Then, place your thumb on top of the ball. This is where the ball should sit before you *place it* in the air. Most people hold the ball in the palms of their hands. That's why they "toss" it, which puts a lot of spin on the toss. Wouldn't you rather hit a ball with virtually no spin on it, as opposed to hitting a ball with a lot of spin on it? It is much easier to control the ball if there is no spin on it.

Release point of the ~~toss~~ *placement*: Put a ball in your left hand. Hold your left arm out, directly in front of you and slightly to the right. Hold the ball at eye level, and then let the ball drop straight to the ground. You would have a perfect ball "~~toss~~" *placement*. Therefore, if you release the ball for the "placement" at eye level, you will have perfect ball "placement" every time, with very little spin, making it easier for you to hit. Most people hold onto the ball too long, which is why it goes too far behind their heads. They just release the ball too late. Conversely, if you release the ball too soon, your ball "placement" will usually be too low.

Height of the ~~toss~~ *placement*: How you "place" the ball depends on what's most comfortable for you. In general, if you stretch your racquet up toward the sky as high as you can, you should "place" the ball at least as high as the tip of your racquet. That is where you should make contact with the ball—it's called the "peak." The peak is the highest point of ball "placement," or the ball toss. You want to make contact at the peak, which is after the ball goes up, right before the ball starts its descent. The moment the ball stops is where to make contact. Your goal is to get all your energy stretching up and reaching up to that point where you want to make contact.

Where the ~~toss~~ *placement* should land: If you put your racquet down on the ground so that the racquet butt cap is in front of your left toe and the racquet is inside the baseline at a 45-degree angle, the tip of the racquet should point toward the right net post. It's on every court, so you will always have the same benchmark to line up your serve. Therefore, your "placement," or toss is always in front and to the right of your center. Or, if you were standing in the middle of a big clock, then the toss should be ***placed*** up to the sky at about where the one or two would be on the clock.

Place the ball up and see if you can land it inside the strings on your racquet on the ground. You can practice this in your own backyard. Put a racquet on the ground, lined up with your front foot, and see if you can get ten balls in a row to hit the strings of the racquet on the ground.

Where your weight should be: When you release placement of the ball in the air, your weight should be on your forward (left) foot or at least balanced between both feet. Most people who struggle to get the ball "placed" in front of them do so because their weight is on the back foot when they release the ball. You can start with your weight on the front foot and rock. You can start with your weight on the back foot and go forward or you can start with your weight balanced. The main goal is that when you release the ball, your weight is on your front (left) foot.

Learn from your mistakes: The good news with your serve is that you get two chances to get the ball into the service box. What a relief! Therefore, use your mistakes to your benefit. Notice where your ball misses and make adjustments from there.

Follow these simple guidelines for where your serve lands and you will always be able to fix your serve if something goes wrong: Contact point #1 is the perfect "placement" or toss for a flat or a slice serve—out in front of the body and slightly to the right of your left toe, a racquet-length in front of your left or front foot. Contact point #2 is parallel to the baseline, where you can sometimes get the ball in. Contact point #3 is behind the baseline, where the serve usually goes long.

Toss, a.k.a. "Placement" 1, 2, 3...

- If your serve goes long, then your "placement" (toss)" is too far behind you.
- If you serve into the net, then your "placement" (toss) is too low or too far in front of you.
- If you "place" the ball (toss) in front and to the right of you, then you will hit your serve "in" almost every time!

Service Stance

Standing on the baseline. Where you stand to serve should generally be the same. Some people stand in different locations along the baseline to hit different kinds of serves from different spots, but your opponent usually figures this out pretty quickly. So the best place to stand for singles is one racquet length from the hash mark. For doubles, stand halfway between the hash mark and the doubles sideline.

Foot placement

- **The deuce court.** Service stance should be the same for all your serves. Your front (left) foot should be at a 45-degree angle to the baseline, and your back foot should be parallel with the baseline, about shoulder width apart, so that the arch of your right foot lined up with your left heel. It should be a comfortable stance. With this stance, your shoulders should be lined up diagonally toward the service box. If not, then pull your back (right) foot back a little bit more until your shoulder position is correct.
- **The ad court.** On the ad court, foot placement is the same, except that I pull my back (right) foot back a little bit more, so my instep is lined up with my left heel. This ensures that my shoulders are pointed more diagonally to my target.

Service Motion

The service motion is very complicated. Rather than go through all the parts involved in the service motion, I will try to keep it as simple as possible. Everyone has individual little problems in their serves, but if we start from the beginning in the simplest way possible, these problems should be easy to fix.

When I was a junior player, I worked so hard in one particular clinic, trying to get my serve in the right box, with perfect form and placement and of course, superb speed—all at once. Needless to say, I was not successful in accomplishing all these individual parts all at once. I got so frustrated with myself; I picked up a tennis ball from the big basket of balls and threw that ball as far as I could (I was really mad). It went flying over the fence.

One of the instructors came over to me (I thought I was in a lot of trouble and was going to have to run sprints or something), and asked if I'd just thrown that ball. "Yes," I replied. "I just can't get this serve at all." He looked at me and said, "Try to throw it over the fence again." I picked up a ball and hurled it into the air, clearing the back fence once again.

He said, "I can't believe you can throw a tennis ball that far." I told him I had a pretty good arm, and I had been planning to be a professional softball player before I'd started concentrating on tennis. He said, "Stop thinking about all the parts of the serve and just throw the racquet at the ball—just like you just threw the ball over the fence."

Amazing...I hit my serve in. My only thought was to throw the racquet at the ball. That worked like a miracle for me. It all made perfect sense. I stopped thinking and did what I could naturally do very easily. That seems to be the simplest way to teach people how to serve.

Many women have trouble throwing the ball over the net at first because they never threw a ball or a football when they were growing up. (Maybe they didn't have four brothers like I did. For me it was a matter of survival). I teach women how to throw a ball properly over the net—not "like a girl." Their serves improve immediately.

There are four types of serves: Flat, slice, topspin and kick (also called the American twist).

#1 Flat Serve.

Flat Serve, First Serve. The flat serve goes faster, but you must be much more accurate about where your strings are really facing. On a flat serve, the ball only touches about four to six strings in the middle of the racquet, so there's not much room for an error.

When we talk about what part of the ball to hit, let's pretend that the ball is the face of a clock. You want to make contact where the hands connect on the face of the clock. That point is right in the middle of the clock, or the tennis ball.

An advanced flat serve is served with a continental grip, panel #2-2. As you swing forward, the racquet starts pronating (meaning it starts moving from inside your body, toward the outside of your body, which creates the pronating motion with your arm). Another way to think about it is that when your hand is by your ear, turn your right thumb out toward your target quickly; that also gets the arm to pronate. Be sure your ball toss is in front and slightly to the right (at the one o'clock position).

Three things I do on my flat serve are: 1) Look at where my target is. My eyes are like the viewfinder in a camera; I must know where I am aiming. 2) Look at the contact point (where I am going to hit the ball). 3) Feel the palm of my hand guiding the racquet to my exact target that I initially saw through my "viewfinder."

Flat Serve, First Serve 1, 2, 3...

- Look at your target
- Watch contact point with your eyes
- Swing to your target

Flat Serve, Second Serve. I know many people have the "blooper serve," the "I've gotta get it in, no matter what" serve, the "rainbow serve" (it looks like a rainbow with no pot of gold at the end) and the "slow motion serve." We'd like to have some kind of spin serve, but when it comes down to losing a point in a match, people do crazy things just to get the ball in that little box.

If you have to hit a flat serve just to get it in, then you should at least make sure your swing speed is the same from the beginning to the follow-through. The mistake most people make is they start fast and then slow down so much when they hit the ball that the ball goes in, but it lands so short inside the box that they get killed on the return anyway. Try to keep your swing speed the same; do not speed up and do not slow down. Another factor to remember is that on a flat second serve, you should aim the ball to cross the net one racquet length over the net. This will ensure that the ball will at least land deep in the service box, so you won't be killed with the return as much.

Flat Serve, Second Serve 1, 2, 3...

- Look at your target
- Watch contact point with your eyes
- Aim one racquet length over the net toward your target.

#2 Slice Serve.

Slice Serve, First Serve. When you hit this serve properly, it will travel fast, curve to your left, and to your opponent's right. On a slice first serve, you must make sure you are using a continental grip, panel #2-2. The service motion is exactly the same as the flat first serve, just as if you are throwing the racquet at the ball, or as if you are throwing a ball. The toss is exactly the same as the flat serve, too, in front and slightly to the right (at the one o'clock position).

When you try this serve for the first time, you may hit the ball way outside of the left doubles sideline. It seems crazy that you need to have your racquet turned on the side of the ball to hit it straight to the service box. The key to hitting slice and getting it in the correct square is that you must swing toward the wrong service box. Yes, that's right; on the deuce side, swing to the ad court or the wrong service box. If you are serving from the ad side of the court, you must swing toward the right-hand net post, or the bench next to the right net post. You must trust the racquet to put the correct amount of spin on the ball so it will go into the correct box.

You must have the same swing speed when hitting the slice serve. When people first learn this serve, they swing too slowly and the ball barely clears the net. The motion on this serve is to swing up and forward. So the edge of the racquet swings up toward the sky first; then your direction is a swing with the same edge of the racquet toward the wrong service box.

We will use the clock as a reference point again, as we did discussing the flat serve. On the slice serve, you want to make contact at the three o'clock number on the clock, which would be the outside, or the right side of the tennis ball. When you hit the outside part of the ball, the ball spins to the left and the spin in the air always brings the ball downward. That's why you must swing up and toward the wrong box in order to get the ball into the correct service box.

The most common mistake people make when they're learning the slice serve is trying to hit at the three o'clock point on the ball, and then their wrists move and they swing "around" the ball. When you do that, the ball travels nowhere. It barely gets to the net. Pretend that your racquet is a hammer and there's a wall in front of you. The edge of your racquet is the end of the hammer. Now imagine you are going to hit a nail into that wall in front of you. That is the motion with which the racquet should travel.

Slice Serve, First Serve 1, 2, 3...

- Toss in front and to the right
- Hit the ball at three o'clock
- Swing toward the wrong service box

Slice Serve, Second Serve. When this serve is hit properly, it curves from your left to your opponent's right. The ball is not quite as fast as the first serve, but has more spin on it. The biggest difference between the second serve and the first serve is that the height of ball when it leaves your racquet is much more in an upward trajectory. Aim the ball one racquet length over the net to ensure clearance and that it will land deep in the service square.

Hit the same part of the ball, three o'clock. Your swing speed is the same. Do not slow down your swing or try to guide the ball into the court. Swing just as fast as you did with your first serve, but much more in an upward motion. Practice this shot by hitting ten of these second serves in a row into the proper box. If you miss, start over from one. It will help develop your confidence to swing up on the ball.

Slice Serve, Second Serve 1, 2, 3...

- Toss in front and to the right
- Hit the ball at three o'clock
- Swing up and toward the wrong service box

#3 Topspin Serve, First Serve or Second Serve.

When this serve is hit properly, it arcs up high over the net and then after it hits the ground, it jumps up high. It's similar to a heavy topspin groundstroke. This gives you plenty of clearance to aim high over the net, and it's a harder shot for your opponent to hit, since the ball is high and out of your opponent's strike zone, or comfort zone.

With this serve and the kick serve, toss (place) the ball slightly behind you, or over your head. This is especially true when you're first learning the topspin serve. Simply release the ball placement (or toss) later and it will go a little more straight over your head. When you are first learning this, it is easier to hit at six o'clock on the ball to swing vertically up on the ball.

You can use a continental grip, panel #2-2 for this serve, but the serve is more effective if you can move your grip slightly toward the eastern backhand grip, panel #1-1. You will get more brushing action up on the ball. It helps you to feel that you can swing up as hard as you want on the ball, and it will not go long.

Topspin Serve, 1, 2, 3...

- Toss, or "place" over your head
- Hit the ball at six o'clock
- Swing up on the ball—*fast!*

#4 The Kick, or American Twist, Serve, Second Serve.

When this serve is hit properly, it arcs high over the net, and looks very similar to a topspin serve. As it hits the ground, it jumps up high and moves to the right. For your opponent, it jumps and moves to his left. It is similar to returning a left-hander's serve. It is a very effective serve; it has to be hit when it is high, out of the person's comfort zone and it moves to the person's left, and most people are not used to a ball moving that way.

The grip is the same as with the topspin serve. It's okay to hit with a continental grip, but the eastern backhand grip, panel #1-1 is much more effective. The ball toss is the same as with the topspin serve—a little over your head, especially when you are first learning how to hit this serve.

As for point of contact, instead of hitting at six o'clock on the ball, as you did with the topspin serve, make contact at seven o'clock, and then swing over toward three o'clock. This is an extreme exaggeration of how you must pronate your forearm in order to get the correct action and spin on the ball. When you have made contact, the racquet face will now face the back fence and the back of your hand will face your target area, the court. After the palm of your hand faces the back fence, it will then come down to regular follow-through position, by the left side of your body. It is a very unusual sensation. It just takes practice and trusting your swing because the ball does not go where the racquet head is facing.

Try this new serve; hold your hand on the top of the grip, so part of your hand is on the throat of the racquet and part is on the grip. Toss the ball over your head and swing in an upward motion, as if you were peeling the skin off an orange. As you feel the ball on your strings, your hand turns and faces the fence behind you. That will get the correct "kick" or "twist" on the ball.

You can use it as a very reliable second serve, but it is also very useful in using it as a first occasionally to throw your opponent's rhythm off because your opponent usually expects a fast, hard serve.

The Kick, or American Twist, Serve 1, 2, 3...

- Toss over your head
- Hit the ball at seven o'clock and swing toward three o'clock
- Swing up and have your strings face the back fence

Serving Rituals.

People have heard over the years that you should do the same ritual every time you serve. It doesn't matter if it is a first serve, or a second serve, you should go through the same thing every time. If you watch basketball players who are getting ready to shoot free throws, you'll see they bounce the ball the same number of times, no matter what. If you watch professional baseball players, they do the same routine every time as they go up the batter's box and golfers do the same routine every time before they swing. If they don't, they usually don't hit the shot as well, or they even miss the shot.

You should use some type of ritual or routine with your serve. If you stick with your routine, no matter what the score is, it will help you work through your nerves that come up during matches. That's why it is essential to practice your routine while you are practicing your serve. Bounce the ball the same number of times before each serve, whatever feels comfortable to you. Whether you are winning or losing, you do the same routine before each serve, no matter what.

One of the funniest routines that I ever saw was that of one of my students, Sue. We had warmed up serves and she was playing singles with Jane. They were working on their serves, and setting up the points for their singles strategies. I asked Sue whether she had two balls to start serving the first point, and she said she did. Sue missed her first serve, and in less than one second, pulled out the second ball to hit a second serve. I didn't even see her reach into her pocket to get the second ball. I couldn't believe how fast she got the ball to serve. On the next point, she missed her first serve again. By then, I was curious to see how she got to the second ball so fast. Once again, within one second, she got the second ball and served it, almost before you could blink. It was so fast I still couldn't see where the second ball came from! Now they were in the third point of their game. Sue served and missed her first serve again (I guess the serving practice did not go very well). Now, my eyes were peeled to see where on earth she was keeping the second ball. In another nano-second, Sue reached into her shirt and pulled out the second ball and served it. In all my years, I have never seen a move executed so fast, with such precision. Sue reached down her shirt, pulled out a second ball from her padded bra and served it over the net quicker than you could snap your fingers!

Well, I had to ask her how she did that so fast. She claimed that years ago, before they made tennis skirts with pockets in them and there was nowhere for her to put the second ball, she was wearing a big padded bra, and it kept the ball in a perfect place for her to get to it easily. So she has been doing this ritual for years. She had it perfected, too! When I asked Jane whether she noticed Sue doing that, she said she never noticed where the ball came from; she just knew that as soon as Sue missed a first serve, the second came very quickly, so she'd better be ready. The moral of the story is stick with your routines or rituals before you hit your serve.

Another unusual ritual was a lesson with a woman named Kaye. She just wanted to work on her groundstrokes. She told me that her serve was fine. In fact, she won most of her games with her serve, because people hated it. So we worked on her forehands and backhands, and at the end of the lesson, we played some points in order to put it all together. She served, and I almost completely missed the return because I was watching her serve. She was about 5'1", and her service toss was barely above her head. Nevertheless, in that amount of time, she had her racquet twirl around her head two or three times, like a helicopter's propellers ready to take off. I had never seen anything like that before. Then when the ball hit the ground, it came up only about three inches. You had to be on your knees to return this serve! Kaye's ritual was very effective for her, as long as she did it the same way every time. She was the "Helicopter Serve" lady.

XI. How to Hit a Return of Serve

To me, this is one of the most neglected strokes in tennis. It is just as important as your serve, but it is practiced the least amount. Why? Why don't people realize that this is as important as the serve? If you can't get the return in the court, it doesn't matter how good your big groundstrokes are, or how well you volley at the net. Personally, I treat the return of serve differently than I treat a forehand or a backhand. People miss returns because they think of them just like their groundstrokes. But they're not the same. The ball is usually coming faster, and from a downward trajectory, and you are generally standing closer than you would if you were hitting a forehand or a backhand. Therefore, you must treat the return of serve differently.

Andre Agassi was one of the best returners of modern tennis. If you want to learn how to hit great returns, study how he returned serve. It seemed he was always ready for the serve, no matter how fast it was. His technique was very simple and compact. That was the key for Andre.

Where to stand to return the serve varies. It depends on where you are the most comfortable when hitting the return. It also depends on how fast the serve is hit. Generally, for a good first serve, stand a few feet back from the baseline, which will give you enough time to see the ball and hit it out in front of you. Your right foot should be close to the singles sideline, in order to be able to get a good slice serve in the deuce court.

If you are having trouble returning the serve, stand somewhere different. There is no rule that says you must stand in the same position. So if something is not working, move more to your left, or try more to your right, or go more forward, or even stand back one more step. Sometimes, when you stand in a different position, the server notices and tries to hit a different kind of serve, based on where you are standing. Then he starts missing because he changed what he was comfortable doing.

The movement is forward and diagonal to cut off the angles of the serves. Your weight should be going forward, not backwards. If you stood in your ready position to return the serve, place two tennis racquets down on the ground, making a diagonal line from each of your feet. They should each be in a 45-degree angle from your body. That is the picture you want in your mind as you make the first step after your "split."

There are two types of returns of serve: The topspin return and the chip, or block, return.

1. The Topspin Return. When getting ready to return the serve, stand in the "new ready position," with your racquet head slightly tilted toward the ground, in a forehand grip, panel #3-3. You must see your opponent make contact with the ball up above his head. Right before he hits the ball, you want to take a "split" (also called a "jump"), so you land on your toes, with your weight forward and low, then turn your shoulders only halfway to where you are going to hit the return from. Then finish your swing over your shoulder. Use the speed of the serve to return the shot. You do not have to think of hitting the ball hard on a return. Again, your core turning will help your follow-through and give you plenty of power on the shot.

When you make your shoulder turn, think of the racquet only going back parallel with your body on either side. It will go back a little more, but that is your thought. Then hit the ball at contact point #1. From there, finish your swing over your shoulder. For the one-handed backhand topspin, finish up above your head.

Topspin Return 1, 2, 3...

- Split
- Turn shoulders halfway
- Finish

2. The Chip, or Block, Return. When getting ready for this return, ***do not wait in your "new ready position."*** You must plan and wait in the continental ready position, as if you are at the net. There is very little backswing on the chip, or block, return. It as though you are volleying the ball back, but it's after the bounce. It resembles a volley, with a little longer follow-through. Use this as a change of pace, or if the serve is hit so hard that you don't feel you'll have time to take a full swing at the ball. More male professional tennis players have started to use this return because the pace of serves has become so much faster for them.

There's not much follow-through after the ball is struck. The finish or follow-through goes straight out toward where you want the ball to land. Use the power of the serve to get the return back. The key is to hit the ball at contact point #1.

Chip, or Block, Return 1, 2, 3...

- Split with continental grip
- Set your racquet, no backswing
- Block the ball, elbow straight

Another great way to help your timing on the return of serve is to follow these steps:

- See your opponent's racquet hit the ball............ SAY "HIT"
- See the bounce in the service box .... SAY "BOUNCE"
- See your hit of the ball .... SAY "HIT"

XII. The Split-Step

The split-step is so important for a great game of tennis. Why not use it when you are supposed to? You burn more calories when you do it correctly and you're even more ready for every shot. Isn't that a good reason to split-step? The split-step was once thought of as a type of footwork to do when you played the net position. That's true, but it is also essential if you are playing at the baseline.

Basically, every time just before your opponent hits the ball, you should be doing a split-step. It's a movement that gets your balance lower, to move you quickly to where the ball is hit.

The split-step is done when you are in ready position, with your racquet in front of your body. It is a momentary pause, which gets your body and center of gravity low and on balance. You take a small jump up in the air and land softly on the balls of your feet, where your heels are not touching the ground.

The split-step occurs just before your opponent hits the ball. Therefore, if you hit five balls in a rally, you will have split-stepped five times. If you have a fifteen-ball rally, you will have split-stepped fifteen times during that rally. This is why fitness plays such a big part on the tennis court.

To master split-step timing, you must watch the ball on the other side of the court, where your opponent is.

If you are at the net and your opponent is at the baseline, you should:

- **Bounce.** See the ball bounce on your opponent's side of the court.
- **Split.** Split-step right after the bounce.
- **Hit.** See the opponent hit the ball.

Right after you split, step with your foot at the exact same time you are hitting the volley.

If you are playing the baseline, and your opponent is at the net, you must: watch your opponent's racquet to split right before your opponent makes contact with the ball. As soon as you split, turn your shoulders and run to the ball, or turn your shoulders and wait until the ball comes to you.

- **Split.** Split right before you see your opponent hit the ball.
- **Turn.** Turn right after you decide if it is forehand or backhand.
- **Hit.** Hit the shot when it comes to you.

Playing the baseline is the same timing of the split. If your opponent is at the baseline, and you are at the baseline, watch the bounce, then split, and then see your opponent hitting the shot back to you.

Right after you split, see which way the ball is coming to you, either forehand or backhand, and then you split, turn your shoulders and run to where the shot is going.

- **Split.** Split right after the bounce on your opponent's side of the net.
- **Turn.** Turn your shoulders to either the forehand or backhand side.
- **Hit.** Hit the ball when it is on your side of the net.

Make sure you do the split on your return of serve. It will happen right before your opponent hits the serve. Therefore, you must watch him toss the ball, split right before he hits the serve, and then turn your shoulders for the return of serve.

- **Toss.** Watch the toss come out of your opponent's hand.
- **Split.** Split right after your opponent tosses the ball, right before he hits it.
- **Turn.** Turn your shoulders to either the forehand or backhand as soon as your opponent hits the serve.

My system uses no more than three things to think about or work on when you are practicing—but not while you are playing. I've found that more people complicate their learning by over-thinking almost every shot they hit. It is mind-boggling how people actually think of so many things while they are playing in a match, or while they are getting ready to hit the ball.

With this book, you also get a FREE bonus that includes more information. Go to my website, **WinningInTennisAndLife.com,** and click on the "Free Stuff" button. There you'll receive instructions for twelve advanced specialty tennis shots. Each stroke has three simple steps to use to bring your tennis game to the next level. These are twelve advanced shots you only see the pros hit. Now, you can learn how to hit them and beat that opponent you have never beaten. It is an extension of this chapter. It will give you more "tools in your toolbox" to use on the tennis court.

FOREHAND VOLLEY

1. SET THE RACQUET

2. STEP & STRAIGHTEN THE ELBOW

3. READY POSTION

BACKHAND VOLLEY / 1-HAND

1. SET THE RACQUET

2. STEP & STRAIGHTEN THE ELBOW

3. READY POSTION

BACKHAND VOLLEY / 2-HANDS

1. SET THE RACQUET

2. STEP & STRAIGHTEN THE ELBOW

3. READY POSTION

FOREHAND GROUNDSTROKE SWING

1. TURN

2. DROP

3. SWING

TWO-HANDED BACKHAND GROUNDSTROKE SWING

1. TURN

2. DROP

3. SWING

1-HANDED TOPSPIN BACKHAND GROUNDSTROKE SWING

1. TURN

2. DROP

3. SWING

1-HANDED SLICE BACKHAND GROUNDSTROKE SWING

1. TURN

2. STEP

3. SWING

STANCES WITH YOUR FEET: FOREHAND

1. OPEN

2. SQUARE   3. CLOSED

STANCES WITH YOUR FEET:
BACKHAND

1. OPEN

2. SQUARE

3. CLOSED

STANCES WITH YOUR FEET:
OPEN STANCE FOREHAND GROUNDSTROKE

1. TURN SHOULDERS

2. BEND & HIT

3. EXPLODE

STANCES WITH YOUR FEET:
OPEN STANCE BACKHAND GROUNDSTROKE

1. TURN

2. BEND & HIT

3. EXPLODE

LEFT-HAND DOMINANT

**1. TURNS SHOULDERS
ON FOREHAND**

**2.TURNS SHOULDER
ON BOTH 1-HANDED &
2-HANDED BACKHANDS**

**3. FINISH ON 1-HANDED BACKHAND
LEFT HAND POINTS TO THE BACK FENCE**

CONTACT POINT:
FOREHAND - OPEN STANCE

1. IN FRONT OF FRONT FOOT

2. NEXT TO FRONT FOOT

3. BEHIND FRONT FOOT

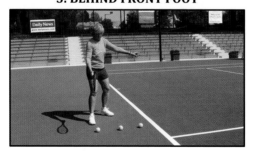

CONTACT POINT:
FOREHAND - SQUARE STANCE

1. IN FRONT OF FRONT FOOT

2. NEXT TO FRONT FOOT

3. BEHIND FRONT FOOT

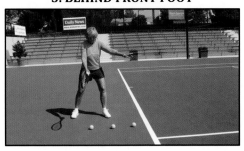

CONTACT POINT:
BACKHAND - OPEN STANCE

1. IN FRONT OF FRONT FOOT

2. NEXT TO FRONT FOOT

3. BEHIND FRONT FOOT

CONTACT POINT:
BACKHAND - SQUARE STANCE - 2-HAND

1. IN FRONT OF FRONT FOOT

2. NEXT TO FRONT FOOT

3. BEHIND FRONT FOOT

CONTACT POINT:
BACKHAND - SQUARE STANCE - 1-HAND

1. IN FRONT OF FRONT FOOT

2. NEXT TO FRONT FOOT

3. BEHIND FRONT FOOT

FINISH OR FOLLOW-THROUGH
FOREHAND - OPEN STANCE

1. IF YOU CONTACT AT#1 -
BACK OF HAND TO EAR

2. IF YOU CONTACT AT #2 -
BACK OF HAND TO LEFT SHOULDER

3. IF YOU CONTACT AT #3 -
VERTICAL OR TO RIGHT SHOULDER

FINISH OR FOLLOW-THROUGH
BACKHAND - 2-HANDED

1. OPEN STANCE - FINISH OVER SHOULDER

2. SQUARE STANCE - STEP-IN BACKHAND - FINISH OVER SHOULDER

3. SQUARE STANCE - STEP-IN BACKHAND - WITH RECOVERY STEP FINISH

FINISH OR FOLLOW-THROUGH
BACKHAND: 1-HANDED

1. BACKHAND - TOPSPIN -
EDGE OF RACQUET POINTS TO THE SKY

2. BACKHAND - SLICE -
EDGE OF RACQUET POINTS TO TARGET

3. BACKHAND - LOW SLICE -
SAME FINISH AS ABOVE - BEND KNEES MORE

APPROACH SHOTS:
FOREHAND - REGULAR - TOPSPIN

1. RUN

2. PLANT

3. HIT

APPROACH SHOTS:
FOREHAND - HIGH ROLL-OVER - TOPSPIN

1. TURN - RACQUET HIGH

2. ROLLOVER - TOP ½ OF BALL

3. FINISH - WITH FACE OF RACQUET
POINTED TO GROUND

APPROACH SHOTS:
BACKHAND - REGULAR TOPSPIN - 2-HANDED

1. RUN

2. TURN & PLANT YOUR BACK FOOT

3. FINISH

APPROACH SHOTS:
BACKHAND - SLICE - 1-HANDED

1. PLANT

2. STEP FORWARD & HIT

3. CARIOCA STEP BEHIND

OVERHEAD:
STEP-IN OVERHEAD

1. LEFT HAND PUTS RACQUET BEHIND HEAD

2. POINT TO BALL WITH LEFT HAND, WHICH IS TO RIGHT SIDE OF HEAD

3. STEP FORWARD INTO COURT WITH LEFT FOOT & HIT

OVERHEAD:
SCISSORS-KICK OVERHEAD

1. LEFT HAND PUTS RACQUET BEHIND HEAD

2. TURN & RUN

3. JUMP & HIT

SERVES:
TOSS OR PLACEMENT

1. CORRECT WAY - HOLD BALL ON FINGERTIPS

2. WRONG WAY - HOLD BALL IN PALM OF HAND

3. RELEASE POINT - AT EYE LEVEL

4 TYPES OF SERVES:
HITTING SPOT ON CLOCK

1. FLAT HIT WHERE
HANDS CONNECT ON CLOCK

2. SLICE - HIT AT 3:00

3. TOPSPIN - HIT AT 6:00

4. KICK - HIT AT 7:00

4 TYPES OF SERVES:
CONTACT POINT ON RACQUET

**2. SLICE -
HIT AT 3:00**

**1. FLAT -
HIT IN MIDDLE OF BALL**

**4. KICK -
HIT 7:00 TOWARD 3:00**

**3. TOPSPIN -
HIT 6:00 TOWARD 12:00**

RETURN OF SERVE:
FOREHAND - TOPSPIN

1. SPLIT

2. TURN SHOULDERS HALFWAY

3. FINISH - OVER YOUR SHOULDER

RETURN OF SERVE:
BACKHAND - TOPSPIN - 2-HANDED

1. SPLIT

2. TURN SHOULDERS HALFWAY

3. FINISH

SPLIT - STEP

1. SPLIT - STEP - HEELS OFF GROUND

2. SPLIT - STEP AT BASELINE

3. SPLIT - STEP AT NET

CHAPTER 5:
DEVELOPING WINNING STRATEGIES

A champion is afraid of losing. Everyone else is afraid of winning.
— Billie Jean King

Winning Strategies as Easy as 1, 2, 3 for Life:

One of the biggest problems people have with their tennis game is that they don't stay focused on the immediate game or serve. They are too busy living in the past, remembering the last time they failed to hit the ball, and focusing on the failure causes success to elude them in the present. This chapter will help you develop winning strategies that will teach you to maintain your focus and improve your game.

Live in the PRESENT.

The past is history,
The future's a mystery,
Being alive in this moment is a gift...
That is why they call it a PRESENT.
If you still have one foot in the past, and
One foot in the future, then
You are peeing on the present.
Stay in the moment. Enjoy the experience.
— Author Unknown

We focus too much if the ball is going in the court (FUTURE)

We focus too much on what happened in the last game, or the last point (PAST)

Instead of focusing on the routine (PRESENT)

Positive Intention, Not Negative Expectation

Imagine in your mind the tennis ball going into the court. That is an image of a positive intention, rather than a negative expectation. Being concerned about what the result will be is different from envisioning a result you intend to occur. There is no tension in the body when you just have an image. In fact, an image of a good shot actually reduces tension.

Worry creates an entirely different feeling in your body and a different focus for your mind. It can lead you further into the future. If you are worrying about the score, then your mind is already there. Think about it; your body hasn't even hit the shot, but your mind is already in the future. Clearly, your body and mind are not synchronized.

Your Brain has Two Parts

1) The thinking side of your brain; and
2) The intuitive side, which controls your motor coordination.

It takes about ten seconds for a message to get from one side of your brain to the other.

Experts say that tennis is ninety percent mental. So your mind is the most important part of your game.

Your mind has different components:

A) The thinking mind, which develops concepts and words

   o Paralysis from analysis

B) The intuitive mind

   o Knowing without thinking or analyzing
   o The basis of our habits
   o Learning through repetition
   o "Muscle memory"

C) The critical mind

   o Evaluates
   o Judges

- ○ Descriptions in terms of good and bad
- ○ Our mind could be our own worst enemy
- ○ Negative talk, self-doubt

Plan with Your Head. Play with Your Heart.

You Must Give Up Control to Get Control.

An example of this is to write your name in big letters on a piece of paper. Now, try to trace it perfectly.

- The ego-centered, self-conscious thinking mind is what needs to give up control.
- The intuitive mind is what gets control. It just goes. The intuitive mind is the expert at running the body.

Change Your Old Habits.

Research says your brain does not know the difference between what is real and what isn't real. This means you can improve your tennis without ever being on the tennis court, physically hitting tennis balls. So if you practice just your tennis swing for twenty-one days straight, you will improve. The key to this change is when you take your practice swings in your living room at home; you have to swing the exact same way that you would if you were physically hitting a tennis ball on the tennis court. Doing this action for twenty-one days straight will change your "muscle memory," thereby improving any of your tennis strokes.

An example of this happened with me. I was taught the "old way" to hold the racquet to play tennis, with a continental, "universal grip, one-grip fits all." I knew I had to make the change to the new modern grips. So I practiced for about twenty minutes a day for twenty-one days in my house, holding the racquet, changing my grip from forehand to backhand and vice versa. I changed to my "new" grip, took three to four running steps over to where I pretended the ball was and set my feet properly. I then imagined I was hitting a ball, swung as fast as if I were on the tennis court, heard the "swish" sound with my racquet flying through the air and shuffled back three to four steps to get back into ready position, noticing where my grip was.

I had to prove to myself that this technique worked. I'd been hitting tennis balls with the "old" grip for many, many years. I knew if this worked for me, it would work for anyone. It's also a great workout, if you actually pretend you are hitting a ball.

It is also a great way to practice your visualization skills. Visualize yourself hitting the ball; see it going into the court, exactly where you planned it. Visualize what you want, and be very specific. Feel it, touch it, smell it, taste it. Visualization is one of the most powerful tools we can call upon. Unfortunately, it is often neglected. Picture the ball going exactly where you planned it. Picture and feel what it would be like to win a tournament and receive your trophy. How would that feel for you? This technique will work with any stroke in tennis. Just be patient and do it for twenty-one days straight. You will be amazed at the improvement in your game!

Visualization Works in Other Areas of Your Life.

What field of work would really make you happy? How would your life change if you had your "dream job?" Children are sometimes much better than adults at visualizing. They have great imaginations. When they tell imaginary stories, they reenact the story as if it were real.

My family went to Hawaii over the summer for vacation and decided to rent a condominium there for the first time. My stepdaughter, Remi, was using an outdoor shower for the first time, surrounded by beautiful trees, birds chirping and the Hawaiian breeze in her face. The outdoor shower was right outside the bathroom. She thought it was one of the greatest inventions she had ever seen.

She said to me, "Pat-Pat, I think we should buy a house in Hawaii. Our house will have two outdoor showers, and in the bathroom, above our tub, we'll have three big pictures of the ocean. They'll be so big that they'll take up the whole wall and it will look like the ocean waves are crashing through the wall. When you open the door to the bathroom, it will sound like ocean waves are crashing on the sand. Every time you turn the handle and open the door, you will hear the wave sounds." It already feels like we bought our house in Hawaii, doesn't it? A six-and-a-half year-old child understands how to visualize. We need to learn from our children. That's why they are here; to teach us some lessons we've forgotten.

A Picture is Worth a Thousand Words.

How many times have you heard that? Watch a professional tennis match on television, and usually the next time you play, your game is better. It really improves if you visualize and see yourself hitting those same shots. Visualize Rafael Nadal following through on his forehand groundstroke, all the way past his shoulder. Picture that and you will duplicate that vision.

If you want to fix a flaw in your tennis swing, have someone videotape your swing. It is a beautiful thing when I videotape my students. I do not have to say the same correction repeatedly; they see it for themselves. Most people learn better visually than audibly. So if you have told someone that his racquet is too high in the backswing, and you have said it at least fifty times, show him a videotape of his backswing. You will hardly ever have to say that to him again. A picture *is* worth a thousand words!

Key Issues that Have an Impact on the Quality of a Tennis Match

Stay in the present and do not be distracted by the results or thoughts of the outcome.

Take it:

One point at a time. One game at a time. One match at a time.

Composure and focus. Have a clear picture in your mind before you hit the shot. Know where the shot is going to land; picture it landing in that exact spot.

Gather yourself; gather a good picture.

Trust your swing and play within yourself.

Nothing special; nothing extra.

Don't be hard on yourself when you make a mistake.

Take care of the process and the results will take care of themselves.

You Produce What You Fear.

FEAR = False **E**vidence **A**ppearing **R**eal – *or–*
Forget **E**verything **A**nd **R**un

Fear creates a magnitude of feelings in your body. Our bodies are geared to freeze and stop breathing when we experience fear. Think of the expression, "You look like a deer caught in the headlights."

When you're playing tennis, and you think to yourself as you're getting ready to serve, "Don't double fault. Don't double fault." You know what will happen—yes you *will* double fault.

Fear creates a feeling of low self-worth and low self-esteem. Fear can make us feel bad about ourselves, where we actually berate ourselves for making a bad shot.

True Fearlessness.

Rather than try to get rid of your fear, go through it...***true fearlessness.***

- Put it all into perspective.
- Perspective = insight.
    - Win or lose, my kid will still love me.
    - Win or lose, my dog will still lick me.
    - Win or lose, my partner will still be my friend.

- You must accept the possibilities of both good and bad results, without taking them on as measures of your self-worth! Avoid thoughts such as:
  - "I am so bad, because I played bad today."
  - "I suck."
  - "I am a loser."
  - "I will never win."
    - The results have nothing to do with what kind of person you are. Nevertheless, many people take on that role. You must separate your task, good or bad, from the kind of person you are.
- Take your tennis seriously, but do not take yourself too seriously.
- Take negative images of what you *don't* want to happen, and replace them with positive images of what you *do* want to happen.
- Which is greater, the fear of success, or the fear of failure?
- Which is greater, the fear of winning, or the fear of losing?

Focus on what you want to happen, not on what you fear might.

Trust.

Trust your body and your mind. When you throw a ball to a partner, do you have to analyze how to do it? Do you have to think about rotating your shoulders, putting your left hand across your body and laying your wrist back to get ready to throw the ball? Do you have to think about how many fingers are touching the ball at the time you're ready to release the ball? Do you have to think about where you should release the ball to throw it to your partner, who is standing diagonally from you? No, of course not. You just trust your intuitive mind and throw the ball to your partner.

When you play tennis, trust that you are playing "keep-away" from your opponent. That's really all you are doing when playing the game. Your instincts know how to play "keep-away." Don't think about how you are precisely moving your body to get to a certain place on the court. Your body will just get there. That is the intuitive mind working. You must trust this process.

If you could trust your body (your intuitive mind) to hit the shot and not care about the results, you would cut down on unforced errors.

Before you hit the ball, mentally say a phrase, such as: "Let it fly," or "It's all yours," or "Take over."

Trust that the swing you have practiced for years will return. It may have just taken a temporary vacation.

We always remember our bad shots more than we remember our good shots. This fear of missing the shot undermines your confidence and interferes with your swinging freely. Let the bad thoughts come and go. Do not hold onto them. Let them blow away like the wind. Experience your thoughts; then let them go.

The Glass of Muddy Water

If you stir a glass of muddy water, it will stay muddy. Take the spoon out and let all the dirt settle to the bottom and the water will become clear.

Like the glass of muddy water, when you struggle with your thoughts over and over, they remain stirred up. Instead, stop giving them energy. Let them come and go in your spacious mind of non-judgmental awareness. After a while, they will settle themselves and your mind will be clear.

Do not give anything that much power!

Extra Baggage

Get rid of all of the extra mind baggage that is holding you back such as:

    A) Lower expectations
    B) Trying too hard
    C) Worrying so much

Play within yourself

On a scale of 1-10, one is the softest you can hit the ball over the net, and still use a full swing, and ten is the hardest you can possibly hit the ball over the net. How many tennis balls in a row can you hit over the net at a swing speed of ten and never miss? At five?

Don't try to "hit the cover off" the ball on every shot. Work on hitting different spins and different paces. Work on variety (it is the spice of life). It's not who hits the ball harder who wins; it is who is smarter.

Practice hitting:

- Three balls in a row. Do five sets of three in a row. If you miss, you must start from the beginning of the set again.
- Five balls in a row. Do five sets of five in a row. If you miss, you must start from the beginning of the set again.
- Seven balls in a row. Do five sets of seven in a row. If you miss, you must start from the beginning of the set again.

Remember, you only have to get the ball over the net one more time than your opponent does.

You receive the same point, if you hit a winner, or if your opponent misses. You do not get an extra point if you hit a winner or if you hit it harder than your opponent does.

If you are struggling with consistency, hit five balls in a row before you try to hit the ball harder (your "big" shot). Be steady for the first five shots, and then you can step up your pace a little bit. If can you hit five balls in a row, that would be a ten-ball rally. Most people miss before reaching that number.

Momentum

Momentum is a very big part of any game or sports event. It is also important in life. You have heard the saying that things happen in three's. I find that true in my teaching: 1, 2, 3. Momentum changes in a tennis match; it changes in a set; it changes in a game; and it often changes during the point. Therefore, if you always stay in the moment, you can flow with momentum much more easily.

There are two times that momentum seems to have a big effect during play:

1) **Focus on the third point in the game.** It is a big "momentum swinger." For example, if the server is serving at 30-love and wins the next point, it is now 40-love. Mentally, most people don't try as hard if they are losing at 40-love. On the other hand, if the server is serving at 30-love and the returner wins the next point, now the score is 30-15. Mentally, there is a big difference in those two scores. The returner now thinks he is back in the game.

2) **Focus on the seventh game.** This is also a big "momentum swinger" for winning or losing the set. For example, if Brad is ahead in the set, 4-2, and wins the next game, the score will be 5-2. But if Larry, his opponent, wins the game, the score is now 4-3. Mentally, this is one of the biggest momentum swingers for winning and losing matches.

Care vs. Worry

Earlier, we talked about not worrying so much. Worry causes tension in your body, and therefore, you cannot perform as well. Worry is using the thinking side of your mind too much.

Care about making the shot or not, but do not *worry* about making the shot.

Strike Zone

When you're playing tennis, you want to feel relaxed and in control of your shots. The more you hit the ball in the same place above the ground and in front of your body, the more consistent you will be as a player. The best players in the world are the players who can hit the ball the same way more times than the other players.

We all have varying degrees of how high off the ground we want to hit the ball. It depends on the player's height, grip, and confidence level with different heights of the ball in the air. The key is footwork. The better your footwork, the better you will strike the ball.

One of the hardest shots for people to hit is a slow, high, loopy ball that goes high over the net. Players feel as if they have three days to hit it. *That's* the ball that people miss. What happens is while they see the ball coming *slowly* toward them, their brains think they have plenty of time to hit it, so they wait longer to turn their shoulders and get ready. Because they don't get ready immediately, they end up being off balance when they hit the shot so they miss it.

The next time you see this high, soft, easy, loopy ball coming to you, use that extra time to move your feet more than you usually do and try to get into perfect position to hit the shot perfectly on balance.

Most people hit the ball most consistently by hitting it at waist level. Some people like to attack the ball more; therefore, they are going to strike the ball at chest or shoulder height. You can also hit the ball at knee level, but you have to spin the ball more and you have to back up much more to let it come down to your knee level.

Strike Zone 1, 2, 3...

- Waist Level
- Chest Level
- Knee Level

Roger Federer is the best person you could watch to simulate footwork for high, soft, loopy balls. He uses that extra time to get into perfect position with his feet so he is always on balance while attacking that shot.

Patterns Prepare Your Strategy

For your singles strategy, remember that most people are creatures of habit; they tend to hit the same shots repeatedly. This is usually because they have the most confidence in those certain shots. So if you can start noticing the pattern your opponent is using with you, then you can anticipate better where the ball will go.

Notice, for example, when you serve wide to your opponent's forehand where he usually hits the return. Try to keep track of where that shot lands. If you hit a short ball, where does your opponent usually hit it— down the line, or cross-court? When you charge up to the net, does your opponent hit a passing shot, or lob every time? Where does your opponent generally serve into the deuce service box? Is it the same on the ad side? Keep noticing where your opponent serves most of the time in the two service boxes. Again, we are creatures of habit. We tend to repeat the same patterns.

You need to have a strategy when you get ready for a match. Know your strengths and weaknesses. A good way to have a plan, or a pattern, is to practice first, then put that strategy into play when you are in a match.

When playing singles from the baseline, here is a formula that works very well:

1) The 3-1 pattern: Hit three balls to one corner (the backhand corner) and then hit one ball to the opposite corner (the forehand corner).
2) The 2-1 pattern: Hit two balls to one corner (the backhand corner) and then hit one ball to the opposite corner (the forehand corner).
3) The 1-1 pattern: Hit one ball to one corner (the backhand corner) and then hit one ball to the opposite corner (the forehand corner).

With these patterns, watch your opponent run as you control the point. It does not matter what your opponent hits back; you stick with your pattern.

Winning Strategies as Easy as 1, 2, 3 for Playing Singles

If you can count to three, then you can play successful tennis!

Where to Stand Playing Singles

Where to stand at the baseline, playing singles:

Stand at least five feet behind the baseline when in ready position. Directly behind the hash mark, is position #2. One little step to the right of it, is position #1. One little step to the left of # 2, is position #3. Being behind the baseline gives you a greater chance of seeing the whole court and you can run on diagonals to intercept the ball. If you position your body behind Circle #1, notice if you looked forward toward the net, you will make a straight line to #1 circle at the net, and the #1 circle on the other side of the net.

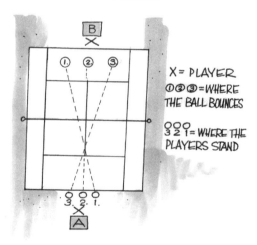

You should hit cross-court most of the time when you are rallying and not trying to put the ball away from the baseline. It is easier to hit the ball crosscourt because:

1) The net is six inches lower in the middle.
2) There is more court to hit toward.
3) You can make your opponent run more.

Where to stand at the net, playing singles:

Stand halfway between the net and the service line, straddling the center service line. This is position #2. The #1 position is one giant step to the left of #2. The #3 position is one giant step to the right of #2.

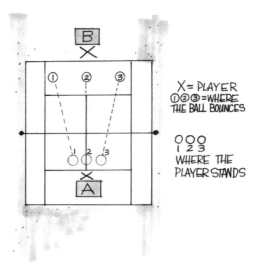

You should hit to the open court as much as possible when in your volley position. Make your opponent run the most, so he has a harder time hitting a passing shot on the run, or so he cannot hit a great lob on the run.

The simplest strategy for singles is when you play the baseline. Line up on the *opposite* side to where the ball will bounce. When you go to the net, you should line up on the *same* side as where the ball will bounce.

If you get a short ball, an approach shot, try to hit it down the line most of the time. The reason for this is that hitting down the line makes your opponent take more steps to the ball, while you have to take fewer steps to get into position to make a good volley—1, 2, or 3 by following the path the ball has gone on the other side of the net. The exception to that rule is if your opponent is standing on the down-the-line side of the court, because that's where the last ball was hit. That's when you hit a crosscourt shot, to make your opponent run more.

Keep your strategy as simple as you can. Now that you know where to stand when you play singles, you will be able to run your opponent all over the court and you will have to run less. That sounds like a great plan, doesn't it?

My 5' 0" Haeja Rule:

There was a student named Haeja in one of my drill classes. She was 5' 0" tall. One day I made her lie down on the court, with her heels at the end of the baseline. We marked off where the top of her head was behind the baseline. When she got up, we charted a dotted white line in an arc that extended from baseline to baseline. At the top of the arc was 5' 0". Now we just refer to the "Haeja Rule."

You should think of the "Haeja Rule" as you are playing a singles point from the baseline. You always want to go back to the 5' 0" foot area. From there, you see the entire court and can easily move forward to cut off the angles. When you shuffle back toward the middle of the court, shuffle back in the arc motion, as seen with the dots in illustration.

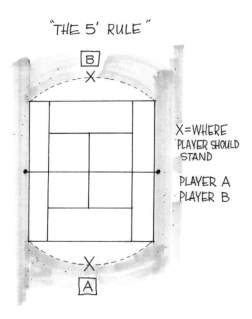

"THE 5' RULE"

X=WHERE PLAYER SHOULD STAND

PLAYER A
PLAYER B

A problem is that people move forward to get a groundstroke and then shuffle back toward the center of the court, standing on the baseline, instead of five feet behind it. What commonly happens as a result of not using this rule is:

- After hitting the serve, you must take two steps back behind the baseline.
- After returning the serve, you must shuffle back toward the middle of the court in the arc formation.

Seven Ways to Get to the Net

For years I have taught that you want to come to the net, when the "party is at the net." (You must say that with a New York accent to get the full flavor of the statement) To come to the net effectively, you should wait for an invitation. An invitation to the net is a short ball from your opponent. You want to know that you can hit this shot, and make your opponent run while you are getting into a good volley or net position. Therefore, if you are going to the net, you are going on an "invitation only" approach.

However, there are more ways than one to go to a party. In high school, we "crashed" a few parties. Here are some strategies you can use to "crash" the party and get to the net without an invitation. By doing this, you are forcing the issue and taking time away from your opponent, who is used to the ball bouncing on your side to get back into a good position toward the center of the court.

Here are some other ways to go to the net:

1) **By you hitting an approach shot.** This is when your opponent hits a short ball to you, which usually lands inside the service line. This is the most common way to get to the net.
2) **By you serving and volleying.** This is when you decide in advance that you are going to assume your serve will go in and you are going to follow your serve in to the net.

3) **By you chipping and charging.** That is done after your opponent hits a serve, mostly a second serve, and you slice the ball to keep it low, down the line, and charge the net.

4) **By you hitting a short-angle roll shot.** You must hit the outside of the ball to make the ball land short and wide, preferably inside the service box, to pull your opponent well outside the singles sideline. (The outside of the ball is the 3 o'clock position on the clock. We'll discuss strokes in relation to positions of the clock at the end of this chapter).

5) **By you hitting a deep moon ball.** You must hit the ball three racquet-lengths over the net with topspin so the ball hits the ground and bounces up toward the back fence. As soon as you see your opponent move backwards to get the shot, you start sneaking in toward the net. By the time your opponent hits the ball back, you've reached the net.

6) **By you hitting a very deep groundstroke that pulls your opponent off the court.** You must hit this so your opponent strikes the ball from a very defensive position. As soon as you see your opponent is in trouble, you start taking one to two steps inside the court.

7) **By you hitting a drop shot.** You hit a drop shot so that your opponent has to run all the way in from the baseline. As your opponent runs in, you are also running forward to guard against your opponent hitting a drop shot back to you. You can split-step around the service line, which is before your opponent hits the ball.

Using the Serve and Volley in Singles

Even though the serve and volley strategy is not used very much in today's game of tennis, it is being used more frequently as a change of tactics to surprise an opponent. It is a good way to attack your opponent and give him less time to set up properly to hit the ball back.

Here are three serve and volley strategies to use occasionally. You can also use these the same way when serving to the ad court.

Strategy #1:

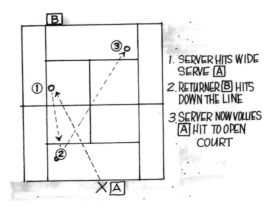

1. SERVER HITS WIDE SERVE [A]
2. RETURNER [B] HITS DOWN THE LINE
3. SERVER NOW VOLLIES [A] HIT TO OPEN COURT

A) The server hits the serve wide.
B) The opponent hits the ball back down the line or sometimes to the middle of the court; rarely does the ball go extremely cross-court.
C) The person hitting the volley hits the ball into the open court.

Strategy #2:

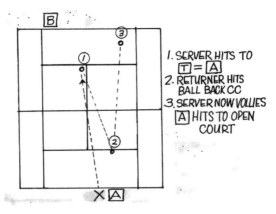

1. SERVER HITS TO [T] = [A]
2. RETURNER HITS BALL BACK CC
3. SERVER NOW VOLLIES [A] HITS TO OPEN COURT

A) The server hits the serve to the "T."
B) The returner hit the ball back cross-court.
C) The person hitting the volley hits the ball into the open court, deep.

Strategy #3:

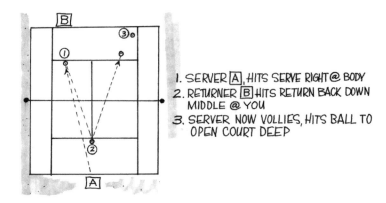

1. SERVER Ⓐ, HITS SERVE RIGHT @ BODY
2. RETURNER Ⓑ HITS RETURN BACK DOWN
   MIDDLE @ YOU
3. SERVER NOW VOLLIES, HITS BALL TO
   OPEN COURT DEEP

A) The server serves directly at the opponent's body.
B) The returner hits the ball back down the middle, directly at the server.
C) The person hitting the volley hits the ball into the open court, deep.

If you do serve and volley, you need to have a definite plan of where you are going to aim the ball. That way, you do not care if your opponent hits the return to your forehand or your backhand; you already have your plan of where to put the volley. If executed properly, you will make your opponent run and you will be set up well for the next volley to put the ball away.

Winning Strategies as Easy as 1, 2, 3 for Playing Doubles

If you can count to three, then you can play successful tennis!

Where to Stand Playing Doubles

Where to stand at the baseline, playing doubles

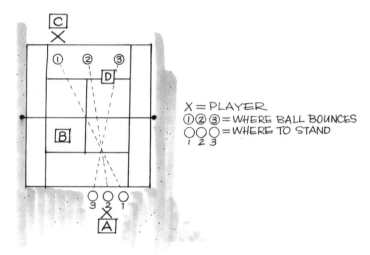

X = PLAYER
①②③ = WHERE BALL BOUNCES
○○○ = WHERE TO STAND
1 2 3

Stand at least three feet behind the baseline when in ready position. Approximately halfway between the hash mark and the doubles sideline, is position #2. One little step to the right of that is position #1. One little step to the left of #2, is position #3. You don't stand quite as far behind the baseline while playing doubles as you do in singles because you are always looking for the ball so you can get in toward the net and attack it. If you play too deep from the baseline, then you may play too much of a defensive doubles game. If you position your body behind Circle #1 at the baseline, and look toward the net, you will make a straight line to the #1 circle on your side of the court at the net, and the #1 circle at the baseline diagonal from you on the other side of the net. You should hit cross-court most of the time when you are rallying. Look for an opportunity to come to the net on any short ball that is hit to you. You should not hit down the line too much because you are very vulnerable if the volley will be hit between you and your partner down the middle for a winner. Only go down the line, generally, if you think you can hit a winner there, or if the court is open.

Where to stand at the net, playing doubles:

Stand halfway between the net and the service line. Make an imaginary "X" in the middle of the service box. That is your #2, neutral, position for doubles. Take one giant step to your left of #2. This is your #1 position. Take one giant step to the right of #2 positions. That is your #3 volleying position.

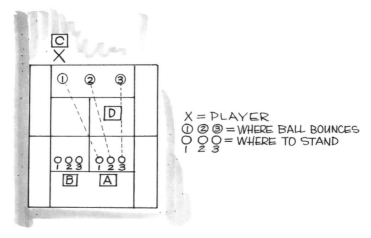

In playing doubles at the net, you and your partner should try to stay as close together as possible for the optimum playing level. If you are at the net at the same time, pretend you are joined together by a rope between your waists. The tighter the rope stays, the better your chances of covering the net well. Your goal is to try to stay the same distance from your partner at all times. That is when you feel you are a team playing together, instead of two people playing singles on a doubles team.

Therefore, the simplest doubles strategy is that when you play the baseline, you line up on the ***opposite*** side as where the ball bounces. When you go to the net, you line up on the ***same*** side as where the ball bounces.

If you get a short ball, an approach shot, you should hit it cross-court most of the time. The reason is if you hit the approach shot to the net person, he can put it away easier. A good cross-court approach shot will many times set up your partner to put the volley away down the middle, if he has moved over to the correct position. Remember, your goal is, "The party is at the net!" Try to beat your opponents there. Whoever gets to the net first usually wins and has much more fun. If you and your partner are at the net, and both people know the 1, 2, 3 tennis by numbers theory, you will have eighty percent of the court covered. Let your opponents win twenty percent of the points. If you are at the net and they hit a few great shots, then that may happen. But that's the only way they will win...with a GRRREAT shot, which doesn't happen very often. They will never win a match if they only win twenty percent of the points.

"THE PARTY IS AT THE NET"

Where to move at the net, playing doubles:

You are the partner at the net when your partner is serving. You should position yourself in the middle of the service box. Make an imaginary "X" in the middle of the box and stand where the "X" connects. That should be halfway between the service line and the net. That is your neutral, starting position. Most people play too close to the net, or too close to the alley.

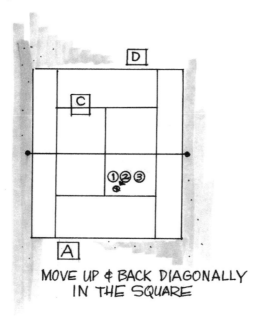

MOVE UP & BACK DIAGONALLY
IN THE SQUARE

When your partner is serving to the deuce court: If your partner serves the ball wide, close to the singles sideline, then you should take one-step to your left, to Circle #1, and split-step. If your partner serves the ball to the T, stay in the middle of the box, at Circle #2, and look to see if you can poach that ball.

After the serve is returned, the net player must move a lot if her partner stays at the baseline. The net player's first objective is to try to intercept the ball at the net. If that player can't reach the shot, she must move back diagonally two steps toward the center of the court, toward the T. She should then focus her attention on the net player on the other side of the court (Player D).

If Player B's partner hits the ball cross-court to Player C, then Player B moves back to Circle #1 or Circle #2. Depending on where the ball lands, you should try to get to Circle #1 or Circle #2 before your opponents hit the ball. That way, you are ready for an alley shot, or you can intercept the ball in the middle of the court. You are at the net in perfect volley position to try to intercept the ball being hit by Player C. If Player C hits a good cross-court shot again, you, Player B, must again move back diagonally two steps, watching your opponent (Player D) in case she intercepts the ball down the middle of the court.

On the other hand, if your partner hits a shot down the line, then you are close to the T, to cut off the middle of the court for your opponent. In addition, it gives you more time to react if your partner does not hit cross-court well enough. By moving in this manner, you are also active at the net and will always play better. Many times, just by constantly moving at the net, your opponents will accidentally look at you moving, instead of at the ball. When that happens, it usually leads to an error by your opponents.

The key to this much moving is that you must do your split-step before your opponents hit the ball, even if you are not in perfect position. You will primarily be moving diagonally forward and backward between Circle #1 and Circle #3, (which is close to the T). If your partner moves up to the net with you, then you do not have to go backward to Circle #3, rather just side to side. That means much less moving for your partner. That is why higher-level doubles teams come to the net much more. They save each other from so much moving up and back.

When your partner is serving to the ad court: If your partner serves the ball wide, close to the singles sideline, you should take one step to your right, Circle #3 and split-step. If your partner serves the ball to the T, stay in the middle of the box, at Circle #2 and look to see if you can poach that ball.

After the serve is returned, the net player must move in the same way she moved, while her partner was serving in the deuce court. The net player is still trying to intercept the ball at the net. If she cannot reach the shot, she must now move back two steps diagonally toward the center of the court, toward the T.

She should focus her attention on the net player on the other side of the court (Player C). If Player A hits the ball cross-court to Player D, then Player B moves back to Circle #3 or Circle #2, depending on where the ball lands. You should still try to get to Circle #3 or Circle #2 before your opponents hit the ball. You will be ready for the alley shot, or try to intercept the ball down the middle of the court. The movement is all the same as it was from the other service box, just reversed.

When you are the partner standing on the service line, and your partner is getting ready to receive the serve, you should position yourself on the service line, a little closer to the middle, or by the T. This actually cuts off the angle toward the middle of the court.

When your partner is returning serve from the deuce court, you must stand at the service line. The first job for the partner standing on the service line is to call the serve out if it lands past the service line. Then once the ball is inside the box, the net person should focus her attention on the net person.

Rule to memorize: If the net person is hitting the ball, stay at the service line and get low and get ready, because the ball is probably coming to you. If the ball goes past the net person (cross-court), then immediately move forward toward the net to Circle #1 or Circle #2, depending on where the ball lands. Now the net person must move up and back diagonally, as previously discussed. The net person always moves up and back diagonally, depending on where the ball is going to land. These movements are very quick and precise.

When your partner is returning serve from the ad court, you must stand at the service line. Again, stand a little closer to the T, to cut off any ball hit toward the middle of the court. Call the ball out if it lands behind the service line.

Once the ball lands inside the service box, watch the net person to see whether she is going to get the ball, or poach. If she gets the ball, stay at the service line and get low because it is coming toward you. If it goes past the net person to the cross-court corner, then move forward two steps and a split-step. You will move forward toward Circle # 3 or Circle #2, depending on where the ball lands.

Do the same footwork as described above. Remember, when you have to move diagonally backward toward the T, look at the net person again to cover up her easiest shot to the middle of the court.

Where to move when serving, playing doubles:

When you are serving, you have two choices where to move afterwards:

1) Serve and volley; or
2) Serve and stay back (behind the baseline).

1. Serve and Volley: The key to a good serve and volley game is to plan that you are going to serve and volley before you serve. You must first assume that your serve is going in the box, and second, split-step wherever you are before your opponent hits the ball. If you map out the steps going toward the net, it is three steps and then a split-step. That puts most people right in front of the service line as they approach the net.

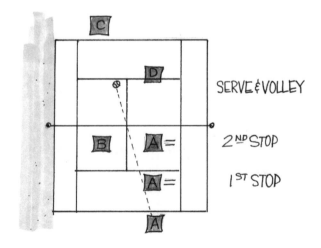

A common mistake occurs when people try to run to the service line before they split-step. The split-step is the most important part of the serve and volley. If you have a proper split-step, then you are on balance to move side-to-side or to go forward or backward, depending on where the opponent hits the ball. How far you get in toward the net depends on how fast your serve is and how fast you run.

Most people think they can only go toward the net after their first serve and then they never go in after their second serve. As long as the second serve is not really short, it is still a good idea to go in after your second serve to take over the net position. Most people serve slower on the second serve, so you have more time to get into a better net position, closer to the net. Don't go in if your serve generally always lands short and the opponent is attacking your second serve, coming forward.

2. Serve and Stay Back: The biggest flaw people have when serving while playing doubles is they serve, watch their serve go in and then they are stuck one or two steps inside the baseline. This is known as "No-Man's Land," now known as the transition zone. If you have decided you are going to serve and stay back, then hit your serve and follow-through by taking a step inside the baseline. Now take two big steps backward, so you are behind the baseline.

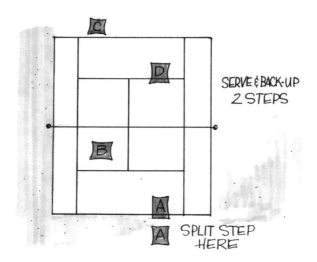

You never want to wait one or two steps inside the baseline. If you take those two big steps back behind the baseline, then you have time to move forward into your next shot. If your opponents hit a deep cross-court groundstroke deep into your court, you have time to back up and still hit it in front of you, to keep it cross-court, away from the net person straight across from you. It is always easier to move forward than to move backward, especially at the last minute. So, remember, after your serve: Take two giant steps backward behind the baseline.

Plan ahead when serving and volleying for doubles.

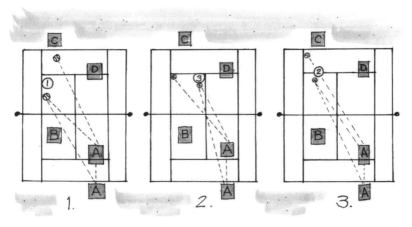

When you step up to the baseline to serve for doubles, you want to have a plan. Plan the shot and then trust your intuitive mind to react to the shot. When you serve and volley, you want to have a game plan so you're not surprised when the ball comes back at you with great speed. Plans can always be altered, but you want to start with your game plan.

When you stand at the baseline, you want to plan:

1) Where your serve is going to go
2) Where return is going to be hit
3) Where you are going to hit your first volley

It's like playing chess. Plan your strategy, knowing where your opponents hit the return most of the time. Obviously, the return will be different at times, but for the most part, we are creatures of habit, and playing doubles, the return comes back to the same area seventy percent of the time.

Depending on where you serve the ball decides where you are going to plan to hit your first volley. Remember, it's like playing "keep-away" from your opponent. You want to hit the ball where your opponent has to run the most to try to return your volley.

1) If the server hits the serve to Target #1 (the wide serve), then hit the first volley to the "T."
2) If the server hits the serve to Target #2 (at the body), then hit the first volley back deep cross-court.
3) If the server hits the serve to Target #3 (the "T" serve), then hit the first volley to the short angle.

Another easy way to think about this strategy is that if you hit the serve wide, to the angle, hit the next shot to the "T." If your opponents hit the ball back again, then hit the next volley to the short angle. If your opponents happen to get the next ball back, then hit the next volley to the "T." The point should be over by then!

The strategy is the same if you serve the ball to the "T." Hit the first volley to the angle. If your opponents get the next ball back, then hit the volley to the "T." If they hit the next ball back, then hit the next volley to the short angle. Again, that point should put the ball away!

Again, play keep-away with one person, so his partner cannot help him, and he feels helpless. When the ball finally does go to the net person, he is not ready for the shot and is in a very vulnerable position on the court.

Where to move when the lob is hit over your head in doubles

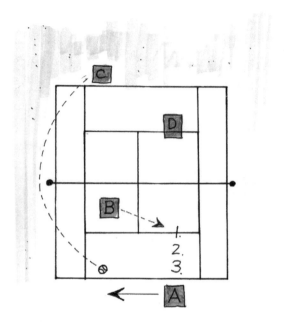

If the ball goes over your head, you must *yell* (or call) out, "Mine." This means you will get the ball. Or *yell* (or call) out, "Yours." This means your partner is responsible for getting the lob. There is really no right or wrong call, as long as you make some call, "Yours" or "Mine," the second the ball goes up high in the air.

If you say, "Mine," then you should be setting up your feet, getting ready to hit an overhead out of the air. Your partner should be parallel to you, as you hit the overhead out of the air. If you hit a good over-head, you and your partner should move back in toward the net.

If you say, "Mine," start running back to hit the overhead out of the air. If the ball happens to be too deep, or if you misjudged the ball's height in the air, and you cannot take the overhead out of the air, then run back behind the ball, let it bounce and then hit the ball back after the bounce as a lob. Do not call, "Mine," then realize it is too far over your head and say, "Yours" for your partner to try to get it. This NEVER works! Your partner cannot run the ball down at the last second and be expected to hit it back with last-second notice.

If you say, "Yours," when the lob is hit over your head, then your partner is now responsible for getting the ball that has gone deep over your head. It is easiest to run back in a diagonal line, let the ball bounce, and hit it back as a:

1) Lob: If you are barely able to get to the ball.
2) Driving forehand or backhand groundstroke: If your partner is fast, and beats the ball back toward the baseline, she can let it come down to her waist level and hit it low over the net, so it is at the net opponent's feet.
3) Overhead: Again, if your partner is fast, and beats the ball back to the baseline, she can let the ball bounce and hit it as an overhead.

If you say, "Yours," then your partner runs back in a diagonal line to get behind the ball. You should *never* just switch directly across to the other service box. You should go to one of three positions:

1) At least (minimum) to the service line.
2) Back to "No-Man's Land."
3) All the way back to the baseline, with your partner.

Remember:

Always move back in a diagonal line. Make sure you split-step before your opponent hits the next shot. No matter how far you go backward, split-step before you hit the shot. Get low and get ready. Do not continue to move backward when the ball is being struck.

Where to hit the ball when at the net for poaching in doubles:

1.   EXCEPTION: LOW BALL

POACHING means taking away or intercepting your partner's shot. This is why you want to put the ball away—so your partner doesn't yell at you for technically "taking her shot."

When you are poaching, if you physically cross the center service line (with your feet), you should keep moving diagonally and switch sides of the court with your partner. If you cross the center service line, your partner is responsible for switching sides with you by crossing behind you because she sees you crossing in front of her.

If you go for the poach, but you technically do not cross the center service line, then you should NOT cross to the opposite side. You should go back to where you were.

If your partner is serving, you should be standing in the middle of the box, at Circle #2.

Things to keep in mind when poaching:

1) Have a plan in your head where you want the ball to land on the other side of the net.
2) Always move in a diagonal line toward the net. Never move sideways to try to intercept the ball. By moving in a diagonal line, you:

- Cut off the angle of the shot early.
- Get to the ball when it is higher above the net, which makes the volley easier.
- Have a better chance of making the shot.

3) Don't leave your "spot" until the ball bounces. If you leave before the bounce, then your opponents will have enough time to hit the ball down your alley, where you just left a big hole down the line.

If your partner is serving and you are at Circle #2, after the ball bounces, go diagonally toward the white net strap (it should be on every net). Hit the poach to:

- First choice—Halfway between the service line and the net, right at the singles sideline.
- Second choice—At the net person's feet, at the service line. Try to land the ball right on the service line. It should *not* land in front of this because it would be too easy to return the shot.
- Third choice—Aim the ball to land past the service line, down the middle, behind the net person.

The exception to the rule of hitting one of these three shots is if the shot you are poaching is below the net level when you hit it. Then you should hit it back as a cross-court, soft drop shot.

Where to hit volley in doubles:

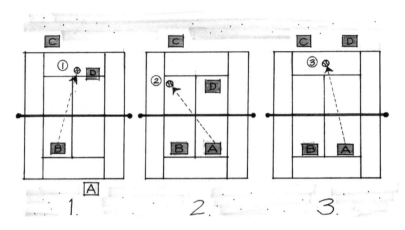

1.   2.   3.

1) If the deep person is directly in front of you, whether you get a forehand volley, or a backhand volley, hit the ball to the "T." (B hits to #1)

2) If the deep person is diagonally across from you and you are in regular volley position, hit the volley to the short angle cross-court. You want to land it on the singles sideline, halfway between the service line and the net. (A hits to #2)

3) If both people are deep at the baseline, and you are in regular volley position, hit the ball deep down the middle, past the service line. The person who plays the ball back should hit the next volley to the short angle that is left open. When you hit your volley down the middle, both players first have to figure out who is supposed to get the shot, and then they still have to hit it over. . (A hits to #3)

Where to hit the ball when difficult shots are hit to you;
Playing the net in doubles

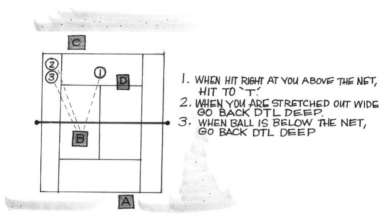

1. WHEN HIT RIGHT AT YOU ABOVE THE NET,
   HIT TO "T."
2. WHEN YOU ARE STRETCHED OUT WIDE
   GO BACK DTL DEEP.
3. WHEN BALL IS BELOW THE NET,
   GO BACK DTL DEEP

How you handle a difficult shot depends on where the ball is hit to you:

1) If the ball is hit directly to you, above the net, and it is either a forehand volley or a backhand volley, then hit the ball past the "T" in a diagonal line. This means the ball should go past and behind the net person and it should land so it is away from the deep opponent, who just hit it to you.

2) If the ball is hit to you when you are stretched out wide, toward the doubles sideline, hit the ball back down the line, preferably deep.

   • It is easier to hit the ball straight back over the net when you are barely able to reach the ball.

   • You are also in a much better position for the next ball because you hit the ball to Target #1; then you have to recover for the ball coming back at Circle #1. It is a lesser distance that you have to get ready for the next shot.

   • It is easier not to have to change the angle of the ball when it is hit wide to you. Hit it back in the same direction that it came from.

3) If by the time you make contact with the ball, it is below the net because it was hit hard and low, that is another time when you should hit the volley back deep down the line. Otherwise, if you

try to hit to the "T," you will be hitting the ball up to the other net person. They will have a high ball they will then kill you with, or hit it to the middle of your side of the net for a winner.

Where to aim the ball so it lands in the proper location, close to the baseline

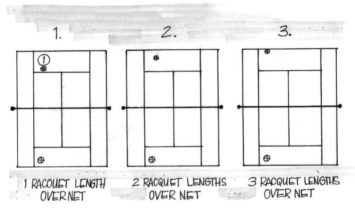

Tennis players used to think that one of their best shots was when the ball barely cleared the net. People have even told me that they try to hit the ball as hard and as close to the net as they possibly can. You have to be *really* good to do that, but people still try to master it. That's why they hit a lot of balls into the net.

You must give yourself some room for error. You will not be perfect all the time. This is not a game of "perfect," and it never will be. There will always be mistakes. What's important is to learn from your mistakes and move on from there to the next point.

The simple *1, 2, 3* rule for where to aim the ball is:

1 = One racquet-length over the net if you are hitting a passing shot, or an approach shot. If you get a short ball from your opponent and you are going toward the net, aim the ball to go one racquet-length over the net to get good depth on your shot. If your opponent comes into the net, aim your ball one racquet-length above the net to keep the shot low at your opponent's feet. This strategy is used for both singles and doubles.

2 = **Two racquet-lengths over the net** to hit a deep groundstroke. Any time you are at the baseline, or 5'0" behind the baseline, aim two racquet-lengths over the net. This ensures that your shot will land behind the service line on the other side of the net. This will keep your opponent(s) pinned back at the baseline, where they cannot hit winners against you. If you hit consistent shots deep in the court, past the service line, you will soon get a short ball that you can attack. This strategy is used for singles and doubles.

3 = **Three racquet-lengths over the net** to hit a moon ball or a lob. If your opponent hits you a very deep shot and you must back up toward the back fence, then always think of hitting the ball three racquet-lengths above the net. The most common mistake made on this shot is that a player backs up to hit the ball, but does not aim high enough over the net to get out of trouble. This is especially true on the backhand side. For most people, the high backhand is one of the hardest shots to hit. If someone hits you a moon ball, or a high topspin shot, then hit the same shot back. This strategy is used for both singles and doubles.

Aiming the Ball and Imagining the Ball In

Aiming the ball and imagining the ball going in are one in the same. Earlier, we talked about how you don't have to think about how to throw the ball to aim it. It's the same in tennis, but slightly more specific because the ball is moving in tennis.

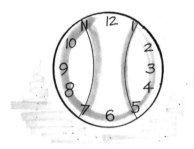

—AS THE BALL
COMES TOWARD YOU.

Aiming the ball. Let's use the face of the clock to talk about how to aim the ball.

- To hit a forehand groundstroke cross-court, hit the five o'clock.
- To hit a forehand groundstroke down the line, hit the seven o'clock.
- To hit a backhand groundstroke cross-court, hit the seven o'clock.
- To hit a backhand groundstroke down the line, hit the five o'clock.
- To hit a forehand or a backhand straight down the middle of the court, hit the six o'clock.
- To hit a forehand volley deep cross-court, hit the five o'clock.
- To hit a forehand volley to the short angle, hit the three o'clock.
- To hit a forehand volley deep down the line, hit the seven o'clock.
- To hit a backhand volley deep cross-court, hit the seven o'clock.
- To hit a backhand volley to the short angle, hit the nine o'clock.
- To hit a backhand volley to the deep down the line, hit the five o'clock.
- To hit a forehand short angle roll shot, that will land cross-court inside the service box, hit the three o'clock and swing up vertically.
- To hit a backhand short angle roll shot, that will land cross-court inside the service box, hit the nine o'clock and swing up vertically.

Hit with Imagination

- Imagine how the ball will land.
- Imagine where the ball will land.

Here is an exercise to try imagining your serve:

Hit the serve. Do not move your head and call out:

1) Net
2) In
3) Long

Keep your head up, looking at where you just hit the ball from, while you call one of those three images. Then see the bounce. See if you can imagine by the feel where the ball went, without looking.

Now picture the ball going exactly where you want it to go. Imagine that is where it will go. Imagine how it will feel when you hit it to that target. Looking at the part of the ball you want to hit to make it go in a certain direction really helps you stay in the moment and trust where you are aiming. You also watch the ball more closely and your success rate will skyrocket!

CHAPTER 6:
FOCUSING ON YOUR GOALS: IN TENNIS AND LIFE

Tennis adds years to your life and life to your years.
— Roy Wilder

Do you have a crystal clear picture of your better future? Particularly the next two years and a rock-solid plan that will ensure you get there? The purpose of this chapter is to help people focus on their strengths, so they can maximize their productivity and income, while enjoying an excellent balance between work and family.

Success isn't Magic or Hocus-Pocus...
It's Simply Learning How To Focus.
— Jack Canfield

The #1 reason that keeps people from getting what they want is a lack of focus!

The Focus Game of Tennis

My experience over the years is that the best way to quiet your mind is not by telling it to "shut up," or by arguing with it or criticizing it. Fighting with your mind just doesn't work. What works best is learning to focus your mind. Learning to focus is an art and will benefit us in almost anything we do in life.

Ability is useless unless it is used. — Robert Half

A person's abilities and the desire to accomplish something can do anything.
— Donald Kircher

Three Exercises to Demonstrate the Power of Focus:

1) Stare at a tennis ball. *Really* stare at it. Notice the fuzz on it; see if the ink is still visible on all the writing of the ball. Focus and see if you notice the shadow underneath the ball. See if the seams are all spaced the same all around the ball. Do not move the ball, keep it still and stare at it for about ten seconds.

Now—*quickly*—add thirty-five and forty-eight. What is the total? Could you do the math? Could you do it without having to move your eyes? Did you have to look away, and think about adding the two numbers in your head and then be able to give an answer?

I do this focus drill all the time with my students. Hardly ever has anyone been able to add those two numbers, or any two numbers that you have to *think* about, without moving their eyes. It is nearly impossible.

The secret behind this drill is that if you are really paying attention, then your entire focus is on staring at the ball; you cannot think about anything else. The rest of your mind is blank, and your focus is the ball. The more you watch the ball, the bigger it seems to get.

In other words, the right side of your brain (Self 2) cannot work properly and focus if the left side of your brain (Self 1) gets involved. So if you are practicing your focus, it is all that you should practice. You should not think about "How to hit the tennis ball." If you do, then you will not be successful playing tennis freely.

2) The "I Can't" Drill. This is a demonstration drill. The student will demonstrate how our mindsets determine results. The student stands with feet shoulder-width apart and puts his left arm out to the side of his body, at shoulder height. Then the student extends the left arm with the palm down toward the ground, and resists the pressure from someone else to move his arm toward the ground. After the strength/resistance, ask the student to repeat to himself, "I can't; I can't" repeatedly while the same pressure is applied to push the arm toward the ground.

This drill amazes anyone who sees it. The arm gets pushed down almost immediately, all the way to the person's side. There is absolutely no resistance to hold the arm at shoulder height anymore. It is a great way to demonstrate how we follow our thoughts. It is stunning!

3) Straight arm drill. The student has the same body position as in Drill #2. Stance is shoulder-width apart, with one arm extended to the side of the body at shoulder height. The student extends his dominant arm with the palm facing the sky. The student tries to resist pressure from another student trying to bend his partner's arm at the elbow. Usually, the arm is bent in some form or another.

Then the student is instructed to imagine a metal rod extending through the arm, and past the arm so the metal rod goes on until infinity. The metal rod extends to infinity from one end of the arm, all the way through the body, to the other end of the arm. Now, the student puts that mental picture in his mind and thinks about it for about five seconds.

Student #2 then tries to bend the arm at the elbow again, and the arm does not move one inch. It is rock solid, totally straight. It's amazing because the same force is used in both instances. However, the power of focus, thinking about a steel rod in the arm, makes the arm locked, and it will not bend.

Different Ways to Focus on the Tennis Court

1) Seam-watching. We discussed this in a little detail in Chapter 4. Toss the ball back and forth with your partner. Does the ball spin more before the bounce, or after the bounce? Count the number of rotations the ball makes before the bounce. Then count the number of rotations the seams turn after the bounce. Which has more? The ball has about twice to three times as many rotations after the bounce.

The irony of this is that most people watch the ball more before the bounce, and do not see the ball hit their racquet after the bounce. We just determined that the ball bounces more after the bounce. Therefore, that's the most important time to watch the ball to see the seams of the ball.

2) Bounce, Hit. See how accurately you are rallying back and forth with your partner. See how accurately you call out loud, "Bounce" when you see the ball bounce, and "Hit" when you see it hit your racquet. Most people are not very accurate when they first try this drill. Your goal is not just to say the words; your job is to say the action exactly as it is happening. To master this drill, see how good you can get saying the words out loud for fifteen minutes. When you practice this drill, your mind cannot think about anything else. You have to stay focused.

3) Hit, Bounce, Hit. When you feel you have mastered Drill #2, then progress and add saying aloud, "Hit," when your partner across the net hits; then say "Bounce" and Hit" on your side of the net. Again, see if your accuracy stays the same, gets better or gets worse, because there is more going on inside your head. You should feel how much more consistently you are able to sustain a rally.

4) Back, Bounce, Hit. If you always seem to hit the ball late, meaning behind your front foot, then this drill will work fabulously for you. Again, with your partner, rally back and forth across the net. You have to say out loud, "Back" when you see your opponent hitting the ball from across the net, then once again say, "Bounce and Hit" when you do that action. The word "Back" represents the action you should do with your racquet. Your racquet goes back, as your shoulders turn, all at the same time. Saying the three words should become almost rhythmic.

5) "Track It to the Racquet." Saying this helps people watch the ball from when their opponent hits the ball. You will see the flight, or the arc, of the ball better when you think to yourself, "Track it to the racquet." When you see the flight of the ball from your partner's racquet to yours, you will get into position automatically.

6) Turn backwards and find the bounce. This drill is fun to do. It is one of the kids' favorites. You can do this with one person, or you can also do it with a group. The instructor feeds the ball. Students stand at the service line at first, with their backs toward you. You tell them to turn when you hit the ball. When they turn and face the net, their objective is to find the bounce with their eyes. If you do this correctly, you will not panic, even though you never saw the arc of the ball, or tracked it with your eyes from the other side of the net. The key to this drill is that it trains your mind to find the bounce, which will emphasize how important the bounce is when playing tennis.

7) Hitting with the opposite hand. We also discussed this in Chapter 4. If you make students switch their racquets to their non-dominant hands, it shows them how valuable it is to focus on the ball. If they try to think about how to hit the ball, because they are using their opposite hands, they will not be able to hit the ball over the net.

8) The ball-calling drill. Divide the court into three sections. Closest to the net is Position #1. Position #2 is halfway between the service box and the middle of No-Man's Land, while position #3 is halfway between No-Man's Land and the baseline. The object of this drill is for the student to call aloud the number: 1, 2, or 3, depending where the ball lands. The student is trying to call the number before the ball actually bounces, while sustaining a rally with his partner. It teaches the student about where the ball is really bouncing and puts his body in the appropriate position if he calls the number correctly.

9) Breathing. This is one of the most important things when playing the game, so you won't pass out on the court. To learn to breathe correctly, you want to have a long breath, to ensure a proper inhale and exhale. No, not as loud as Maria Sharapova. When hitting a groundstroke, your breath needs to be longer, and when striking a volley, your breath needs to be shorter. So when you are hitting a groundstroke, say the word, "Finish." Say it every time you hit the tennis ball. Listen to your breath; it is a rhythm. When you go to hit a volley, say the word, "Hit." The stroke is shorter. Therefore, the breath must also be short.

After you have mastered breathing through saying those two words, you can now just do the breath, instead of saying the words. It takes two or three weeks to get the hang of saying the words exactly at the moment of impact of hitting the tennis ball. Your breath should be as long, or as short, as the words you say.

Any of these drills will work to improve your power of focus while playing tennis, no matter what distractions come your way. You need to practice focus drills just as much as you practice how to execute your other shots. Remember, when you are practicing focus, do not try to analyze how you hit the shot. Self 1 should be rather quiet. You are simply "in the moment."

Any of these drills will work to help you master staying focused. Pick the one that works the best for you. Good luck, and embrace the power of focus!

With this book, you also get a free bonus of more information. Go to my website, **WinningInTennisAndLife.com** and click on the "Free Stuff" button. You will receive six additional advanced "Focus Drills" you can use. You will learn as easy as *1, 2, 3*. Take your tennis game to the next level. These are six advanced "Focus Drills" you only see the pros use. Now, you, too, can learn how to imitate them and beat that opponent that you have never beaten. It is an extension of Chapter 6. It will give you more "tools in your toolbox" to use on the tennis court.

Focus on Golf

I just have to share this story with you. Over the summer, my family and I went to Hawaii. When I go there, I always play golf. I love playing golf. Besides playing tennis, golf is my next love. I just never get to play often enough. You cannot have a bad day of golf in Hawaii. If you are having a bad day, just look out into the ocean and appreciate the beauty.

On the plane ride over, I was writing this chapter. When I went to play golf the day after we arrived, I decided to try an experiment. I decided to try the tennis focus techniques on the golf course. I was playing alone, which I like to do there. So, it was a competition between my Nike ball and my Callaway golf ball. I hit two balls on every hole and then I keep score for both of the balls. It is quite a challenge and lots of fun.

What do you think happened? I am usually a 12 handicap. That means that I usually shoot somewhere in the mid 80's. My lowest score ever was a 78, a few years ago. I worked on staying relaxed and staying in the moment. I did not figure out what my score was on every hole, and therefore did not try to figure out what the end score would be.

My focus was in watching the "dimples" of the ball, just like I watch the seams of the ball in tennis. It is a little easier in golf, because the ball is not moving. That was my entire focus that day. I actually stayed with that focus for 18 holes. When I was finished, I added up my scores: Nike: 79; Callaway: 73. I immediately added again, because that couldn't be right. I had never even come close to that score, except on miniature golf. It was incredible. I knew I was not missing anything; everything was straight and the ball almost always went where I wanted it to go. I had shot a 73! I saved that scorecard. I played again that week and the result of the focus was the same.

So, if you are playing golf, use the tennis focus techniques on the golf course. You will be amazed, as I was. Now I should retire, right? Happy hitting!

The Tennis Game: "Self 1" vs. "Self 2"

In Timothy Gallwey's book, *The Inner Game of Tennis*, he talks about the right brain vs. the left brain. To simplify that process:

1) Self 1 (the left-brain) is THE TELLER; the talker, the critic, the controlling voice.
2) Self 2 (the right-brain) is THE DOER; the self that has to hit the ball.

It becomes apparent that the less controlling, judgmental conversation from Self 1, the better the shots will turn out. The more I trusted in my Self 2 potential, the better I played, and in turn, the quieter the Self 1 conversation was. This part of the Inner Game has not changed and will never change as long as human beings are vulnerable to fears, doubts, and distractions of the mind.

Self 1 has more persistence and inventiveness in finding opportunities to get in the way.

Self 2 is also the doer; it has a great capacity to learn. It is capable of a range of feelings that are the most human characteristics of life. These feelings can be explored in sports, the arts, business and countless other activities. Self 2 is the acorn that, at first, seems quite small yet turns out to have the uncanny ability not only to become a magnificent tree, but if it has the right conditions, can generate an entire forest.

While learning to play tennis, there seems to be an internal conversation (or committee) going on. Some of the conversation is based on fear and self-doubt.

Trust in Yourself. The ability to approach this state is the Inner Game. While learning tennis, you begin to learn how to focus your attention and *how to trust in yourself.* This trust is far more valuable than hitting a good forehand. A good forehand is important on the tennis court, but mastering the art of effortless concentration is invaluable in whatever you set your mind to do. It could be another sport, it could be focusing in school or it could be focusing at your job. This concentrated focus brings you to great levels of performance, learning more efficiently and enjoying your task.

Playing "In the Zone" or Playing "Out of Your Mind"

When you are playing in a tennis match and you are playing "In the Zone," your mind is quiet. You have heard people use expressions like, "She is playing out of her mind," or, "He is over his head," or, "She is unconscious out there," or "He doesn't know what he is doing." The common theme in each of these sayings is that some part of the mind is not active. Athletes use similar phrases and they know their peak performance never comes when they are thinking about it.

Someone "playing out of his mind" is more aware of the ball, the court and when it is appropriate, the opponent. However, he is not aware of giving himself instructions, thinking about how to hit the ball, how to correct past mistakes or how to repeat what he just did. He is conscious, but not thinking and not over-trying. A player in this state knows where he wants the ball to go, but he does not have to try hard to send it there. It just seems to happen. It requires energy, yet the results happen with greater accuracy and power.

Can you play "out of your mind" on purpose? How can you be consciously unconscious? A better way of saying it is the player who is "unconscious" is a player whose mind is so concentrated, so focused, that it is *still*. He becomes one with what his body is doing, and the unconscious, or automatic, functions work without interference from thoughts. The concentrated mind has no room for thinking how well the body is doing, much less about the "how-to's" of doing. When a player is in this state of mind, there is no interference, and he will play to his full potential and skill.

Take Time Off; Play Great. Have you ever noticed that when you take time off, for whatever reason, the first day you return to the tennis court, you actually play very well? Usually, much better than expected. Why is that? You go away on vacation and you come back after not playing in two or three weeks and you cannot believe how well you play. The reason this happens is before you even arrive at the tennis court, you do a lot of self-talk.

This kind of self-talk is usually positive, such as: "Don't expect too much today because you have been away on vacation," or "We ate like pigs on our vacation, so I may not move well today, so I'm not going to worry about it," or "I am not going to worry about winning or losing; I am just going to be happy to be out playing tennis again; I really missed it when I was gone." With this, you set yourself up for success. You're not putting any pressure on yourself when you go to play because you talked yourself into that before play even started.

You started with the positive self-talk before you even hit one tennis ball. Most people usually watch the ball much better when they come back after not playing. They are excited to be there and they are enjoying the moment. They are staying in the "now" with no expectations and no tension in their muscles. Therefore, they swing freely.

On the other hand, the second day back after time off is usually a disaster because the first day back you played great, with no expectations. But, on the second day back, you expect to play as well as you did the last time you played. So, you have higher expectations.

The self-talk before you arrive on the tennis court may be something like this, "I am going to kick Fred's butt today because I played so well last time." We now care about the results too much. We also try to hit the shots more perfectly and are thinking too much about how to hit the shot. We should just watch the bounce instead. Now we "try too hard" and are optimistic that we are going to play better than before. That is a definite recipe for failure.

So the second time out after not playing tennis for a while, you should make it your goal to see how well you can see the bounce and hit of the ball. That's all you should work on the second day. Don't have any other expectations. You still need Self 2 to play freely.

Don't Try So Hard. How many times have you heard, "Don't try so hard?" I think that was my motto growing up. I did not have all this great information back in "the olden days." I wish I had. Imagine the possibilities. To me, if I did not try hard, I was giving up. At that time, it was hard for me to find the balance between trying too hard and not trying at all. So now, I am "trying" to save you years of aggravation.

If you really want to see how this theory works, the next time you are playing in a social match, when you are changing sides of the court, say this to your opponent. "Hey Jane, you are playing so well today. What are you doing that is making your forehand so good?" As soon as Jane starts thinking about "how" she is hitting her forehand so well, she is doomed. You should now win the match. That will happen, especially if Jane goes so far as to try to explain to you what she is doing differently in her forehand. Now, she will be "thinking too much" and "trying to hard" to impress you, since you noticed how good her forehand was. I have tried this with many people. I'm telling you, it is as good as already winning the match.

Examples of tennis players "trying too hard":

- I have many, many students come for tennis lessons. The first thing they tell me is what they would like to work on. They explain how they have a terrible serve, and how they cannot hit more than two backhands in a row over the net. So they hit some backhands and some serves. Every time, without fail, they barely miss either of those two shots after they just went through all of the details explaining their problem. Why does that happen? Because they just took all of the pressure off themselves, explaining that their shots will be bad. When that happens, Self 2 takes over, and just hits the ball with no thought or interference from Self 1. When they tell me how much trouble that they are having with a shot, they are not trying to impress me. They have already given in to being unable to hit the shot the way they want to hit it, so they have given up trying to control the ball, and the result is they hit it better than they ever had.

- Conversely, when I have a students come to my court and tell me how well they hit their serves in their last matches, or how they never miss their forehand; well, you can guess what happens. Yes, that's right, they miss almost every ball. That is because they are "trying so hard" to impress me and show me how well they are doing. When they "try too hard" in that circumstance, Self 1 has totally taken over. Then Self 1 starts analyzing every shot because they cannot believe they are missing all their forehands, especially after telling me how good they were.

- The last example of "trying too hard" comes when you are returning a serve. Have you ever noticed that anytime your opponent hits a serve long (past the service line), you call the ball out and then return the shot back over the net? No one misses that return. Even if the ball is well past the service line, the returner doesn't miss the return that actually doesn't count because the serve was out.

Why can we hit every return in the court when we have called it out? Then when the server gets the ball in the service box, we "try" to make a good return and we miss. No expectation, no pressure. We have already called it out, so we know that it does not count. When we call it out, we relax and just swing easily, no tension in our body at all. When we know it is in, our body tenses up more, "trying" to make it in the court.

Time Well Spent. If you play in a singles match, how much of that time is actually spent hitting a tennis ball? Twenty-four minutes.

If you play in a doubles match, how much of that time is actually spent hitting a tennis ball? Seventeen minutes.

That's incredible, isn't it? So, what are you doing during the rest of those sixty minutes of play?

- Walking back to get a ball
- Changing sides of the court
- Sitting down for a three-minute changeover
- Walking from the deuce side of the court to the ad side of the court
- If the point ended at the net, walking back from the net to the baseline
- Waiting for the other person to serve

Therefore, most of your time is thinking time. That could be a good thing or a bad thing if Self 1 tries to take over and be in charge, or if Self 1 is quieter and Self 2 is in charge.

Three Generations of Gilberts. I cannot be that old. Over the summer, I realized I am teaching my third generation of a family. (I must have started teaching them when I was ten). Needless to say, this is when I realized that tennis has no age limit. That's why it is the sport of a lifetime, even three generations! I believe that the Gilberts are the clients I have been teaching the longest. Yes, they are all still playing tennis with me.

That's what I love about my job. I can make a difference in someone's life and I get to be around to see it blossom and grow, with both adults and children. The children then become adults, and then they have children and introduce them to the great sport of tennis. The Gilberts are one of the nicest, most generous families I have ever taught. They passed those wonderful gifts to their children and grandchildren, too. They are also very close friends after all these years.

Lessons the parents learned on the tennis court have been transmitted to the next generations. What a beautiful thing that is. Here is Janice Gilbert, the mother's (and now, the grandmother's), story:

"Mary Pat has taught tennis to three generations of our family: My husband and I, our three children, and now, our grandchildren. How lucky we are! Recently I had the pleasure of watching her teach our five-year-old grandson to play tennis for the first time. He learned the volley, groundstrokes, serve and ran a lot, all in one hour in 100-degree weather. How did she do it? With a lot of positive reinforcement, appropriate progression of each skill, a quick pace, and fun 'games.'

"At the end of his lesson, our grandson said, 'I love tennis; can you wake me up early in the morning for another lesson?' That is the best part of this story: He loves tennis. We all do and we have Mary Pat to thank for that. As our children were growing up, I think tennis helped them build a certain 'mental toughness, self confidence, and self esteem.' We have Mary Pat to thank for that.

"Mary Pat is an incredible teacher because of many years of experience, research, caring, and this amazing intuitive instinct about how to adapt her approach to teaching each individual person.

"I have often said, 'Who needs a psychologist when they have Mary Pat!' After a private lesson or drill class, I feel aggressive, proud, positive, and upbeat. The lessons I learn on the court are valuable strategies in life as well. For example, "KEEP SELF TALK POSITIVE."

"Tennis is as easy as 1, 2, 3. MP uses these three numbers in her teaching. Just having to remember three things helps bring the focus where it belongs. For example, a lesson on the serve: She would divide the return-of-serve box into thirds, then say,

1) **Think** where you want to serve the ball, spot # 1, 2, or 3.
2) **Watch** the ball hit your racquet.
3) **Palm of hand** pointing to the target.

"For example, a lesson on groundstrokes:

Say out loud:

1) *"Hit"*
2) *"Bend" on the bounce*
3) *"Hit"*

"That reminds me of one of her latest teaching techniques:

"DON'T JUDGE, JUST <u>REPORT</u>

"This takes all the pressure off having to do it right; all you have to do is <u>report.</u>

"Forehand and Backhand Volley:

"Report (out loud)

"1" if you hit the ball in front of your foot
"2" at your foot or parallel
"3" behind your foot

"DON'T JUDGE, JUST REPORT 1, 2 or 3 when hitting Forehand or Backhand ground strokes."

"Say out loud 1 if you hit the ball early, 2 a little less early and so on."

"No judgment just reporting. If you keep saying, 2, either back up so you can hit earlier, or get in ready position sooner so you are ready to hit it sooner. This is a great plan when I have been away for a while. Instead of beating myself up, I just report."

"I have the greatest respect for Mary Pat's ability to teach tennis, or anything else, to adults as well as children. She is bright, she is honorable, she has made a difference in all of our lives, and I hope she will continue to do so."

Mental Focus: Cheat Sheets

Key issues that can impact the quality of your play:

1) Staying in the present and not being distracted by thoughts of the outcome. "If I win this match, I will play Charlie, whom I have always beaten in the next round." With this, you are thinking of either the score or the outcome of the match.

2) Establishing composure and focus. Have a clear image of where the ball is going to land, or where the serve will land before you serve.

3) Trusting your swing. Stay clear of negative self-talk. Be the little leprechaun on your shoulder. Only say positive things you would say to your best friend. Stay out of the self-sabotaging tendency to mess up after things have been going well for a while.

4) Not being so hard on yourself if you make a mistake. Manage your strong feelings, such as anger, excitement and frustration. Let it go...let's go!

I have my students write little "cheat sheet notes." At the end of the book, there is a little chapter titled, MP's 1,2,3's Cheat Sheets. You can visit my website: **WinningInTennisAndLife.com** and print them out to keep in your racquet cover to use while you are playing your next tennis match.

When you are changing sides on every odd number game, you have three minutes to have a drink of water, have a couple bites of a power bar, banana or nuts. So, during this period when you have some "down time" read your little "cheat sheet notes."

I used to write notes after all my lessons when I was a teenager. When I wrote something down right there on the court after I took a lesson, it was fresh in my mind. In addition, by writing it down, I remembered it better. I could hear it, audibly, from my coach, write it down, and read it again. That's three different ways I remembered what helped me the most at that particular lesson. As you might expect, my little notebook filled up quickly. It was portable and easy to carry around. I stuck it in my racquet cover. Half the time, my opponents looked at me reading and wondered what it was, maybe my magic "secrets" for how to beat them. It just made them think I had more weapons than they did—even if it wasn't true. Now, you can carry your own "cheat sheets" in your racquet bag to use at any given moment. Also remember to read them before a match and you will feel like you just had a little mini tennis lesson. Your focus will be there from the very first point of the match.

So, here's an example of a small and compact "cheat sheet" for these four qualities that would influence your game mentally, or your swing, or your confidence.

1) **For staying in the present:** One point at a time, one set at a time, one match at a time. Most importantly: Play one point at a time.

2) **For composure and focus:** Gather yourself. Good picture. Visualize the shot going in and to the spot where you want it to land.

3) **For trusting and playing within yourself:** Nothing special, nothing extra. Do not go for any big shot unless the opportunity presents itself. Be patient and wait for the right shot.

4) **For not being so hard on yourself after a mistake:** Let it go...let's go! It's only one point. Do not let one point stay with you so you miss the next three or four shots. One point has *never* made or broken a match. So let the mistake go in your mind. Take a practice swing of the shot that you just missed; picture the swing in your head. Then let it go and move on to the next point.

To dream anything that you want to dream. That is the beauty of the human mind. To do anything that you want to do. That is the strength of the human will. To trust yourself to test your limits. That is the courage to succeed. — Bernard Edmonds

There is no such thing as can't, only won't. If you're qualified, all it takes is a burning desire to accomplish, to make a change. Go forward, go backward. Whatever it takes! But you can't blame other people or society in general. It all comes from your mind. When we do the impossible we realize we are special people. — Jan Ashford

Almost all world-class athletes and other peak performers are visualizers. They see it; they feel it; they experience it before they actually do it. They began with the end in mind. You can do it in every area of your life. Before performance, a sales presentation, a difficult confrontation, or the daily challenge of meeting a goal, see it clearly, vividly, relentlessly, over and over again. Create an internal 'comfort zone.' Then, when you get into the situation, it isn't foreign. It doesn't scare you. — Stephen Covey

Success

Mark David Peters says, "Everybody wants to be phenomenally successful, no matter what endeavor they choose to pursue in life. Unfortunately, most people have a grandiose dream of what they would love to accomplish, but fail to realize they lack the necessary traits and qualities to make their dreams come true. Their habits do not align with what they want to accomplish. In the end, these people end up with broken dreams and a life that is very different from what they would love to do."

"The term, success superstars is a broad term that encompasses everybody who's successful. Success superstars range from the average guy who lives down the street with the perfect family, to the award winning actors and actresses of today. If we study and figure out what makes them so successful, we could discover the traits they all share. Once we do that, we can apply those traits to our own lives and achieve the same results that they have. The people, who we talked about earlier, would then have fulfilled dreams and lives."

You cannot tell your heart what it wants.
Your heart will tell you
— Barbara Sher

If you realized how powerful your thoughts are,
you would never think a negative thought.
— Peace Pilgrim

The ability to love oneself, combined with the ability
to love life, fully accepting that it won't last forever,
enables one to improve the quality of life.
— Bernie S. Siegel

Tennis is just a game,
friends and family are forever.
— Serena Williams

When one door of happiness closes, another opens;
but often we look so long at the closed door that we
do not see the one which has been opened for us.
— Helen Keller

If you want to get somewhere you have to know
where you want to go and how to get there.
Then never, never give up!
— Norman Vincent Peale

There is always an inner game being played in your mind,
no matter what outer game you are playing. How aware you
are of this game can make the difference between success
and failure in the outer game.
— *Tim Gallwey*

Inner Game – From Sports to Life

Did you ever have one of those "MAGIC" days on the tennis court? Did the ball ever seem like it was the size of a grapefruit? Did it seem like you were always at the right place at the right time when playing in a match? Did you ever have that feeling in your office? A day where everyone got along, where all projects were accomplished in record time? Where everyone was happy with what they were doing? Have you had one of those days where work felt effortless and everything just flowed into place?

With this formula, performance can be enhanced either by:

1) Growing "p" = potential OR
2) Decreasing "i" = interference

Most of us have experienced days when our self-interference was at a minimum. Whether on a sports field or court, at work, or in some creative effort, we all have had moments in which our actions flowed from us with a kind of effortless excellence. Athletes have called this state, "playing in the zone." Generally, at these times our mind is quiet and focused.

Nevertheless, whatever it is called, when we are there, we excel, we learn, and we enjoy ourselves. Unfortunately, most of us have also experienced times when everything we do seems difficult. With minds filled with self-criticism, hesitation, and over-analysis, our actions were awkward, mis-timed, and ineffective. We are striving to have more of the "playing in the zone."

When individuals work together in teams, both their potential and their "self-interference" can combine. When the self-interferences of team members play off one another, the interference multiplies and the effective work of such a team is greatly diminished. We have all had experiences like this.

It has been on the sports playing field, it has been working on a project together with a group of people for school, and it has been having a group effort for a deadline at the office; we all know that feeling. When the potential of team members is combined and a minimum of interference is brought to the table, the team is capable of producing results well beyond the mere sum of the potential of its members.

"The Inner Game" provides principles, methods and tools to learn to get out of your own way so you can express your full potential in whatever your chosen activity. The fundamental methods for overcoming self-interference are similar, no matter what outer game is being played.

For example, if a person learns the art of relaxed focus of attention in one activity, that skill can be applied to any other activity. This provides great advantage for anyone attempting to maximize excellence in any field: sports, school, creative arts, or work.

Tim Gallwey's "Inner Game" approach has helped corporations that are looking for better ways to manage change. In his lectures, consulting, and seminars, Gallwey has directed the approach to managing change at 3 targets:

1) Helping all individuals in a company learn how to learn—and think for themselves.
2) Helping managers learn how to coach.
3) Helping leaders learn to create "learning organizations."

The inner game is about a simple way to develop certain "inner" skills that can be used to improve any "outer" game of your choice. It is about learning to get out of your own way so that you can learn and perform closer to your potential.

Corporate Athlete Focus in the workplace:

- Work, life, balance. Your stuff? Could mean you benefit from a more flexible, loyal and motivational workforce. You may also notice tangible benefits:
- Reduction in absenteeism
- Recruitment costs and staff turnover...down...
- Attract and retain a talented and happy workforce.
- Benefits from developing our practice and understanding of the focus process:
  - More effective communications
  - Beginnings and completions
  - Increase in positive feelings and a decrease in negative feelings
  - Increased self-coaching ability
  - Increased problem-solving ability
  - Greater ability to help others
  - Put insight learning into action
  - Greater flexibility
  - Improvements in performance, attitude and the quality of experience toward competence, ease, and more fun.

Making the Transition from Athletics to Academics to the Workplace

I am a prime example of what athletics can teach our children, adolescents and even adults. Athletics teach you:

- determination
- discipline
- the will to win
- a never-give-up attitude
- personal courage
- goal-setting
- to be the best you can be
- persistence

- how to balance stress and recovery
- how to balance family and work
- mental toughness
- hard work
- the importance of repetition practice

I developed leadership qualities that have helped me throughout my life. I developed self-confidence, self-esteem and learned teamwork, which taught me how to get along with others, no matter what it took.

Studies have shown that good tennis players are good students. To play tennis, you must be flexible, think on your feet, change strategies and be able to handle adversity. Other qualities of a good tennis player are that you become very proficient in your time management skills, which are essential in business, you must be organized, and you must be smart and study your opponent's strengths and weaknesses. Those same qualities are extremely useful to you in the business world.

When I was fifteen, I asked my parents if I could take tennis lessons because everyone else on the tennis team took lessons. My parents told me that if I wanted to get serious and have them help pay for my lessons, I would have to quit every other sport I played competitively and focus just on tennis.

I was good at all the sports I played, but I was not great at one particular sport, which was the only way you could get a scholarship to college. At the time, I thought my parents were the meanest in the world. In hindsight, it was one of the best decisions they ever helped me make.

My father told me that I probably wouldn't get a scholarship to play softball, volleyball or basketball, and I would have to play on a good team in order to get enough recognition. That's when it all started to make sense. I did give up my other sports and focused on tennis.

When I was seventeen, someone told me that I'd started playing tennis too late in life, and that I wasn't good enough to get a college tennis scholarship. That was all I had to hear. I could have believed what I heard, or I could have been more determined than ever to prove that person wrong. I guess I just needed a little incentive. I chose to be more determined than ever.

I developed better discipline to work and practice harder so I would achieve my goal and get a full tennis scholarship to a Division I school. I did just that; I proved them wrong. I did receive a full tennis scholarship to a Division I school which led to some of the best memories I have, growing up in college.

I am now a successful entrepreneur because of athletics. I run my own business and have the freedom to decide when and how much I work. I developed the discipline to set and reach goals and I translated that into my career. My tennis has allowed me to travel throughout the United States, and I have built lasting meaningful relationships along my path. Just think of all of the opportunities I would have missed if I'd let someone else's negative thinking deter me from following my dream.

Tennis has enabled me to touch the lives of so many people, to help them transform their lives so they become winners in both tennis and life. What a gift I have been given! I am eternally grateful for this gift of tennis that has so magically transformed my life into a fulfilled, magical destiny. I hope that in reading this book, it will start you on your journey to executing your strategies on and off the tennis court. I hope this will be the start or the continuation of a blueprint for your healthy life.

Dan Jensen summed up his quest for the Gold Medal by saying:

It's never over till it's over. Never stop fighting. Never give up. Never surrender. No matter how bad it gets, no matter how deep your pain; persistence, faith in yourself, and an undeniable spirit will eventually break you free.

Exercise:

What qualities have you taken from tennis and used in academics or in the workplace?

1._____

2._____

3._____

4._____

5._____

6._____

List three of your best qualities that you can attribute to athletics:

1._____

2._____

3._____

Never talk defeat. Use words like hope, belief, faith and victory.
— Norman Vincent Peale

SECTION THREE:

THE GAME OF LIFE

CHAPTER 7:
EMBRACING CHANGE

'But how do you learn?' The way a tennis player learns to play tennis, by making a fool of yourself, by falling on your face, by rushing the net and missing the ball, and finally by practice...
— May Sarton

Change Starts from the Inside

This is an inside job. If you do the work on your insides, the outside will match.

The ability to do something, whatever it is, is in your *belief* that you can do it. It is not in your legs, your arms or your will. It is truly believing you *can* accomplish whatever you want. It does not matter if it is riding your bike up a steep hill. The steep hill is not the problem; it is your belief about how steep the hill is.

You must try to think about how to attack the hill and ride up it, being relaxed and comfortable. It does not matter if you are playing the number #1 seed in a tennis match. It is not the fact that someone is seeded #1. The question is do you *believe* you have put the practice and effort in to win that match, no matter what number seed you are playing?

At the Olympic Games, records are broken, even smashed because that particular athlete BELIEVED he/she could break that record. The statistics may have shown differently on paper, but it is the BELIEF in oneself that can overcome any obstacle.

The new language of working out and training is, "It is so important to work your core." When you work your core, everything else stems from that workload. Twenty-nine different muscles encompass your core; it's not just your "six-pack abs."

When you strengthen your core, every other body part becomes strong as well. That is the paradox with our life lessons. If you work from within yourself, in your core, the outside will match the inside. The beauty is within.

All the work on you comes from within. Finally, it is all about *you!* Work on yourself and people will seem to change magically around you. Do not worry about how someone treats you; think about how you treat others. Do not worry about what someone thinks about you; concentrate on what you think about yourself. Remember, it is an inside job. Happiness comes from within and then transcends to the outside.

When you work your core and start from within your body, and then let the energy flow out to your appendages, you will receive enormous benefits. You do not want to waste your efforts, so let the energy flow from within and work throughout your body. Your core is strong; you must use it and engage it more. It is just a matter of "paying attention" to things you do every day.

Paying attention can range from engaging your core to engaging your total commitment in every aspect of your life. It should happen in everything you do. So many people go through life just getting by or just doing the minimum in any kind of work. If you are going to put effort into your tennis, your job or getting in shape, shouldn't you do it with the maximum amount of effort? Don't you want the best results you could possibly have? The effort you put in is usually what you get out of anything in your life. Why would you only work out a little bit? Why would you do the minimum amount of work on a project you are sharing with your co-workers when you are responsible for one of the parts? Wouldn't it make sense to be fully engaged since you are putting forth the effort anyway?

While you are practicing for tennis, make it your goal to practice hitting the ball by exploding your energy from your core and then just let the rest of the stroke happen. The racquet will come around and hit the forehand, but try to make the initial energy come from your core.

We struggle too hard in sports, in relationships and in our daily work instead of putting the effort in and then just trying to let the rest happen. It will happen if you believe it will happen. If you trust your stroke in practice, you will trust it in a match. You will believe in your game, fully. Be fully engaged; let the energy flow!

In the past, most coaches have told me that I "try too hard." How can that be? I always thought that the harder you tried, the better you would be. In recent years, that philosophy has changed. You may be "trying too hard." This simply means you do not trust the work you have put in. Your belief system is not fully working yet. My body was working against my effort; I was not letting the energy just flow. It is a hard concept to grasp, but you can do it with practice. When you "try too hard," you are working against your energy flow. A way to counteract "trying too hard" is to relax when the effort becomes harder.

Embrace the effort; feel your core engaged but relax with your arms. Let me give you an example of this: If you tighten up your grip on the tennis racquet, which tightens up your elbow, which tightens up your shoulder muscles, and try to swing as hard as you possibly can, you will swing fairly fast. If you do the same exercise and relax your grip on the tennis racquet a little—keep your elbow and shoulder loose and swing fast, with *relaxing* as your emphasis—the racquet will swing about twice as fast, with half the effort.

Another example of "trying too hard" happened to me when I was in junior college. I was the athletic trainer, which meant I taped the ankles of all the football players and helped with any injuries with all other athletes of other sports. So, if the football players were mean to me, I taped their ankles with no pro-wrap tape underneath the athletic tape. That meant when they took the tape off after practice, they pulled all the hair off their ankles! So, needless to say, the football players were very nice to me.

During football games, I was on the sidelines with the football coaches. During one game, Coach Fenwick screamed, "Mike, get over here! Go in there and take Jim's place at running back." Mike strapped on his helmet, looked at Coach and said, "I'll try, Coach." Mike started running onto the field.

Coach Fenwick yelled back at Mike, "Mike, get back over here and sit down. Jim is in there *trying*. I wanted you to go in and just do it. To get the job done!" Mike sat back down with a look of bewilderment. From that moment on, I understood better the phrase: "You can try too hard." When that happens, everything in your body tenses up. Your muscles tighten up, and your breathing becomes labored and short.

You do not think properly; the oxygen doesn't flow to your muscles as easily and some people have even experienced the feeling of "choking" when they try too hard. The moral to this story is don't try so hard, just relax and breathe through hard efforts, whatever they may be. Focus on your breathing with a big effort and let the rest happen.

How to Make Small Changes That Can Improve Your Life

How many times in your life have you said, "This is the year for big changes for me?" How many times have you promised yourself that you will keep your New Year's resolution? How many times do you fight "a change" in your life? Why is it so hard to accept change as, "This is what is supposed to happen in my life," and embrace it?

It sounds so easy and logical, but it is not. Our life is a work in progress. Our tennis game is a work in progress. Our business is a work in progress. We are always trying to make it better, always trying to improve some aspect. We are always changing, learning, exploring and responding to new situations. How we deal with change is always a big issue for most people.

When something new arises in our path, we immediately think, "Well, I better make this big change." Instead, it might be more beneficial to make very, very minute changes. Then, once you make a little change, it is easier to make another little change, instead of thinking, "I must make this big change right now." That is when most people seem to fail with their goals and desires. As soon as a big change does not happen instantly, people get discouraged; they get the attitude that, "See, nothing really changes; it has been that way for most of my life." For example, "I am going to lose twenty-five pounds, I am going to exercise everyday and I am going to change all of my eating patterns and be healthy." How many times have you heard that? It usually does not work like that.

A better way to approach wanting this change might be, "I want to lose twenty-five pounds and I will exercise four to five times a week for a minimum of thirty minutes. I need to start changing my eating habits. I will not eat past 7:00 p.m. All my snacks will be healthy snacks of protein or fruit. I will do that for two weeks. Then I'll reassess." That at least sounds like something that is attainable. If you make small mistakes and eat past 7:00 p.m., then you can start again the next day. Do not give up all hope and all your eating healthy habits.

Everything should happen in small increments, or small changes. It seems like the more proficient you are at something, the smaller and more delicate the changes. That is why we don't tend to see the improvement right away—because the change is so small. That is where transition comes in.

Transition happens constantly in our lives. For example, transitions happen going from an infant to a child, from a child to a teenager, from a teenager to a young adult, from a young adult to an adult, to then maybe a parent, to then possibly a grandparent. Transformation comes from these small transitions. Transformation isn't always planned; it evolves out of small transitions. Sometimes these events happen in a short time; sometimes they take a long time. They happen if we are patient and willing to take the journey. The problem is we usually get in our own way. We are our own worst enemies, our own worst critics, and we are the ones who really doubt our abilities to make changes, even if they are for our own good.

It was early January 2000; we had just celebrated the millennium. I used to run in the early morning, before the sun even came up, with a friend, three or four times a week. My hip was starting to hurt the more

I ran, since I was on the tennis court for eight to ten hours a day. So I decided to transition from running outside to bike riding inside, which was much easier and had less impact on my hip.

I decided to start doing a spin class. Spin class is an indoor cycling class on a stationary bike with great music, an instructor and crazy friends all around you. It was becoming very popular and it's very addicting. I decided it was a good thing to get addicted to. It was much warmer inside a building in the cool winter months (it really does get cold in California in the winter mornings...30-40 degrees), than bundling up to run outdoors. I got a great workout, was with friends and had all my exercise done, was showered and ready to start my day in ninety minutes.

After spin class one day, Melinda, a friend of mine, told me that she was going to do the AIDS Ride in June and that I was going to do it with her. I laughed right out loud and told her she must have been smoking something very good. She did not even have a bike to do the ride. It was an entire seven-day, weeklong adventure. It started in San Francisco and ran 585 miles to Los Angeles. Melinda really was out of her mind. I asked her where she would stay at the end of the day. She replied, giggling, "You set up your own tent and sleep on the ground in the tent!" I roared with laughter. Melinda is the perfect "princess" in every sense of the word. Her nails are perfectly manicured; her hair always looks like she has just come from the nearest salon and her jewelry is always shining. Melinda has the word "princess" personified.

As I talked to her, I thought if she, "the princess," could do this, then so could I, the professional athlete, a jock since the day I was born and the person who never backed away from a challenge. She also said she was doing the ride in honor of her brother who had died of AIDS just a few years ago. I also knew several people who had passed away from this deadly disease, so I thought it might be a good way to give something back to the community.

It was, in fact, San Francisco to Los Angeles. My geography has never been very good, so I thought that the ride would at be least downhill.

San Francisco starts up above Los Angeles on the map, and it *looks* downhill the whole way. Heck, maybe there would even be a tailwind. If nothing else, I had to see Melinda set up a tent and sleep in it on the ground. That was cause enough to say, "Yes" to this challenge. This was definitely a new transition in my life. This change was certainly not something I was comfortable with at all since I did not even consider myself an outside rider. I just did spinning to stay in shape.

So, that night we signed up online to do the ride. Melinda also got a couple other friends of hers to join. I guess she thought we could whine in unison throughout the week. Anyway, we had six months to train. The ride was the first week of June. We had to get our butts on our saddles and start training right away.

I always seem to do better when I have specific dates for goals, or deadlines. I have always been good at knowing when the test date was, procrastinating until the last minute and doing well in that test. But this was not one of those times where procrastination was going to work. Besides training to do the ride, you also had to raise $2,500 for the event. That's how the event raised millions of dollars for the AIDS charity.

Immediately, I wrote a letter about the adventure I was about to embark upon, and gave it to all of my tennis clients and mailed it to other friends and family. I was shocked and surprised at the unbelievable response I received from everyone I knew. Many people said that fundraising was the hardest part of getting involved in the ride. For myself, I did not find that to be the case at all, quite the opposite. I actually ended up being the highest fund-raiser of the event. I raised $12,600! The feeling of raising money for such a great cause was so rewarding. I had never done any fundraising of that magnitude before, at all.

As a group of us traveled up to San Francisco for the start of our journey, we had to go to an enormous building for check-in the day before the event started. Hundreds of people were sitting outside the building with cardboard signs with amounts of money written on the signs. I asked someone in the building what all those people were lined up for, and she told me that they had been training, but the amount of money on their signs was the amount of money that they still needed in order to qualify to do the AIDS ride. I said, "They did all the training, and they can't do the ride until they come up with $2,500?"

The woman explained that was the rule for the benefit. She said they were waiting outside to see if people had any extra money that they could transfer into their accounts to qualify. I said, "You can take your own money raised from the ride and give it to them?" The woman explained that you could, as long as you still had checks made out to the AIDS ride. I promptly marched outside and felt like I had just won the lottery. I had an extra $5,000 that I handed out to people who were only short a few hundred dollars, and to a young boy, who was short $1,000.

I really felt like Santa Claus, counting out the extra amounts of money into their hands with checks I had raised and then donated to these people. I couldn't imagine them having done all this training and then not being able to ride because they did not have enough money raised. I had such a gratifying feeling, and the ride hadn't even started yet.

Doing the ride for those seven days was one of the most life-changing experiences I have ever had. I came back a changed person. Events happened on the ride that caused me never to take things for granted again. People decorated their helmets and their bikes and wore crazy costumes. Most people had pictures on their jerseys of people they were riding for who had died from AIDS. One woman did not have one inch of space left on her jersey because it was covered with so many pictures of people. I said to her, "Excuse me; are all those people on your jersey sick?" I had to ask because I thought it odd there were so many pictures of little children. The woman told me, "My daughter died of AIDS from a blood transfusion and all of these are other children we met while we were in the hospital when she was sick. So, they have all died, too." I started crying right there.

People tend to think that this disease has just affected the gay population. It has affected all populations—young and old, gay and straight, men and women. That's what made us get up every day, tackle all of eighty miles of hills, endure the aches and pains and push through the cramping that our body went through—to bring awareness to the world.

On the second day, I was a little sore starting and I knew we were going to face many hills that day. It was the longest day of the ride, a distance of 101 miles. At about mile 60, I was trudging up another hill, thinking it would be nice to get a push or find an engine to put on my bike, when I saw a little bike tracking up the hill in front of me a few hundred yards.

As I approached the little bike with a flag on the back of it, I saw a man, in his mid-50s pedaling up the hill, using just his arms. He had no legs. He was doing the entire 585-mile ride using just his arms. His name was David and he was one of the most grateful men I had ever met. I never again thought about how sore my legs were. I was grateful that I had legs that could be sore.

Another reminder every day that kept me grateful was that we rode by people with red flags on the backs of their bikes. This meant they were infected with the AIDS virus. Everyone was in different stages of treatment. Any time I thought I could not pedal one more stroke, I somehow happened to pass one of those red-flagged bikes, and then I would thank God I was not infected and that I was able to do something to help fight the disease. That was a big change for me, to get out of my own head and help other people while I was riding.

The fourth day, I'd been warned, would be one of the hardest days in the ride. The ride included the steepest and longest hills of the ride, "Evil Twins." They named hills that you had to ride up. Or walk up, as the case may be. My lunatic riding friend, Georgene, had done the ride the year before so she had told me about "Evil Twins." For most people, it was the hardest day because of the exhaustion level most people felt by then. She told me she'd gone up and down the hills three times to help people who were struggling. So that was in my mind as we all approached "Twins." And they did look daunting. They were extremely steep and seemed never-ending. You could not even see the top of the hill.

There was a party at the top of the hill, though. People stopped and cheered you up the hill; they rested and gave you and everyone else struggling up the hill their support. When we heard people screaming at the top of the hill, it was encouraging and a great energy boost. That morning, as we left camp, they gave us little whistles, just to make more noise. On our journey up the hills, about ten of us were riding together that morning (we knew power in numbers would be the easiest way to get up those "Evil Twins"). At the top of the first hill, we felt like we had just climbed one of the biggest mountains of our lives.

Then for the bad news: That was only the first "Twin." Just when we were done with one, the other "Evil Twin" appeared. It was a much slower ascent up "Evil Twin" #2, so if you paced yourself, it was not quite as bad. Nevertheless, your brain told your body to hurry up with this hill to get it over with as quickly as possible. But if you did that, there was nothing left in your body to continue pedaling by the middle of "Evil Twin" #2. By the time I made it to the top of "The Evil Twins," I felt surprisingly good. I had paced myself up the mountain.

As the top of the hill approached (and the festivities were phenomenal at the top of the hill), I decided to ride back down the hill and come up again, to see if I could help anyone who was struggling with this workout. I could share with them that it is not so bad if you pace yourself. So I said goodbye to my friends, told them I was going down again and I would see them at the lunch stop. They all thought I had completely lost my mind to do that torture again. Nevertheless, they knew I was a little "over the top." So downward I went. What a glorious downhill ride that was! I blew my whistle all the way down the hill to the travelers on the opposite side of the road, still in the middle of ascending the hill. I was yelling, screaming and whistling encouragement; I was in my element!

Going down, of course, was spectacular, but now going uphill was on the horizon again. As I turned my bike around and sped over to the other side of the road, I started riding with people I had never met. They were nice and had their own fascinating stories that made the ride up the hills go very quickly. At the top of the hill, I said my good-byes and again crossed the street to blow my crazy whistle and sizzle down the hill again to repeat that "free as a bird feeling." Not that I was competitive—Georgene had done the "Evil Twins" three times the year before, so I at least had to equal her great feat.

By my third time, I felt really good. I think some extra endorphins had kicked in. Each time I flew down the hill and then went back up the hill, I met more people, with more captivating stories, and my words to them were just those of encouragement, that this hill really was not so bad. It was helpful to remind all of them that we have all been through worse tragedies in our lives. I was still blowing my crazy whistle on the way down the hill. The more times I went down the hill, the more people seemed to welcome my help riding up the hill with them.

Toward the end of the day, many people were the slower riders, or those who were sick, or those who just were not having a good riding day. So, it was more satisfying for me the longer I did this. Finally, my legs started to feel a little bit tired, and I still had the entire day left to ride—another sixty miles or so. On my last journey down the hill (that's why you endure the pain of riding up—to experience the exhilaration of riding back down the hill, going about 30-40 miles an hour with the wind in your face), very few riders remained to tackle the "Evil Twins."

One girl was at the bottom of the hill, off her bike, crying on the side of the road. I rode up to her, asked whether she was okay and whether there was anything I could do. She replied, "I cannot do this hill. It's impossible. I'm just gonna quit and have a bus pick me up." She was a little overweight and already looked like she could not pedal one more stroke. In her mind, she was finished, but there was still a lot of riding left to do. I told her I would climb the hill with her; all she had to do was to follow my wheel. I would do all the work and she could draft off my wheel. That was her only job, just stay on my wheel. I assured her we would go as slow as we needed to go. It didn't matter how long it took us; we would do it together. Then she asked me whether I was the crazy person coming down the hill from the other side, blowing my whistle. She had seen me, or heard me, coming down the hill. She exclaimed, "You've already done this hill, and you're back here to do it again? Are you out of your mind?"

I had to smile, and then I said, "Yes, I have been told that by many people. That just seems to be my nature. The hill does look daunting, but I can assure you it's not as bad as it looks. I've already done it. So, come on, get up and follow my wheel. I will talk to you all the way up the hill." She obliged, saying that since I had already done it once, she would believe me and go up the hill, following my wheel. I talked to her the whole way up the hill. We talked about where she was from, why she was doing the ride—anything I could think of to try to keep her mind off the fact that this was a "mother" of a hill. I wasn't going to tell her that it was my *seventh* time up the hill.

Yes, I was a little out of my mind; I did the "Evil Twins" seven times! And every time up the hill was a better experience than the one before. The experience with Sara, the last time up the hill, was the most gratifying of them all. As we traveled toward the clouds, the cheering section was still there, yelling and screaming as we approached the top. Sara happened to have a fan club there, which started chanting her name to keep going. It was very emotional.

She let me help her change her mind, her attitude and her ability to believe she could accomplish something that once seemed greater than she was. A person is capable of change, even if it takes some encouragement from a stranger. With the power of positive thinking, and never giving up, great changes can occur in people's lives all the time. I never saw Sara again during the ride, but a few days later, I received an e-mail from her; it went to everyone who participated in the ride. She was trying to find the girl who helped her ride up the "Evil Twin Hills," so she could thank me.

I didn't need her thanks. I learned more from Sara that day than she learned from me. It is all about determination, grit, overcoming fear and breaking barriers in your life. Change is good for all of us. Don't fear change. Instead, face it, head on.

The big change for me was I had been working so hard to make enough money, to be successful, to save enough money to buy a house, buy my car—to buy all the things you are "supposed" to have.

I had never raised money for another cause, other than trying to better myself in my business and personal life. It was such a rewarding experience. Words cannot explain the feeling you get when you give of yourself. The more you give to charities, causes, and to others, the more you receive. This is especially true with how you feel inside from your core to your heart.

Exercise

List three positive changes you can make in your life today:

1._____

2._____

3._____

From Tennis to Real Estate

Have you ever heard the saying, "When one door closes, another door opens?" The problem is most people do not believe that another door will open. The fear of change is so great that they are paralyzed into doing the same things over and over. The definition of insanity is, "Doing the same thing over and over and expecting a different result." This is why many people stay in jobs they do not like where they are not fulfilled, or stay in relationships where they're not happy. What would it take for you to look for a new job? Have doors been closed before for you that you've tried to pry back open? Did you not trust that another door was going to open? Are you worried about the economy and looking into other avenues of income? Are you in a field of work where you are following your passion? What can you do to win in life?

Instead of thinking that change has to be a bad thing, change your thoughts and focus on thinking that change can be for the better. Let another door open. Many doors are closed and other doors open as we move from one transition to another in our lifelong journey. People are sometimes unwilling to pay attention to these subtle changes. Or they move through life with blinders on, unable to notice these changes that could make their lives better.

What challenges have you had to overcome to make changes happen? Were you willing to give up some stability to trust that the next change in your life was for the better? How much risk were you willing to take? Are you willing to change careers to start your own business? Are you willing to follow your passion? What will it take to make you happy?

In 1988, I was teaching tennis full-time, seven days a week. I was a little obsessed, but it was my passion. It was what I loved to do. At that time, my right arm was getting sore. It got to the point that I had to take off and not teach so many days in a row. Of course, it directly affected my income. Still, the pain was there all the time. I had already had an ulna nerve transposition when I was in college. They moved my "funny bone" nerve so it did not feel like I was hitting my funny bone all day long. It took two years for me to recover, so I wasn't willing to do it again.

I had been teaching tennis since college. I did not know what I would do if I couldn't teach anymore. The thought of that was pure fear. Remember what FEAR stands for? Forget Everything And Run. On the other hand, it can also mean False Evidence Appearing Real. That's how I felt at that time in my life. I had a mortgage, car payments, other bills, etc.

I decided to take a course that would allow me become a real estate broker. I took the prep course over two weeks, eight hours a day. I had to tell my clients that I wouldn't be teaching for the next two weeks. I studied until all hours of the night to take the real estate license test. I passed it on my first try and then I interviewed and got a job with a local real estate firm. I sold real estate four days a week and then I taught tennis the other three days. I had to be at open houses on Sunday afternoons, dressed in nylons and heels.

Being inside was one of the hardest things I had to do, especially when the weather was beautiful outside. It was like being in a torture chamber. I sold some houses, got some listings and made some money to help supplement my income from teaching tennis. It was hard not to be at tournaments on the weekends with the juniors I had coached during the week. With rehabilitation and taking more time off, my arm eventually got better.

For me, that seemed to be my life...all or nothing. It was that way in my playing, working and recreation. For me, slowing down was not very comfortable. I had done it so rarely that I almost did not know what to do with myself. Sit down and relax? Those two things did not really exist in my daily life. Since I had such a hard time mentally relaxing, my body did the talking for me. I could not continue teaching that many tennis hours if I wanted my body to hold up for years to come. My body taught me that I had to slow down and take some time to relax.

Even though I only sold real estate part-time, after a year and a half, I realized I was born to teach. My job became learning to work smarter, not harder. I started doing more group tennis lessons, which provided more money per hour. I mixed up my teaching methods by using the ball machine more and videotaping both adult and junior lessons and matches. I also used some of the very good juniors to play against other juniors who were not quite as good, which helped both players.

The moral to my story is that when I thought I might not be able to teach anymore because of my arm, I opened up other doors so I could at least make a living. In doing so, my arm got some rest and I recovered. I learned I could once again do anything I set my mind to, and I set small goals for myself, such as getting a real estate license. I also got a great education in buying and selling homes and then bought my dream house with a tennis court on it. None of this would have happened if I hadn't had some belief that I needed to take a different avenue to get to my destination. Even though I was not sure what that destination was going to look like.

Every setback in life teaches you something...it could be to slow down; it could be to look at what is important to you; it could be to pay more attention to your health, your eating habits or your exercise. It could be to get your life more in balance. Whatever the situation is...when one door closes, another door opens, as long as you are looking for that door.

Keep your mind open; do not think everything has to be the way you planned it. Some of the best plans are spontaneous. Sometimes we try to control people, places and things too much. Let go. Let it happen. Trust the process. Live in the moment. If we are so focused on something having to be a certain way, then we may miss all of the gifts that are there for us on the way to achieving our goal. Is that what they mean by "Stop and smell the roses?" Maybe, but you have to be still and quiet sometimes to find out. If you are running through the roses too fast, you may just get pricked and not enjoy the experience at all.

Lessons Learned

If I look back at all of my setbacks, and I seem to have many of them, they have all taught me invaluable lessons. I guess I sometimes needed to be hit with a two-by-four to stop and listen to either my body or my subconscious. Here are some crazy examples:

1. In high school, the day before our city championship playoff for the finals, I was practicing and leaned over the net to get a tennis ball. The net broke; I fell flat on my face and broke my thumb on my right hand. Yes, I was right-handed. I cried quite a bit. I called my doctor and went over to his house, where he bandaged it up for me, with my tennis racquet in my hand, into the shape of the grip, so I would at least be able to hold the racquet and play the next day for the finals. He, of course, was against the idea, but I assured him I would take full responsibility. I just needed my thumb bandaged enough around the width of the grip so I could hold the racquet for the match. It was, of course, the biggest match of my tennis life. I just *had* to play. We won the Los Angeles City Championships that next day.

Lesson learned: No amount of pain can keep you from your goals. When you are winning, the pain is never as bad.

George Vecsey said this about Pete Sampras beating Alex Corretja on September 6, 1996 at the U.S. Open: "It was not a pretty sight, but somehow deep in his stricken system, Sampras found the strength to stagger back. Pale and wan, propping himself up by his racquet between the points, he literally staggered to victory."

2. In my first year playing college tennis, the women's tennis season was in the spring, so I asked the men's tennis coach if I could work out with the men's tennis team during the fall season. He said, "Absolutely not; no woman has ever practiced with my men. Women aren't good enough. That's why there are men's teams and women's teams." That didn't go over very well with me at all. Didn't he remember the match with Billie Jean King and Bobby Riggs? Equal rights for women? Anyway, my approach was to be one of his assistants as he taught tennis classes to other students at the school.

I was at the tennis courts every free second I had. I made sure I jumped rope right where he could see me. I always practiced my serve so he could see me. I ran sprints, did lunges, ran the stairs...I always made sure Coach saw my extra effort. I just knew I could wear him down. I had to do it. After all, I was one of the hardest workers I knew in any sport! I wanted to go on to play professionally, and I knew he could help me with his coaching and playing because of the international men's state championship team he had built for years. Anyway, about once a week, I asked him if I could work out with the men's team. He said no over and over, until finally one day, he said, "I will let you work out just this once. I'm going to put you on the last court and I will *not* coach you—I'm not going to say one word to you—and I won't allow any other girls to hit in, so don't think all of your friends on the team can come."

I politely replied, "Thank you, Coach. I'll see you tomorrow." The next day at practice, before we ever hit a ball, we had calisthenics for more than an hour. That's what they called them at the time. I have never been so tired, sore and invigorated at the same time. I know he thought I would quit after the first hour. That is how he always got his team whittled down to the "real" players. They could not take the conditioning. As promised, he put me on the last court, hitting with a new guy. Again as promised, Coach did not say one word to me, but I didn't care. I was playing and working out with the men's team. Many of the guys weren't happy about me being there, since it was, of course, the men's team practice, but I did not care.

At the end of three hours of hitting tennis balls, doing drills and playing sets, I was leaving and Coach called me into his office by myself. He said, "You can come tomorrow if you want." I walked out of his little office, so excited. Coach never said very much to anyone, so that was like having a half-hour discussion about how good my tennis game was. After that, I never missed a day of men's tennis practice in college. After the two years I spent there, I learned many great things from Coach about playing and teaching tennis. It was probably one of my best experiences ever. I grew in leaps and bounds as I learned more about self-discipline, being in shape and the art of practicing specific shots for hours until I mastered them. I stayed good friends with Coach for years after college, and I felt that he actually respected me as a player and later as a good tennis coach, even for a girl.

Lesson learned: Hard work and being persistent never goes to waste. If you want something badly enough, then don't stop fighting for it until you get it.

Billie Jean King said, "A girl did not get an athletic scholarship until the fall of 1972 for the very first time."

3. In my third year of college, I received a full tennis scholarship to the University of Alabama in Birmingham. I loved the South, and got to practice with the men's tennis team. That was one of the reasons I chose that Division I school. I played #1 singles and #1 doubles that year. Then during the spring, I had a lot of trouble with my elbow. They have a great sports medicine department there and three doctors agreed I needed to have elbow surgery. I needed to have an ulna nerve transposition. The nerve was pinched between the bones and the muscles in my elbow, and it felt like I was hitting my funny bone all the time. Not very funny, I might add. I did everything I could to avoid the surgery, but it was inevitable. I had to have the elbow surgery.

In the meantime, I was in a sling, trying to rehab my arm and elbow, and we were playing a tennis match against Auburn University. Two of our players were hurt, another player was sick, and we were going to lose in the #6 position because we did not have enough players to start the match. My coach gave us this information right before we started the match. Well, I volunteered to go in and just play left-handed, with my sling on my right arm. I knew we were going to lose that position anyway. He said, "Okay, if you feel up to it." Now, I was not ambidextrous at all. I figured it would be good exercise. My style of play was a lot like Martina Navratilova's—serve and volley to get the point over with quickly. I used the same strategy starting this match. I was not a very patient player from the baseline. When we went to take practice serves, I stopped dead in my tracks. I had to change how to stand, throw the toss-up with my arm in a sling and think how my other arm was going to go down my back, and hopefully up, to hit the ball above my head without me looking like a complete idiot. I actually laughed at myself because I hadn't thought about all of these factors. My serve took about three minutes to go over the net—it was that slow. I knew it could be a real ugly match, but the good news was it would be over with quickly. So we started the match. I served and volleyed and immediately watched the ball sail by me without me even touching the ball. "Okay, she got lucky," I thought. I served and volleyed again and another winner whizzed by my racquet. That game took all of four minutes, only because I tried to walk slowly in between the points.

After about ten minutes, I was losing 5-1. My left arm was so tired I knew I could not stay out there very long and I certainly could not play three sets. So I started talking to my opponent on our changeover. She talked back, since she was killing me and knew the match would be over in only a matter of a few more minutes. She finally asked me why I was wearing a sling. I told her I was getting ready to have elbow surgery and we would have lost this match because we did not have enough players. I told her that I was the #1 singles player, but I was playing #6 position since we would have forfeited anyway. I saw her eyes getting huge. She said, "You play #1 singles and now you're playing me at #6? This is so embarrassing. You shouldn't even be getting points against me."

Now, in my mind, I was thinking, "I have her. She is going to go crazy if I can just get a few more points and then maybe a couple more games. I totally need to change my strategy and decide that I am in great shape and there is no one in better shape than I am. I'll just stay at the baseline, run down every ball and hit it high over the net. My strategy is never to miss a ball. Don't even hit it hard, just high and no misses. I can stay out here all day." Really, I didn't think I could do this for three sets. Anyway, as you may have guessed, my strategy worked perfectly. My opponent self-destructed when she realized she should be killing me and wasn't. I reeled off the next six games and beat her in that set, 7-5. I also won the next set, 6-2. I knew I could not go three sets; my arm was too tired. That's a perfect example to prove that tennis, or any sport, is ninety percent mental. There is no way I should have won that tennis match that day. But as soon as I changed my mindset, and the girl changed hers because of the circumstances, the entire match changed.

Lesson learned: Tennis is ninety percent mental. Believing in yourself is stronger than any forehand, backhand or serve you may have. If you work on your mental game, then the physical part of the game is not as important.

Martina Hingis said, "I did not have the same fitness or ability as the other girls, so I had to beat them with my mind. The first point is always to believe in it when you go on the tennis court and then you have chances to win."

4. After elbow surgery, I could not play for three months. So I traveled with all the other sports teams as an athletic trainer. Part of my job was to tape all the players up before practices and games and help take care of the athletes' injuries, etc. It was a great experience. I learned many mental factors by being around coaches from other sports, which made me mentally stronger.

Each coach taught me different ways of mentally preparing for matches or games. I learned the importance of preparation—how you must do your homework by scouting your next opponents to exploit their strengths and weaknesses. I learned how to focus on what you want to achieve. What does it look like? What do you want it to look like? How do you want it to feel? Can you see it and play it out in your mind? Can you see it in your mind, vividly? Can you touch it in your mind? How do you see your dreams? Create the vision in your head...down to every detail. Dream big; no dream is too big!

At this time in my life, especially when I couldn't play tennis, I learned valuable lessons, such as how to practice mentally, how to focus and how to achieve my dreams. These lessons came from traveling with the other teams and their coaches. I also realized how much I loved playing tennis. I missed it so much. When something is taken away from you, you learn how important it is, or is not, to you. For me, tennis was in my blood. I could not wait to get back to playing. While I was not playing, I started teaching some juniors—left-handed! I realized how much I like teaching tennis and how rewarding it was to watch some-one get better under my tutelage. It was really gratifying.

Lesson learned: You sometimes realize your passion when seemingly bad things happen. For me, mental strength came from losing something, albeit temporarily. Elbow surgery changed the direction of my life. I think I was destined to teach and help people. I can touch so many more people's lives and share my experiences with them. I can try to save them some of the agony I went through. Through teaching, I can help shape people's character, values and build their self-esteem and self-confidence, which they will continue to use in the rest of their lives, not just in tennis.

Billie Jean King said, "Sports teaches you character, it teaches you to play by the rules, it teaches you to know what it feels like to win and to lose...and it teaches you about life."

5. In 2001, I was heavily into bike riding for my health, recreation and fun. I was going out with some friends early one Sunday morning, and I had to be back to teach a big junior program in the afternoon, so I knew I could only ride for about four hours. That was one of our short, early rides.

We were in the middle of our hilly journey, climbing up steep mountain roads; it was a beautiful, crisp day. Then, I decided to go first down a very steep hill. I was going a little too fast when I hit a rock. I was told that I went flying over the handlebars, doing a few somersaults. Luckily I don't remember much about the fall. Fortunately, one girl's cell phone happened to work in that mountain area. Any other time we had been there, or have been back there since, cell phones have never worked. Coincidence? I do not think so.

Anyway, the location where I was, and the fact that I could not move my neck or head, was somewhat of a concern for the emergency dispatch woman. As a result, I ended up having my first helicopter ride. The paramedics were really cute (I think). I thought I was going to be in one of those baskets like you used to see in the TV show, "MASH." I thought I was going to be swinging in the wind back and forth. It didn't seem like a great idea to me, since I kept saying I was "fine" and I had a tennis event at the club at one o'clock. The very cute paramedics assured me I wouldn't be attending any tennis event that day. "Ma'am, I cannot leave here until you get in that helicopter with me." So I was airlifted to UCLA on a perfectly gorgeous Sunday afternoon. And that was my first experience in a helicopter.

Unfortunately, I did not see much scenery and I don't remember too much about the helicopter trip, since I was a little out of it. I was very lucky. I'd only separated both of my shoulders, which is hard to do. I knew I was in trouble when my mom and dad took me home to their house and they got out of the car and went inside. I was in two slings and couldn't move any of my upper body. I was also quite sore from the fall. Finally, my dad came out of the door, hysterically laughing, after realizing I couldn't even unbuckle myself to get out of the car. I didn't think it was so amusing. The reality of how helpless I was hit me again as I was sitting, ready to have some soup, and I couldn't even feed myself. "Oh my," I thought. "It's going to be a long few weeks." I also had a little trouble going to the bathroom, if you know what I mean. The experience was one I had never had, being totally helpless, like a newborn infant. I went to work with a portable ice machine for both my shoulders and people helped set me up. Then they played matches while I watched and coached from the sidelines. Once again, I had to look at different ways to teach without physically being able to hit tennis balls with my clients.

Lesson learned: It is okay to ask for help. People like to feel needed. You don't have to do everything by yourself. Get a good support team so you never feel you have to be in any battles or hardships by yourself. This is true in accomplishing your goals or in getting through some of life's daily struggles.

Althea Gibson said, "No matter what accomplishments you achieve, somebody helps you. No matter what accomplishments you make, somebody helps you."

6. In December 2001, my left hip was really getting bad. I could hardly run on it anymore to teach tennis. Bike riding was getting hard to do, especially climbing hills, which I loved to do. I had gone to a doctor a few years before and he said that I would need a hip replacement in the next few years. I thought he was crazy. He said I had a lot of bone degeneration from years of pounding on my hips with all of my activities. I thought I might need a hip replacement when I was seventy-five years old, not at forty-one.

I went to another specialist who did nothing but knee and hip replacements. He also was a tennis player, so I knew he would understand about me wanting to get back on the court as quickly as possible. I also assumed since that was his specialty, and he saw hundreds of patients, that he would tell me I could wait for a few more years. When I walked into his waiting room in Santa Monica—I was the only one who did not have blue hair, a walker or a cane. I immediately walked out of the waiting room in shock that I was actually contemplating having a new titanium hip put into my body. What if the operation did not work? What if it came out of the socket after he replaced it? What if I could not walk or run, as I used to? What if I could not teach tennis anymore? Or bike ride? Or water-ski, or snow ski? Or go for a hike? Would I have to have another replacement in ten more years, which is what another doctor told me a few years earlier? I was really terrified. I walked back into the waiting room, and saw the doctor. He took an x-ray of my hips and said that the left one needed a total replacement right away and the other one might need a replacement in a few years. Conveniently, they had an opening in two weeks. I had the surgery. It happened to be at a good time, right before Christmas. It's always a slower time for my business, with all the holiday activities.

I recovered pretty quickly, even with this major surgery. Because of how young I was, I had a cementless hip replacement. My recovery took a little longer, but I was told if I was good and let myself recover well, I should not need another replacement for the rest of my life. Needless to say, I was a very good patient, as I did not want to repeat this process, even if the drugs were good. I was back to teaching, slowly at first, then increased my hours gradually. Within three to four months, it was business as usual, with no pain.

At this time, I started teaching more about the mental side of the tennis game, the "focus" part. I asked students, "Which side of your brain controls your focus—your right or left side of the brain?" I did extensive work on that. Tim Gallwey years ago wrote his book, *The Inner Game of Tennis*. I used some of what he says in his book and added other steps I have learned over the years. I conducted clinics called "The Focus Blast," just working on the mental part of the game. We did not discuss how to hit the tennis ball, but how to clear your mind of really thinking so you can play the game, and play freely.

Lesson learned: You must take care of your body as you get older. Do not ignore signs if something is wrong. Your health is the most important thing you have...treat it with great care. Being in good shape going into major surgeries, your recovery time is cut in half. Work smarter, not harder. An entire new arena of teaching was introduced to me through this major injury and change in my life, which added another dimension to my teaching. By sitting still in my recovery, I learned to be better with myself in sitting still, reading and reflecting on my life and the next level of teaching.

Steffi Graf said, "I appreciate being injury-free. I never look back; I look forward. I knew that maybe I wouldn't be playing again, but I just wanted to get into good physical shape."

7. By now, you must think I am done with major injuries, right? Haven't I learned enough lessons? I hope you have learned some lessons from my experiences!

I'm not quite finished. In March 2006, I was on another bike ride, very early on a Sunday morning. No one else was on the road and I was riding in the bike path lane on the street, going downhill. I was being very careful and paying attention to the car in the driveway stopped in front of me. The driver claimed never to have seen me coming down the hill, and she pulled out in front of me to turn left. I had quick reactions, slammed on my brakes and turned the bike as she hit me with her car. Again, I was very lucky. I only had a torn right rotator cuff (remember, I am right-handed), and no, I did not get a helicopter ride, only a ride in an ambulance. Again, I told the paramedic I was not getting in that ambulance because I was, "Fine." When I could not move my right arm in any direction, once again he said, "Lady, I am not leaving until you come in the ambulance with me."

"Okay," I said, "But I am not lying down on that gurney. I will just sit." Again, being in good shape is what cut my recovery time in half. I did not have to have surgery. I healed with physical therapy. However, again, I had forced time off to sit still. I am assuming that it takes me a long time to learn the lesson of slowing down since I have had many instances where I was forced to slow down and evaluate what I am doing. I guess I take a little longer to learn than most people.

Again, I wasn't able to teach tennis for a couple of months. When I am hurt or injured, it's also the time when I realize how much fun I have teaching and playing tennis. Life is still about fun. I realize how I can make life fun for somebody else. You have to have fun in whatever you do. That is when I started writing this book. I realize how much I like doing what I do and how I can teach it to other people as well. It also made me realize once again how vulnerable I am. In my job, if I am not able to work physically, I have no other income. I realized, at this time in my life, I needed to start adding other ways of generating income.

Do you have more than one source of income? Have you looked at your long-term goals for the future? Do you have at least six-months to a year of savings if something major happened to you or your family?

Lesson learned: Have fun at what you do. Life is about having fun and laughing along the way. Save and plan for the future. Something good always comes out of something seemingly bad.

Monica Seles said, "That's the key to success, isn't it? It has to be fun."

Jana Novotna said, "When we don't laugh and when we don't have fun, we play very bad. So, in order for us to play well, we need to enjoy it and have fun. You know, there were some great shots. It was entertaining for all of the players and the public to watch, so why not laugh occasionally?"

Exercise:

List five times in your life when one door was closed and another door was opened:

1._____

2._____

3._____

4._____

5._____

What lessons did you learn?

1._____

2._____

3._____

4._____

5._____

Change is Mostly in Your Own Mind

Look at the 2008 Summer Olympics. So many world records were broken, even shattered. Why was that? Why are records broken every year? Why don't world records hold up for a very long time? One example of breaking world records is, obviously, Michael Phelps. One cannot say enough about this phenomenal athlete. Eight gold medals and seven of them were for world records. That is unheard of, and it will probably not be challenged for many years to come. Mark Spitz had set the bar high, and his record could not be broken for thirty-six years until Michael Phelps came along. Spitz won seven gold medals in the 1972 summer Olympics.

Another world record that was shattered in the 2008 Summer Olympics was the men's 100-meter dash. It is common knowledge that most sprinters are about 5'10" or shorter. If you are any taller than that, then you are a hurdler, or a high jumper, or a long jumper, certainly not a short distance sprinter. However, in the 2008 Summer Olympics 6' 5" Usain Bolt changed the sport forever. He ran it in 9.69 seconds, with daylight to spare. He actually slowed down before he even got to the finish line. He literally dwarfs the other sprinters, and yet, he shattered the world record. My guess is that coaches will now look differently at athletes for sprinting.

Another example from the 2008 Summer Olympics was the female swimmer Dara Torres. She won two silver medals, even though she was forty-one years old. People think your age limits what you can and cannot do. You hear all the time, "I'm too old to do that anymore." What does age have to do with anything? Your body may need more recovery time, but it should not limit you to things you can or cannot do. Dara Torres made people realize that just because you are a certain age, you're not limited in your abilities, in sports or business. You can accomplish anything, no matter what your age. Dara squashed, eliminated and terminated all the thoughts and perceptions that people once thought.

We are always put into a certain mold. We are conditioned at an early age to believe certain myths as "truth."

For example:

- "If your parents were fat, you will be fat."
- "You should just look for a job with good benefits to be *secure*."
- "You do not have the speed, or the hand-eye coordination, or the athletic ability to be a great tennis player, but you could be a good social player."

Instead, *always* remember the *solutions*:

- Listen to your voice deep down in your soul.
- NEVER let anyone tell you what you can, or cannot, do.
- There are really no limits. The only limit is your own mind.

For me, being a coach, I try to instill confidence in my players by telling them, "Just believe in yourself because I believe in you. Then later you will learn to trust that belief, and start to believe it yourself. But, for now, just believe that I believe in you." That seems to be easier for some people to handle, since they have low self-esteem when taking on what seems to them to be an impossible task or an impossible goal.

I started late in my teenage years to try to become a good tennis player. I always remember hearing that if I did not step in (or forward) with my left foot on my forehand, I was going to miss the shot. I don't remember where it started. I do remember having to run many laps around the tennis court each time I didn't step into a forehand shot with my left foot. Right or wrong, still, to this day, I remember that. At that time (in the olden days of learning the game), Chris Evert had the most beautiful strokes in tennis. Every girl tennis player tried to emulate her form, gracefulness and effortlessness in hitting a forehand or a backhand. Needless to say, every time I went to hit a forehand, especially in a tournament, and I was not stepping in, I missed my shot. Shocking, eh? It then became my most dreaded shot, instead of my most favorite shot. In my mind, if I did not have time to step into the shot, I knew I was going to miss. That became reality. Without knowing it, I set myself up for failure a good portion of the time. This was especially evident under pressure, in a tournament, or a big match.

This is an example of a how a myth becomes reality. The myth became my reality because I started believing it. My mistake always seemed to be the outcome. If I did not step into my forehand with my left foot, I would miss. It became a reality because before I even hit the ball, I had so much doubt whether the ball would ever go over the net that I never gave myself a chance to think it "might" go over the net. My myth became my reality. I had myself talked into missing my forehand as soon as the ball came toward me. I hadn't even tried to hit the ball yet. Can you imagine how good I could have been if my thinking had been, "Yeah, here comes a forehand. I hit them great. I know this one is going cross-court."

Exercise

List three things you learned as myths, either about sports or life:

1._____

2._____

3._____

List three solutions you could tell yourself about these myths knowing what you know now:

1._____

2._____

3._____

The Power of Positive Thinking

A coaching friend of mine and I have had numerous discussions on the importance of positive thinking. So many people have grown up with limits placed on them—being told as children what they can and cannot do. The power of positive thinking outweighs the power of negative thinking, 100 percent.

I once was very curious about the answer to this question: Does what you think in your mind control how you react in a given situation?

I decided to do an experiment on the tennis court. I had twenty-five of my best juniors all on one tennis court. At the time, each was ranked either in Southern California or nationally. As a coach, I thought most of the comments said out loud while competing tended to be negative. That made me think negative thoughts were in the players' heads while they are actually playing the point. They were not thinking positively about what to do out on the tennis court.

My experiment went like this: One player lined up and was fed twenty balls. The goal was to get all twenty tennis balls cross-court in a specific area sectioned off with ropes. It was a generous area, which most tennis players hit with great competence. This does not sound like a hard task to perform. A parent, writing down the results, was to record how many of the twenty balls went into the designated area.

I put the other twenty-four juniors on the tennis court, behind the player who was about to hit a forehand. I gave each player a different phrase to say over and over. First, I gave each junior a negative thing to say out loud while the ball was being hit, such as, "You're gonna miss," "You suck," "You're terrible," "You always miss this shot..." (I think you get the point). All twenty-four juniors were to say these phrases at the same time, the entire time the other player was trying to hit the twenty forehand cross-court shots. We did this with all twenty-four players. They each got a turn trying to hit twenty forehand shots cross-court, while everyone else stood yelling negative sayings. Can you imagine how everyone's efficiency was? The kids thought it was one of the funniest things they'd ever done. The noise level was tremendous.

I then reversed the exercise and gave the juniors positive phrases to say while the same twenty forehand cross-court shots were hit. A parent recorded how many of the twenty balls landed in the designated area. Some of the positive phrases were, "You can do it," "You can make this ball," "You're great," "You've practiced this shot a hundred times..." The juniors liked screaming the negative phrases more. I guess that's where they were more comfortable—because they say them so often to themselves.

Anyway, we totaled up the results and it was astonishing. I'd assumed there would be a difference, but I was shocked. For the totals from all twenty-five junior players, when they heard negative phrases, they only made twenty-five percent of the balls into the cross-court area. When they heard positive phrases, they made eighty-five percent of the forehand shots. That's sixty percent—and that's the difference between winning and losing a match. Wouldn't you agree? That is an astonishing figure. You did not have to work on new forehands, or a new back-hand—all you had to do was change what you thought about in your mind. That is powerful. Why doesn't everyone do that? When is the last time you heard, "Great job," "You were fabulous," "You tried your best; that's all anyone can ever ask," "Thank you for all of your hard work," "Thank you for everything," or "That was an excellent effort."

As colleagues, practice partners, friends, family members, teachers or coaches, we must remember that a positive statement far outweighs a negative statement. I once heard that when you say one negative thing, it takes 100 positive things to replace that one negative thought. If you have to confront someone about a situation, always try to start with a positive point first; then talk about the problem. An example might be, "Your attitude out there on the court was great, but we still need to work on your consistency during the point," or "Your work was very well organized and it was a great idea, but can you be more specific about the problem we had with this company?" If people hear the negative statement first, they usually do not hear anything you say after that. They are still dwelling on the negative comment. So, make a conscious effort to start from a positive point of view. People will be more apt to change something you suggested and you will have more success in anything you personally do, too. Wouldn't you rather make seventeen forehand cross-court shots rather than only five forehand cross-court shots in a tennis match?

In conclusion, with positive thoughts, students were successful eighty-five percent of the time, and with negative thoughts, students were only successful twenty-five percent of the time.

Exercise

List three negative things you say when you are on the tennis court:

1._____

2._____

3._____

List three positive things you can say instead:

1._____

2._____

3._____

List three negative things you say to yourself in everyday life:

1._____

2._____

3._____

List three positive things you can say instead:

1._____

2._____

3._____

Louise L. Hay is one of the founders of the self-help movement. She is an author of numerous books, including, *You Can Heal Your Life*. She has written about how positive affirmations can change so many different aspects of your life...Picture the ball going right into the middle of the service box.

F = False		F = Forget
E = Evidence	OR	E = Everything
A = Appearing		A = And
R = Real		R = Run

So, take it easy, take it just one-step at a time. Relax and breathe while you are in the midst of being fearful.

Exercise

List three fears you would like to overcome:

1._____

2._____

3._____

Use affirmations to replace negative images of the past with positive messages of the future.

Affirmation Prayer

Just for today, I will respect my own and other's boundaries.

Just for today, I will be vulnerable with someone I trust.

Just for today, I will take one compliment and hold it in my heart for more than a fleeting moment. I will let it nurture me.

Just for today, I will act in a way that I would admire in someone else.

I am a child of God.

I am a precious person.

I am a worthwhile person.

I am beautiful inside and outside.

I love myself unconditionally.

I can allow myself ample leisure time without feeling guilty.

I deserve to be loved by others and myself.

I am loved because I deserve love.

I am a child of God and I deserve love, peace, prosperity and serenity.

I forgive myself for hurting myself and others.

I forgive myself for letting others hurt me.

I forgive myself for accepting sex when I wanted love.

I am willing to accept love.

I am not alone; I am one with the universe and myself.

I am whole and good.

I am capable of changing.

The pain that I might feel by remembering cannot be any worse than the pain I feel by knowing and not remembering.

I am enough.

— Affirmations from Al-Anon

May you be at peace.
May your heart remain open.
May you awaken to the light of your own true nature.
May you be healed.
May you be a source of healing for all beings.
— *The Metta of the Buddha*

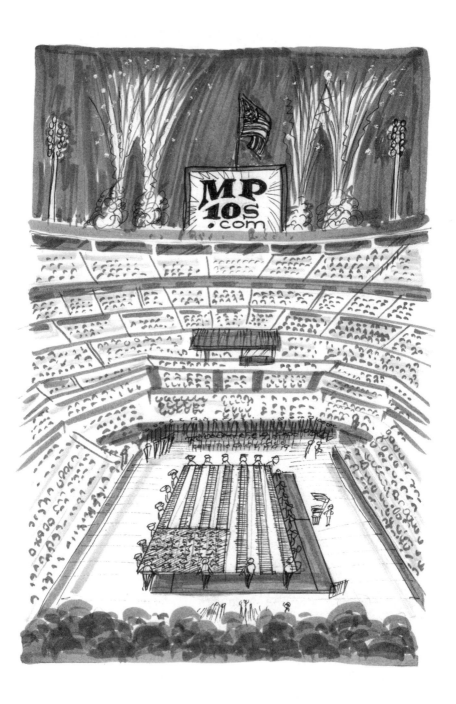

CHAPTER 8:
LEADING ON AND OFF THE COURT

Experience tells you what to do; Confidence allows you to do it.
— Stan Smith

Bring Yourself into Everything You Do

In Billie Jean King's book, *Pressure is a Privilege*, she writes, "Bring all of yourself by completely committing yourself to whatever you do. Take things one-step at a time, and break your challenges down into manageable goals and objectives so you do not get overwhelmed. Stay in the now by embracing each moment, being aware, noticing the right details, prioritizing, staying focused. Avoid dwelling in the past, but also avoid looking so far ahead that you cannot see the next step in the process. Finally, learn the difference between letting it happen and making it happen. To enjoy life and make the best of it, try to recognize when it's time to try a different approach, and when it's time to just walk in a new direction."

Know yourself. As the saying goes, "To thine own self, be true." I have tried to live by that statement. You must find your own truth. Self-awareness is the foundation of all these life lessons. Self-awareness is probably the most important step on your road toward being a champion. Know your abilities and know your limitations. Continually work on your weaknesses and stay on course with your strengths. Trust yourself. Knowing yourself is knowing your truth.

Leadership

The very essence of leadership is that you have to have a vision. It's got to be a vision you articulate clearly and forcefully on every occasion.
— *Rev. Theodore Hesburgh,*
President Emeritus University of Notre Dame

What qualities are needed to be a leader? What leadership qualities do you want your coach, your boss, the CEO of the company you work for to have? What qualities can you develop to help your teammates on your sports team? Have you worked for people who had great leadership qualities? Have you ever played for a coach who made you reach higher limits than you ever thought possible? What does it mean to be a dynamic leader in sports? What lessons from sports leadership can be translated into our own leadership journeys? What lessons from sports leadership can we directly translate into our daily living, including our jobs and teaching our children some of these traits that are so important? Sports and leadership go hand-in-hand. When people learn these skills while playing sports, they are more proficient in the business world, as the qualities are similar.

Great Leaders:

1) Have good ethics and values. What they do, and what the team does, emulates good values and ethics. They can be trusted.

2) Do many good things. To get the best results, leaders train their people; they coach their people; they mentor and they support their people. They lead by the positive example of "See something; do something." In this way, they become people of action and they are strong in their convictions.

3) Good communicators. They help people resolve problems quickly. They have an open door policy for all team members. They do not bully or harass team members to try to get something accomplished. It is not the, "Do as I say, not as I do" theory. It is quite the opposite.

Great leadership qualities start with the concept of being good at guiding people, coaching and mentoring people to be all they can be. In this process, it causes you, the leader, to be better too.

Lead by Example:

Leading by example is one of the greatest attributes a leader can possess. I think that sometimes we do not realize the impact we, as leaders can have on people, no matter how small the example. Children are constantly watching their parents, and doing or saying exactly what they see. They are the best imitators. Many times, when we see children do or say something, we stop dead in our tracks, and realize they were just imitating us, as parents. Sometimes it is not for the good, either.

I was driving with my stepdaughter, who was two-and-a-half years old, in her car seat in the back of the car. A man in another car was in the lane next to me, and turned in front of me, as if I were not even there. I slammed on the brakes and the car swerved a little. From the back seat I heard, "_ _ _ _." Well, I had to laugh out loud, but then we had a conversation about how that is a bad word and we do not use that word.

Another story of leading by example happened when I was teaching a group of beginner kids, between five and seven years old. They were at the net, learning how to volley, to ensure being successful by getting the ball over the net. All six children were spaced apart all along the net. They were talking, and so excited to have tennis racquets in their hands. They were waving them over their heads like great batons flying through the air. I instructed them to put their racquets down so they did not hurt anyone. In one quick second, every child dropped his or her racquet and all six racquets landed on the ground almost at the exact same time. Wow...talk about trusting what you say. I was hysterical. I really meant just to put their racquets down in front of their bodies, and not wave them in the air. So, I learned a great lesson. Be careful what you say to children, as they will do *exactly* what you say. That is a good thing, and sometimes, not a good thing.

Another funny story happened as I was giving my stepdaughter, Remi, a tennis lesson. Before we start every lesson, we do a little warm-up. She was six years old at the time. So, we started our little jog around the perimeter of the tennis court together. For years, I've always had my ChapStick readily available because my lips tend to be sunburned if I do not apply ChapStick repeatedly during the day. If I'm not wearing shorts with a pocket in them, and I am wearing a tennis skirt, I have to put my ChapStick in a place where I can get to it easily. Tennis skirts are made with shorts sewed into them with little pockets for the tennis balls on the outside of the shorts, under the skirt. That's a perfect hiding spot for my ChapStick, so I always keep it there. So, when we started our little jog, Remi was running right next to me, and all of a sudden, I almost tripped on a little tube of cherry ChapStick. I stopped and picked it up and continued running. Two seconds later, a little toy brown bear was lying on the tennis court. I picked it up and said, "Where did this come from?" Remi laughed as a little Polly Pocket doll fell onto the ground right where we were running. With another running step, Polly Pocket clothing was splattering all over the court. It was everywhere. "Remi," I said, "Where did all this stuff come from?" She was still laughing, and said, "Pat-Pat, I put it up my skirt, just like you do. You put things that are important in your skirt." I could no longer run. I was almost peeing in my pants. That is the funniest thing I think I ever heard on the tennis court. That is a perfect example of how we are always examples to our children. In every action we do, in things we say, and in ways we treat other people in front of our kids, we're leading by example. Do so with great care!

As I mentioned earlier, when I was fifteen, my family moved from Chicago to California. I was not happy with that situation, to say the least. I thought I was in my prime. I was on every varsity team in Chicago, even though I was a freshman in high school. I had all of my friends; I was a "star" in any athletics offered in my high school. I thought I was going to be an Olympic athlete in softball. Then when we moved to California, the first sport I tried out for was tennis. I had played tennis a little in Chicago, whenever tennis season came around but it was not my best sport at the time. I was astonished when more than seventy-five people tried out for the tennis team. We did not even have seventy-five people who played sports in my entire high school in Chicago, let alone try out for just one sport.

In California, everyone on the varsity team was nationally ranked, had her own private coach and even had a tennis court in her own back-yard. I was surely outclassed. Many of the girls on the team were members of a private club, the Warner Center Racquet Club. They took private and group lessons there. One day, I took the bus with a few friends from the tennis team to the tennis club. It was like visiting a magical place. The two stadium courts were magnificent, with stadium seating on either side. The grounds were beautiful; the Olympic size swimming pool looked like a lake; the indoor racquetball courts were gigantic and there were twenty-seven tennis courts on ground level. I had never seen anything like it before! You could even give the woman behind the glass partition your member number and order food right there at the tennis club. I thought I had died and gone to heaven.

A friend I had met on the tennis team, Janet Farrell, was a member there. She also took private tennis lessons. She told me about all the tennis pros at the club. Their teaching styles differed dramatically. I wanted the hardest coach, the coach who did not fool around—the one who would make me sweat the most. His name was Bob Collins. Every junior thought he was the meanest coach at the club. That's why I specifically asked him to give me lessons. I had a lot of learning to do in a very short period. Everyone at my high school was so much better than I was, so I needed to improve at a rapid rate. I took my first tennis lesson from him, and I remember almost throwing up. That's when I knew he was the coach for me. I came from a big family, six children, and when I told my parents about this club, we joined it as a family, which meant I could go there and play any time, day or night. My dad and I spent hours practicing and playing there every Saturday and Sunday. Thank goodness he liked tennis as much as I did.

We could not afford all the private lessons the other girls on my team had. My parents said they would pay for half the cost of the lessons, and I had to come up with the other half. I talked with my coach, Bob, about that dilemma. He made a very generous agreement with me. He told me he would teach me for that amount of money, but in return, I had to hit with all of the other juniors he taught, and I had to drive his students to some of the tournaments and watch them play. I also learned to string tennis racquets at the club. I made extra money that way, also. He taught me how to watch a player play and to evaluate her strengths and weaknesses in a very short period. He made me chart players' tennis matches, plan a strategy of what I would do if I were playing them and how I would correct their strategies if I were coaching them.

In those years of Bob coaching me to become a better tennis player, I learned more than I ever thought I would. His leadership taught me how to mentor young students, who looked up to me as a better junior player, how to feel part of a unique group of coaching his junior tennis team and how to make money to accomplish my goal. He taught me how to set goals by writing them down on a piece of paper and then set deadlines for accomplishing them. He taught me the commitment I needed to have to him and to his students. I had to become a great analyst to see the "cause" of the problem with a student's stroke. Then I learned to be a great communicator to make the simplest correction and have the student understand the correction immediately.

Bob used to stand behind me as I was hitting or feeding balls to his students, and ask me what was the number one thing wrong with that student's stroke. I would tell him what I thought the problem was, and he would correct me by explaining there was something more important. He explained that if you fixed the number one problem, the other four (or more) things would fix themselves. I learned very early how important it was to find the number one cause of a problem because then the rest will take care of themselves.

In those years, the students also had to trust me. I was their sounding board. They could tell me anything, about any situation and they had to know the conversation would go no further. That's a big quality in good leadership. The trust I developed with those juniors was never broken. Many great players developed from that program. It was a combination of all of these leadership qualities, and the integrity of the program. It allowed everyone to grow and become more successful than any of the juniors could have been on their own. These gifts were given to me, without me even knowing at the time what I was learning for my later career choices. I am so thankful I had that opportunity when I was young to learn and develop all of these qualities.

Exercise

List at least three people who were leaders to you when you were growing up:

1._____

2._____

3._____

The most important words a leader can say:

The six most important words: "I admit I made a mistake."

The five most important words: "You did a good job."

The four most important words: "What is your opinion?"

The three most important words: "If you please."

The two most important words: "Thank you."

The one most important word: "We"

The least important word: "I"

Leadership in Sports:

Examples of leadership can be seen in the boardroom, the workplace, management level firms, coaching teams, team owners, general managers, and grades that are received in high school. Coaches and players feel the pressure to succeed in sports, more than ever before in history. Why are dads from opposing Little League teams getting in fistfights over a baseball game? Why are coaches at the professional level fired and hired on an annual basis? Why is winning and losing so important? What happened to good sportsmanship being so important? If children are taught at a young age that winning is the most important thing in sports, then many leadership qualities will not be taught. Many of those attributes will go by the wayside, never to be used or contemplated. We need to focus on children having "fun" again in sports.

A sport that has gone back to the basics of "fun" is in the entry level American Youth Soccer Association (AYSO). At the entry level, no score is kept. The kids play soccer, and of course, the object of the game is to score a goal, but no "official" score is kept. The boys and girls learn to have "fun" playing their sport, while learning the game week to week. At the end of the season, every participant on every team receives a trophy. Their season concludes with earning a trophy, not just winning or losing.

Julie Foudy, former captain of the USA Women's Soccer Team, two-time Olympic gold medalist and two-time World Cup Soccer Champion, has started a Sports Leadership Academy for girls ages twelve to eighteen. According to her web site, www.juliefoudyleadership.com:

"The program helps girls learn strategies and techniques that will lead to improved self-concept, team building, and leadership qualities in all of the players. Our focus is to teach our students the ingredients it takes to be a leader on the field and a leader in life. Our students get the best of both worlds: They learn soccer from some of the best women's players in the world and they are exposed to a multitude of leadership concepts they can cultivate for life."

Billie Jean King. When you speak about leadership in sports, one person's name stands out more than any man or woman...Billie Jean King. She has done more for women's sports and equality than a thousand people combined. In 1971, she was the first female athlete to win more than a hundred-thousand dollars in prize money in a single season. BJK spoke out for women and their right to earn comparable prize money in tennis and other sports. Her constant lobbying and commitments have broken many barriers.

King was ranked number one in the world for five years. Her 1973 "Battle of the Sexes" match against fifty-five-year-old Bobby Riggs, who claimed the women's game to be inferior, highlighted King's campaign for equality. The match drew a worldwide television audience of some fifty million, and King beat Riggs, 6-4, 6-3, 6-3. In 1974, she became the first president of the Women's Tennis Association and headed up the first professional women's tour, the Virginia Slims, in the 1970s. Between 1961 and 1979, she won a record twenty Wimbledon titles, including six singles titles in 1966, 1967, 1968, 1972, 1973 and 1975. She also won thirteen U.S. Open titles (including four singles), four French titles (one singles) and two Australian titles (one singles). She was elected to the International Tennis Hall of Fame in 1987 and served as captain of the United States Fed Cup Team in the 1990s. King founded tennis clinics for underprivileged children. She started a women's sports magazine and a women's sports foundation. She became the director of World Team Tennis after retiring, and she became an announcer, coach and author.

"In the '70s we had to make it acceptable for people to accept girls and women as athletes," Billie Jean King said. "We had to make it okay for them to be active. Those were much scarier times for females in sports." She was involved in the passing of Title IX for women in sports in schools. It created equal scholarships for female athletes, just like male athletes. If it were not for King's determination and hard work, I would not be where I am today. I would not have received a full athletic tennis scholarship to college to pay for my education.

"She has prominently affected the way 50 per cent of society thinks and feels about itself in the vast area of physical exercise," Frank Deford wrote in Sports Illustrated. "Moreover, like (Arnold) Palmer, she has made a whole sports boom because of the singular force of her presence."

Martina Navratilova said of Billie Jean King, "She was a crusader fighting a battle for all of us. She was carrying the flag; it was all right to be a jock." It was because of her crusading that in 1990 *Life Magazine* named King one of the "100 Most Important Americans of the 20th Century." Not just sports figures, but Americans. She was the only female athlete on the list, and one of only four athletes; Babe Ruth, Jackie Robinson and Muhammad Ali were the others.

Leadership Characteristics. In one sense, solid leadership is a subjective thing; in another there are certain characteristics that are, by consensus, typical of quality leadership. What does it take to be a leader? There are certain characteristics that are a typical quality of a person with good leadership qualities.

Karlene Sugarman, M.A. defines in her book, *Winning the Mental Way*, "Leaders must possess the qualities they are trying to incorporate into their team. For example, if you want members to be confident, have self-control, be disciplined, etc. then you must first possess all these traits. One of the most powerful things you can do is lead by example. You serve as an influential role model for your players and everything you do will be watched."

Vince Lombardi said, "Leaders are made, they are not born and they are made just like anything else has ever been made in this country—by hard work."

Six Rules That Apply to All Leadership Situations— At the Workplace & In Sports

1) Treat players with respect and you will earn their respect.
   * All players should be treated equally.
2) Identify each player's strengths and weaknesses.
   * Know the players well enough to see these differences.
3) Lead by example.
   * If you expect players to be on time, then you should never be late for a meeting yourself.
4) Share your strategy with your players.
   * It is much easier for players to support a strategy if they understand it first.
5) Be decisive and confident.
   * A coach's confidence can be contagious. If the players know you believe in them, they will start believing in themselves.
6) Always instruct in a positive way.
   * Tell them what they want to do, not what you do not want them to do.

As a coach, you must understand your role is more than to be a good judge of a player's abilities. If you want to maximize the team's chances of winning, then you need to apply the same leadership qualities that exist in today's workplace. This means treating players with the respect they deserve. It also means understanding that the same leadership techniques do not apply to all players. This is also the case with workers of different degrees of strengths and weaknesses.

The concepts that apply to the workplace are pretty much the same as those found in sports. As a coach or a manager, you are trying to motivate your "players" to reach their full potential. In addition, when everyone on the team understands the direction and strategy the manager/coach has developed, success is much easier to achieve.

Exercise

List three characteristics or qualities you can work on to be a better leader:

1._____

2._____

3._____

Self-Confidence

Arthur Ashe stated, "One important key to success is self-confidence. A key to self-confidence is preparation."

Walt Disney said, "Somehow I can't believe that there are any heights that can't be scaled by a man or a woman who knows the secrets of making dreams come true. This special secret can be summarized in the four C's. They are: Curiosity, Confidence, Courage and Consistency. The greatest of all of these is confidence. When you believe in a thing, believe in it all the way, implicitly, and unquestionably."

People who are self-confident are those who know they have the skills and ability to achieve, and most importantly, they take action! They do not rely on the approval of others to affirm their existence. It is enough that they know they have the capacity and the potential to achieve what they want to achieve, and they can see that what other people think is trivial.

What is self-confidence? Is it the ability to speak in a loud voice so you can get people's attention? Is it power dressing? One of the things that seems to hold people back from pursuing their dreams for many years is the fear of failure...and the lack of self-confidence that is needed to overcome that fear. It is something I think everyone has faced, at various times in life, and in various degrees. The question then is, "How do I overcome that fear, and gain my self-confidence?" By working on your self-confidence and your self-esteem, you will overcome that fear.

It may take some work, depending on what degree of fear you currently have.

One way to improve self-confidence, feelings of self-empowerment, self-satisfaction and fulfillment is to set goals. It is very important to set small goals, so they are reachable. Then, keep setting more small goals, until the main, big goal is achieved.

True self-confidence is not an overnight instant change that will occur. You may have had something traumatic or dramatic happen in your childhood that has greatly affected your self-confidence as an adult. It is not too late to make changes. You must be willing to do the work. You will receive the benefits and keep excelling in other areas of your life.

If you have low self-confidence or low self-esteem, it is nearly impossible to make time for your dreams, to break free from the traditional mold, and truly to be yourself. You must learn to take control of your self-confidence.

Taking Control of Your Self-Confidence

Do you think it is possible to do things that will change your feelings of low self-confidence? Is your self-confidence in your control? It is not genetic, and you do not have to rely on others to increase your self-confidence. You can change your thoughts. What do you think about yourself? Are you not attractive enough? Do you fear you are not very smart? Are you a positive person? You can become someone worthy of respect, and someone who can pursue what he/she wants despite what other people say to you.

Is there a big difference between self-confidence and self-esteem? They can be used interchangeably, but there is a subtle difference in them. The difference is:

1) Self-esteem is whether you believe you're worthy of respect from others.
2) Self-confidence is whether you believe in yourself.

You can take control of your life, and you can take actions to control your self-confidence. By doing these steps, you can improve your self-image and your competence, which will increase your self-confidence, without the help of anyone else.

A good example of taking pride in your self-image to build self-confidence happened to me recently. I took my stepdaughter to the children's "Lollicut" hair cutting salon. All the stations are designed for cutting kids' hair, including a Barbie car, a Batman car, a rocket ship and a pink Cadillac. I have never seen a child walk in there and mind having a haircut. The children's personalities change dramatically when they walk into the haircut place. The kids also strut out of there. I'd never noticed the changes in the children until today.

My stepdaughter has beautiful shoulder-length blonde hair (yes, people would kill for her hair). She needed a little trim to get ready for the new school year. She received just a little trim and they trimmed her bangs, so you could see her beautiful green eyes. Everyone comments on how beautiful her eyes are and how gorgeous her hair is. They put little curly ribbons in her hair, following the length of her hair, and she was looking in the mirror the entire time, smiling at herself. Her entire personality changed after getting her haircut, and now she really looked beautiful. She was exuding self-confidence. She went to the playground area after her hair was done and helped a little boy get on a truck.

I noticed so many other children who came in from soccer practice, or a crazy Saturday, and by the time they finished with their haircuts, their entire personalities changed for the better. It almost looked like a transformation happened from the time the children climbed into the chair to when they left the chair, with their hair all done beautifully. Boys and girls alike. All the children knew that they looked good. All the hairdressers, the mothers, the fathers, the receptionist, everyone gave them lots of compliments as to how great they all looked. Each kid's posture even changed. They walked straighter, taller, with their heads up. They even said "Thank you" after they received the compliments.

A small event, such as getting a haircut, showed me how much something that little can change a person's self-confidence. Those children took pride in their appearance after noticing how good they looked. They stood taller, looked you in the eye and were generous in their helping other children. They looked in the mirror and smiled a lot. Their entire demeanor changed just because they got a haircut. This is a perfect example to show that just by doing some of the simple actions on the list above, a child's self-confidence was dramatically changed. We need to instill this in the hearts of all young children. They need to gain self-confidence in their day-to-day existence.

The action of being prepared struck home with me. I think I do a good job as a tennis coach in preparing my junior tennis players for tournament play. About fifteen years ago, I was coaching a twelve-year old boy named Jason. He was new at junior tournaments. He had been playing tennis with me as his coach for about a year and a half. He was a great athlete. He had been an outstanding baseball player, and while playing little league baseball, he was pitching and a line drive ball came flying off the bat, and he was struck squarely in the side of his forehead. The ball had hit him so hard that the baseball ended up at first base. Jason was rushed to the hospital, and countless tests were done. He was very lucky to be alive. His skull had shattered in thirty-two places. Anyway, he was told he could no longer play baseball or any contact sports. That is why he chose tennis. Being the great athlete he was, he learned the game quickly, had great hand-eye coordination, and was fast. Within a year, he had sectional ranking, and was beating boys that had been ranked higher and had played for many more years than him.

It was the beginning of the summer, and after having a spectacular southern California junior sectional tournament, Jason was ranked high enough to be invited to the Boys National 12 and under tournaments, one held in Texas, the other in Florida. I had one month to prepare him for these tournaments, where the competition was fierce, even at the age of twelve. I do not know why they choose these states to have the most important tournaments of the year. It could not have been hotter or more humid. Jason had never played at this level, or in those parts of the country, so preparation was extremely important.

Since I'd played tennis in Alabama, I knew how hot and humid conditions could be. I had Jason practice every day for about three hours, during the hottest time of the day, to try to get used to the heat. In addition, that month during practice, he had to wear a rain suit, the top and the pants, to practice. That way, his body would get used to sweating profusely and he would understand how much fluid would have to be replaced in his body daily. He was not very happy with me; he thought I was out of my mind. I was in a tank top and he was sweating as if someone had turned the hose on him. He played many practice sets, did tons of wind sprints, lots of recovery drills, hit thousands of serves and returns. He practiced with kids much older than him so he could get used to the much heavier topspin on the ball. By the end of our month, I felt he was ready to play anyone. He still thought I was a little off my rocker.

We traveled to Texas and he played very well there. No one knew who he was—he was a virtual unknown to all those who had traveled on the national circuit during the year. He had many good wins against players who were better than him. He played even better than he practiced. That was a rare and great gift. We then flew to Florida. We arrived a few days early, so we could practice on the courts where the tournament was to be played. Jason could not believe how hot and humid it was. He recovered day to day because of his preparation in California.

The first day of the tournament, Jason and I looked at the draw on the big scoreboard. He was so mad, he was complaining, "We come all the way here to Florida, and I have to play the number one seed? That stinks! That is not fair! There's no way I can win." Well, it was not exactly the kind of attitude you want your student to have. Here was the perfect opportunity for me to show him the significance of, "Is the glass half empty, or half full?"

I was really excited that he had to play the #1 seed in the first round. I said, "What could be better?" Once again, Jason really thought I had lost all of my marbles. I then explained to him that if you have to play a seed, the perfect time is in the first round. No one knows who you are and no one knows how you play. The #1 seed is usually very cocky in his first few rounds because he is so good and experienced he thinks no one can really threaten him. This was actually the perfect scenario for Jason to play in one of his first national tournaments. I had scouted the number one seed and watched him practice. I knew his strengths and weaknesses, shared them with Jason and then put our game plan together for how he would beat this guy. I believed deep in my heart that Jason could win no matter how much more experienced was his opponent. I think I convinced Jason of it. When Jason stepped onto that court with the number one seed, he knew he could win. I told him if he did not believe he could win, it would be a waste of his time even to walk on the court with him. He had to believe he could beat him.

Jason looked pretty confident in the warm-up, but so did the other guy. More cocky than confident. As the match progressed, Jason executed the strategy perfectly. He won the first set, 6-1. The guy did not know what had hit him. He did not know who this "no name" guy was who'd just killed him in the first set. The next set was much closer and Jason lost in a tiebreaker.

Now I could talk to him for ten minutes. He came off the court a little discouraged. He said, "Now the guy knows my strategy; he figured it out." I replied, "He did not know your strategy; you just stopped using your strategy in the second set, which allowed him to play his attacking game. You must go back to the strategy you came in here using. He'll start missing because all of the pressure is on him. He's also exhausted. Look at him—he is sweating as if he just got out of the shower and you look fresh as a daisy. You can stay out there all day with him if you have to. Just be willing to stay out there for as long as it takes. You've done all the work and preparation to get here; now it will pay off." Jason trusted my judgment because he saw how it had worked in the first set. We talked about a few more little adjustments, and he was ready to go back onto the court.

Meanwhile, the number one seed's father was over on the other side of the court, literally screaming at his son for losing to this, "no name." You could hear him from anywhere around the court.

The third set worked like a charm. It was like watching a chess match. Both players knew what to do, but it came down to who wanted it more, and who executed better. Jason won the third set 6-3. He was so excited. It was definitely the biggest win of his short tennis career. The number one seed shook his hand after the match and told him what a good match he'd played. He was a very gracious loser. In the meantime, the boy's father was acting like a crazy man. He did not take his son's losing in the first round of a national tournament very well. Jason's self-confidence grew in leaps and bounds from that win and many others like it. He had the preparation, trusted the strategy and process and acted and thought positively. This is a perfect example of how a person's self-confidence can take him farther in whatever career path he is on...whether it is tennis, climbing the corporate ladder or feeling good about yourself for who you are—it all comes from having self-confidence.

Another example of how a person's self-confidence can grow by being successful happened to me a few years ago when I volunteered to help teach tennis at the Special Olympics, being held at UCLA. If you have never been to the Special Olympics to watch, or volunteered to be a part of it, you have not lived. It was one of the greatest days I can remember. I picked up my volunteer nametag and headed to the tennis courts. At this particular area, there were six courts. We were told that we were going to get kids who wanted to play tennis and we would teach them for about half an hour. Then we would get another set of children. The age ranges were five to eighteen years old. Some had played a little tennis before; some had never played at all.

All the athletes were sitting on the bleachers as we took roll call to find out who was there and what tennis experience each one had so we would know how to place them on the tennis courts. We had only a small group of twenty kids for the first round. We split up the athletes into the appropriate courts, but there was one boy left on the bleachers. He raised his hand and asked, "Can I play tennis? I have never played before." I said, "Of course you can. Come with me." You would have thought I just told him he'd won the gold medal. He jumped out of the bleachers and started screaming, "I get to play tennis; I get to play tennis!" He did not have a tennis racquet, but I had one for him. I asked him, "What is your name?" "Charlie," he replied, with great enthusiasm. I said, "Let's go then, Charlie." He said, "You have to come and get me. I can't see, I'm blind." "Hhhmmmm," I thought as I walked him down from the bleachers to the tennis court, "Now what am I supposed to do? I certainly can't tell him he can't play just because he is blind."

Charlie, who was sixteen, did not seem to think he had a disability. He had more self-confidence than almost anyone I had ever taught. I had a great-uncle who was blind. He had the most spectacular German shepherd dog, Champion. I brought Champion to school once as my "Show and Tell" to the class for what it was like to be blind and travel with a seeing-eye dog. One of the important things I remembered from my uncle was that when you lose one sense, all the other senses take over and become hyper-sensitive. That was my thought as I was holding Charlie's hand, while walking onto the court.

The other tennis instructors asked whether I was okay or needed any help. I told them I was fine. I decided to use as many senses as I could to get Charlie accustomed to his surroundings. I took him around the perimeter of the tennis court, so he would have a sense of how far he had to hit the ball. I made sure he touched the fences and touched the lines on the ground to show him the boundaries, because the lines feel different than the cement. We touched the net all the way from one end to other, so he could get a sense and feel of how high he had to hit the ball over the net.

Then I put a racquet in his hand. He said he could get the ball over the net; just hit it to him. He had a lot of confidence. Some of it may have been slightly exaggerated. He did not care. When I tossed the ball to him, he swung like a wild man in the woods. I thought he might hit himself on the head. We then went back to my way of small steps to accomplish a goal. The goal in my head was to assist him by holding his hand on the racquet to help him hit the ball over the net. In my mind, he would have been a success. I did not know Charlie had a different idea. I showed him how to hold the racquet; I stood behind him and helped him swing the racquet through the air.

Charlie was a big sixteen-year-old. He was very nervous being out on the court. It was not a comfortable environment for him. He kept ducking his head and I did not know why. He kept hearing the noise from the ball machine making a popping sound, like a small gun going off a couple of courts away from us. I told him what the noise was and he calmed down. I did not even hear the noise and to him it sounded like it was right next to him. His swing was very stiff and mechanical, so to fix that, I had him listen to the difference when he relaxed his arm—how the racquet made a "swoosh sound" as opposed to when he tightened up, and when he swung the racquet, there was no sound. He had to work very hard to swing, but he did not get the "swoosh sound." That exercise taught Charlie how to relax to get the real benefit of the swing.

I then bounced the ball while standing right next to him. His job was to say the word, "Bounce" when he heard the bounce on the ground. We then worked on the timing for when to say, "Bounce" and then he said the word "Hit" right after the word "Bounce." This sounds simple, but Charlie had never done anything like this before. Charlie was blind, and mentally handicapped, so getting the synchronization of saying both words with the correct timing took quite a long time. When he finally understood when to say it, I added the challenge of bouncing the ball right next to him and he had to say the words, "Bounce" and "Hit" and then swing the racquet to try to make contact with the ball.

By now, we had been on the tennis court for more than an hour and Charlie did not want to go back with his group; he wanted to stay and play tennis with me. A crowd was watching Charlie's determination in trying to make contact with the tennis ball to get it over the net. Just making contact was a big accomplishment. Touching the frame of the racquet with the ball was almost as exciting as hitting it over the net because some kind of contact was made. I bounced the ball right next to Charlie so he would get the "bounce and hit" theory at least 400-500 times—and that is no exaggeration. He never got discouraged and I certainly did not, since he didn't. He kept on with the task until he FINALLY hit one ball over the net. It was the sweet sound of the perfect impact of the ball hitting the strings. It was magical. Charlie felt it; he jumped up and down. He screamed with pleasure; he hugged me and the crowd started clapping and yelling words of encouragement. Charlie had hit the tennis ball over the net, for the very first time.

"Let's do it again!" he shouted. He continued with the success of the racquet hitting the ball, which made it go over the net. Once he got the hang of that feeling, he started hitting the balls over the net in a row. The crowd got bigger and more vocal. They started counting out loud every time Charlie hit the ball over the net. The chanting increased. Charlie had the biggest smile on his face the entire time he was playing. You could see his confidence growing with every ball he successfully hit over the net. He started counting with the crowd. He knew it was going over by how it felt on his racquet. He hit fifty-five tennis balls in a row over the net without missing. It was quite a change from the hour before where he'd swung and missed 400-500 times and not even made contact.

The transformation was incredible to witness. I wish I had videotaped this event. It showed how determination, perseverance, tenacity, and the never-give-up attitude can have people soar far beyond their wildest expectations of success. Charlie had some self-confidence when he started, just in being able to start the activity, but the growth of his self-confidence, feeling good about himself, feeling like he could conquer anything, all came from the progression of accomplishing small goals first, then moving on to accomplish another small goal, etc. The self-confidence that was beaming from every ounce of his being was contagious.

I then moved to the other side of the net. If he could keep the same rhythm of the swing when I bounced the ball in the right spot, he could actually feel like he was playing tennis, just like a person with sight. He was full of confidence to tackle the next challenge. He performed it very well. It took a few swings to realize he did not have to swing hard to be successful. Once he heard that sweet sound in the middle of the racquet, he started yelling out how many times it went over the net. As you can imagine, the crowd was now counting with him. He hit it over the net 102 times without missing. The crowd went wild. Charlie went wild. I went wild. I had never experienced anything like it in all my life! With the sounds of yelling and cheering, you would have thought Charlie had won the gold medal. In Charlie's mind, he *had* won the gold medal. It was the greatest success he had ever accomplished. With this success, in the relaxed, proper form, Charlie had the perfect forehand swing. If someone just looked at Charlie hitting forehands, they would have had no idea he was blind and handicapped. His form was better than mine.

It was an incredible lesson to see how building someone's self-confidence can lead that person to heights he never thought possible. Thank you Charlie, for teaching an incredible lesson that has stayed with me for years. Still to this day, I feel there is no one I cannot teach the game of tennis to in this world. The game of tennis teaches you about life and yourself.

Exercise

What are the principles upon which your life is built?

_____

_____

_____

_____

What three steps can you take today to give yourself more self-confidence?

1._____

2._____

3._____

Parental Support and Acceptance

People begin to develop confidence while growing up. The role of parents instilling self-confidence in their children is very important. Parents who are always critical of their children without acknowledging their strengths unknowingly dampen the development of their self-confidence. On the other hand, parents who are always willing to give support while encouraging their children to take a step forward will most likely rear self-confident children. Parents who make their children feel loved and accepted despite their imperfections will most likely encourage self-confidence.

Lack of self-confidence is not proportional to a person's abilities. In fact, there are people who are extremely talented and able, but they lack self-confidence to show off these abilities.

If you are seeking self-confidence, then you must continuously do things that will help you gain your confidence.

Identify your strengths and weaknesses and capitalize on that. Make full use of your strength and gather positive points. This will help you gain self-confidence. Do not expect everything to be perfect because you are bound to do something wrong along the way. Nobody is perfect and everyone makes mistakes.

Acknowledge your abilities and talents. Do not underestimate yourself. Try to recognize every little thing you have done which has become successful. Try to learn a new skill, and try to learn new things, as this will make you a better person, thus leading to better self-confidence.

Look for things that make you feel good about yourself. It can be photos of achievements such as if you won a tennis match, a race, or a debate; it can be a poem you wrote that was acknowledged in a book. Concentrate on things you have achieved and take it from there. This will give you more confidence to do other things in life.

Avoid things that will discourage you from gaining confidence. Do not dwell on past mistakes or failures because they will make you feel insignificant. Learn from your mistakes and try to move on from there.

Concentrate on the positive things you have accomplished and make them your inspiration. In time, you will have more faith in yourself, and hopefully, more confidence.

I was teaching a lesson to a little girl named Samantha, who had just started playing tournaments. She loves playing tennis and watches tennis on TV every time it is on. She is only nine years old and wants to play every day. She was having trouble running forward for short balls. This weakness was starting to appear when she played practice matches against other kids. I had to figure out a drill to teach her to see the ball sooner. She had to call out a certain number, 1,2,3,4 or 5 that corresponded with where on the tennis court she thought the ball was going to land. At first, she was not correct with calling the number because she never noticed where the ball was actually landing.

This particular drill was great for her, starting to watch the flight path of the ball from when I hit the ball to where it was going to land. As you might imagine, it took at least a half an hour for her finally to understand where the ball was going to land, in relation to how high the ball was coming over the net. Her mother watched the entire lesson from the sideline. I allow parents to watch lessons, as long as they just watch and say nothing. The longer we continued this exercise, the better and more accurate Samantha became. Her body language was positive, her smile was bigger and her entire attitude changed toward being positive because she was really accomplishing the goal we set up at the beginning of the lesson. The more accurate she got, the faster she ran up to the ball and the better she hit the approach shot.

It was the perfect domino effect. When you do the first part correctly, the rest of the stroke and the shot, fall into place. Samantha looked at her mother almost every time she hit a good shot, wanting her approval. Her parents had been very hard on her, recounting her matches by telling me what had happened. Her mother told me how she *never* got to any short balls, how she was slow and out of shape. Any time her opponent hit short balls to her, she missed because she was so slow getting to the ball. Part of my job is to change how parents talk in front of their children about their tennis. My guess is that how parents talk about their child's tennis is how they also talk about other areas of the child's life. In my experience, when a child hears a parent talking in front of them about what they do wrong, their self-confidence, their self-esteem and their self-worth is severely damaged. Samantha interpreted her mother's words to mean she was slow and fat, did not try and never got to short balls. So, when a short ball was hit to her in a match, those negative thoughts caused her to miss every time. Therefore, the mother had set the daughter up for failure, with no self-confidence, all stemming from the way she talked about a certain tennis shot. Isn't that sad?

We continued with our drill of calling the numbers and Samantha improved rapidly. She was so proud of herself. I told her every single time she was successful, and she acknowledged the progress. We played a game with this same drill to play points so she could see how it would work in a match or a tournament. She won that game and was successful almost every time in getting to the short ball with much more ease.

At the end of the lesson, I said to her mother, who was still sitting on the sideline, "Didn't Samantha do great? It is unbelievable how much she improved in getting to the short ball, and then could place it where she wanted." Her mother said, as Samantha was standing right there, "In her tournament, she is so slow and doesn't get to short balls. Last week in her match, she lost every point when the ball was short." I had to calm myself down before I spoke, "Jane, you cannot take everything we just did in the last hour and smash it to pieces and talk about what happened last week at the tournament. You must help Samantha's self-confidence and self-esteem and tell her how much better she got in this last hour. She needs that from you, not the criticizing parent who is still stuck in the last match. I need you to tell her what you thought about her playing in this last hour of practice. She needs to hear it from you. She has been hearing it from me for the entire hour. If you have one foot in the past and one foot in the future, then you are peeing on the present. You just peed over all the work we did in the last hour. So, if you want *me* to help your daughter, *you* have to help her as well, and be positive about what is currently happening." Oh, the fire was burning under my skin, but I think I got my point across. I hope I did—for Samantha's sake.

Parents have such a big role in creating or destroying their children's self-confidence. In my career as a tennis professional, the juniors who were highly ranked and did well in tournaments had very supportive parents who praised their children for all their efforts. The juniors whose parents were very critical and hard on them did not progress as far in the rankings and eventually quit the game altogether. To them, the pressure from their parents was just too much. So, help your children build their self-confidence and self-esteem from a young age; it will help them in every aspect of their lives. You can never give too much praise to your children. Try it; it works wonders.

Exercise

If you are a parent, list three things you could say to improve your child's self-confidence:

1._____

2._____

3._____

Self-Esteem

Where does self-esteem come from? How do we develop better self-esteem? How can we have good relationships with other people if our self-esteem is low? How do we feel about ourselves? Can we improve our own image of our self-esteem? What does a good person look like? Who are the role models our children look up to? What kind of example are these role models setting for our children?

Self-esteem is how you regard or value yourself in terms of your job, your accomplishments, your relationship with your peers and your family and your place in society. It is actually the image you have of yourself. Having high self-esteem means you have a high regard for yourself while low self-esteem means you perceive no value in yourself.

One way to improve self-esteem, self-confidence, feelings of self-empowerment, self-satisfaction, and fulfillment is to set goals and reach them.

Parents need to convince their children that it's what is on the inside that matters, not how much "stuff" you have. Parents need to believe that, too, so they can instill these values in their children. Children are constantly bombarded by superficial, outside factors. The mantra that you want them to remember is, "What is on the inside is what matters most." So much of kids' success and character these days is defined by their possessions, rather than their personal power. The key to success is a solid sense of character.

Athletes, teachers, coaches and other adults inspired me to be the very best I could be. I felt a sense of obligation to use the gifts I had. While I was growing up, my job was to be the very best I could possibly be. I tried to follow the examples of the people who taught me, people who inspired me. They taught me important values such as honesty, integrity, truth, good sportsmanship and compassion.

For a child, self-esteem is like a three-legged stool:

The first leg is a sense of belonging.

The second leg is a feeling of being worthwhile.

The third leg is a feeling of being capable.

If one of the legs is missing, the stool will fall over and not be able to stand up properly. It's the same as a child's self-esteem. If children do not have all three of these qualities, they will fall over and not feel a sense of completeness. A parent's job is to keep the child standing with good balance. This can be accomplished if the child has a high sense of self-esteem.

Qualities of High Self-Esteem. I have my students do an exercise called "Act As If." I have them print out those three magical words on a piece of paper. Then, I have them tape it onto the side of their tennis racquets. If they are playing a match, they can look at that little saying, and remind themselves to "Act As If" when things are not going their way.

There are many things you could fill in the blank with for "Act As If." Some of them include:

Act As If...

- You are winning.
- You are the better player.
- You can come back, even if you lost the first set.
- You are calm, cool and collected.
- You have a great serve and can win points with it.
- You have a great volley and are a threat every time you go to the net.
- You are willing to stay on the court for as long it takes to win the match.

That is the power of the mind—if you "Act As If" just as if it is really happening, then your brain will believe it and your emotions will follow the signal from your brain. You will start winning, if you "Act As If" you are winning. You must believe that statement, and not just say it for the sake of saying it.

Exercise

List three phrases that could help you in tennis or in life that could begin with the phrase, "Act As If:"

1. Act as if..._____

2. Act as if..._____

3. Act as if..._____

List three qualities you have that help your self-esteem:

1._____

2._____

3._____

To help a child's self-esteem, have children elect to take the stairs instead of an elevator. They can also ride their bikes instead of always getting rides from their parents. A healthier child will feel more energetic and willing to take successful risks, as opposed to a couch potato child who will learn the habit of taking the easy way out in life. That is why sports are so good to help a child's self-esteem issues. In a sport, you address losses just as you will have to do with failures in life. That is what makes you stronger and successful. If you didn't win the championship game, but the team learned how to be unselfish players, then the team just won an award.

I really began to understand how important physical exercise is for children when I went to college in Alabama. For one of my classes, I volunteered at a juvenile prison for kids ages ten to eighteen, for the entire semester. I had to go there a couple of times a week, write a paper on what I observed and what changes I thought I could make at the prison.

The first day I went was a Saturday morning. The prison was heavily guarded, so I had to show my ID, get my picture taken, explain why I was there and talk with two different supervisors to get the proper clearance. When I went down to where the kids were kept, there were three rooms. There was an all-glass room in the middle, with four guards sitting inside, watching TV. Another room was an all-glass room through which the guards could see where they kept all the girls in the jail. There were eight girls in that one room. The other all-glass room was a larger room where all the boys stayed. About forty of them were in that one room. When I opened the door and entered the guardroom, no one even looked up to see who I was. I finally told one of the guards I was there as a volunteer. He said, "Okay by me." Then he went back to watching TV. I asked him what I should do, and he said, "Do whatever you want to do, but I'd suggest just staying in the girls' room. Don't go in the boys' room. If the girls start to fight, don't try to break it up. It's good for them to fight to get it out of their system." What a shock. I figured this visit would turn out to be an adventure.

I got brave and went into the girls' room. All eight girls were hovered around a little, tiny black-and-white TV, watching a cartoon a four-year-old would watch. Their ages ranged from ten to seventeen. I stood next to them as they watched their little, tiny TV, and no one even looked up. It was a repeat of what I'd encountered in the guardroom. I said hello to them and they just grunted at me. The youngest one did ask me what I was doing there. I said I was here from the university and would be visiting often. The sister of the youngest one said, "You won't be back. They never come back."

I asked what they were going to do that day; it was Saturday, after all. They said, "This is it; this is what we do; we watch TV." I said, "You can't just stay inside all day; don't you go outside at some point during the day?" They said, "No, we only go outside maybe once a week."

"Are you kidding me?" I asked. I could not believe it. "Once a week? I would go crazy in here." They laughed. Then, they began asking me questions like, "Are you married?" "No," I replied. "Do you have any kids?" I said, "No, I'm not married, remember?" One of the girls said, "That doesn't matter. Most of my friends have kids and they aren't married." (She was fifteen).

"How many abortions have you had?" they asked. "None," I replied, looking at them like, "You are kidding, right?"

"How many times have you been in jail?" "None."

"How many times have you been arrested?" "None."

One girl, who had not said a word to me yet, looked up from the TV and said, "What is wrong with you? Haven't you ever been in trouble with the pigs?" "No, I guess I have had a pretty boring life compared to all of you." They actually smiled. Even though I was so straight-laced and square, they started telling me about their lives. I wanted to cry. Most of the girls had been in that juvenile hall more than once. Some of the older girls had been arrested at least seven times. There was no rehabilitation for them—after their trial, if they got out of jail, they would go back and do the same things that got them in trouble in the first place.

The girls were all in there for different crimes, from stealing at liquor stores, to robbing people's houses, to being in a stolen car. Those were their lives. It was a revolving door from the streets, back to jail, to court, back to the streets. It did not change for any of those girls. They all came from broken homes. Some of their parents were in jail, too. None of the girls had ever played a sport. They had barely watched any sports on television.

I asked what kind of physical activity they did since they only went outside once a week—that was still hard for me to believe. They said that for one hour per day, they all went to the gymnasium, and it was coming up in an hour. I went with them to their gymnasium. There was one tiny gymnasium for both the boys and the girls to go for one hour. The girls sat on the floor against the wall because if you were not against the wall, the big boys playing basketball would have trampled on you if you got in their way. There was barely any room at all on either side of the basketball court. You could only sit next to the wall. In one corner was one bench press with one barbell where ten big boys took turns working out. This was the jail's idea for the boys and girls to blow off some steam. There was not even a ball for the girls to throw around or play with.

When we went back to the girl's room, it was almost time for lunch. Right before lunch, a big fight broke out with two of the girls. It was nasty. They were kicking, slapping and pulling each other's hair. Of course, with my instincts, I went over to the girls and tried to break up the fight up and immediately got punched in the face by one of them. I don't even know which one hit me. I fell to the ground and then the guards came in and broke up the fight. The guard yelled at me and told me that I was not supposed to interfere when there was a fight. In the boy's room, fights broke out about every thirty minutes. The guards hardly ever broke up their fights, either. After the girls calmed down, both were sorry I was hit; they wanted to make sure I was not mad at them and would come back. I said I would and asked each of them whether there was anything in particular they wanted. Of course, they all laughed aloud and said what they'd really want.

I got the strangest requests from them. The requests from the girls were a jump rope, the card game Uno, a boom box, a Rick James album, Lay's potato chips, dill pickles, a basketball, a deck of cards and a tennis racquet. All of them made me promise I would really come back the next day. They wanted an exact time I would be there. They said people who came to visit all said they were going to come back, but they never did. These girls didn't trust anyone, never mind themselves.

Actually, I had plans for the next day, but changed them so I could go back to the prison, as I had promised the girls. I went as promised, with an armful of goodie bags with all their special requests. Each gift had to be screened by the guards, and then they let me take them in to the girls. I could not take my tennis racquet in because it could be used as a weapon. Everything else I brought was allowed. When I arrived at 10:00 a.m., as scheduled, every girl was standing at the window waiting for my arrival. As I walked in with my hands full, they all started cheering. (For Lay's potato chips?) Anyway, it seemed to make their day special. They all had grins on from ear to ear when I walked into their room. In the meantime, many of the boys from the opposite room were standing at their window watching all of this activity, and all the little gifts I was bringing the girls. Of course, they asked the guards if I could go into their room. I was not ready to tackle that by myself yet.

I turned on the boom box, put in Rick James' "She's a Very Special Girl," and started to dance with the girls. It was a great day. We played Uno, cards and ate Lay's potato chips with dill pickles (I do not think anyone was pregnant). I taught some of them how to jump rope and we played jump rope games together, just as if I were back in grammar school. I also taught them how to bounce a basketball. None of them had ever dribbled a basketball before. So, we danced, ate, sang, exercised and laughed a lot. There were no fights that day from the girls, not even any big disagreements. The girls thanked me repeatedly for bringing all their requests to them.

It seemed as if no one had ever followed through on any promise to them before. That was a big cause of their low self-esteem issues. They also did not have any trust for anyone. They were unhappy on the inside, so they acted out, crying for attention. They had never had any goals set for them to accomplish, so there were no feelings of self-worth. We set goals that day. Every girl had to jump rope twenty times. Every girl had to make five basketball passes to each other around the circle without dropping the ball or we had to start over. None of them had ever done simple little tasks like that. These small activities help people develop more self-esteem.

I returned later in the week. I felt like a rock star when I entered the girls' room. They were happy to see me, some of them still not thinking that I would come back. They actually had a teacher come to the room to teach them math on the day I was there. I stayed in the room with them to help them with their match studies. They were doing math problems at second grade level and were struggling with those problems. Again, I was shocked. That's another reason they had no self-esteem, no self-confidence. They had never been successful in anything, sports, math, or reading. The only thing they were successful at was crime, so when they got out of jail, they went back and did it again. It was a vicious cycle.

I was only required to volunteer at the jail five hours a week, but I sometimes spent more than five hours a day there. In fact, I spent most of my semester there. After three weeks, I talked with my professor and told him what I had observed at the jail. The one injustice, I thought, was that there was no physical activity for any of the girls, and for the boys, the only ones who got any exercise were the really good basketball players. Everyone else just stood on the sidelines doing nothing. So I implemented an exercise program that included going outside for fresh air. The jail was fenced in, so I didn't see why the activities couldn't be done outside. Within the month, there was physical activity every day, outside, and the girls played their own games of basketball, volleyball and tetherball. Jumping rope was a big sport for them, along with just walking the grounds. Many of the boys started playing other games on their own, too, since the space was much bigger outside.

Less and less fights took place each day. The kids seemed much happier. They certainly started to develop a little different outlook on life. We talked about what they could do differently when they got out of jail—things they could do to help themselves, and consequently, feel better about themselves. Most of the girls did not return, but a couple of them did while I was still there.

I finally ventured over to the boys' side after a few weeks. I had a guard with me at all times. That was the rule. They felt slighted because I'd spent so much time on the girls' side and did not bring them Lay's potato chips. On occasion, I did bring massive amounts of potato chips. I played a lot of cards and Uno on the boys' side of the jail. I also started bringing other board games to help them occupy their time. They could use the games to help them learn how to count. Many of the boys did not know how to count or read. It was so sad to witness.

I believe their lives became a little better because we started an exercise program outside the jail for girls and boys. I believe their self-esteem was enhanced because of that physical exercise program. Once their self-esteem was higher, they thought more of themselves, they trusted themselves and they had a better sense of right and wrong. Those kids tended not to return to juvenile hall.

Other Qualities That Lead to a Better Life

Character. The key to life is a solid sense of your own character. Who you really are. What you really stand for. What are your beliefs.

Trust. A funny story about trust happened to me this summer. My family was in Hawaii, where my six-and-a-half year-old stepdaughter loves climbing up the rock wall. She had only done it two or three times. At this location in Hawaii, the rock wall was high, about thirty feet, straight up. I went to watch her climb the wall that morning, and we had talked about when she gets scared trying something new, she can say always remember to say to herself, "I think I can. I think I can," from the story, "The Little Engine That Could." I love that saying. Therefore, we talk about using it frequently.

While she was climbing up the wall, and starting to get tired, she yelled down from midpoint, "I think I can. I think I can." Her little voice carried all around the wall. We were all amused. She kept climbing further up the wall, and then she yelled, "Trust the rope. Trust the rope." I had never heard her say that. She looked like she was not going to make it to the top, but she kept trying. The instructor on the ground said to her right before she got to the top, "Trust the rope, Remi." She finally made it all the way to the top, rang the bell and then climbed up to look to the other side.

After she'd rappelled back down, I gave her a big hug and told her how proud of her I was that she'd made it all the way up to the top. She said, "Did you hear me talking up there?" I said, "Yes, Rem-Rem, of course I did. Where did you learn about trust the rope?" She said her climbing wall instructor taught all the kids that. "Trust that you will not fall; the rope will hold you up there on the wall. Even if you have to take a break while climbing, that is okay, but make sure you trust the rope. It will not let you fall." Remi and all her friends learned a great lesson that day, and it was a good lesson for me as well. We do not always trust ourselves, or people. Trust, and it will not fail you.

Integrity. Be true to your word. Do as you say. This means what you say and what you do are one and the same. What you show when your bosses or others in leadership are around must be the same when they are not around. The values you speak are what really determine your behavior. If you give your word, it is as good as done.

Honesty. People need to trust that what you say is the truth.

Generosity. You must give back. You will always feel better when you help someone in need. The more you give of yourself, the more you receive in return.

Pride. Youngsters who have pride in accomplishments are more anchored.

Self-empowerment. Grant yourself the power to assume responsibility for your own life. Advance your life and reach your full potential. Many of us have formed the habit of depending on others for what we think, what we do and who we are.

Values. What is important to people today? What car they drive? Are they keeping up with the Joneses? What name brand of jeans are you wearing? What music is on your ipod? What happened to working for things that you really want? What happened to buying things for yourself rather than expecting your parents to give you everything you want? What happened to doing chores to earn an allowance? Do we still have any of those values? What is the value of money? Does it still mean the same to kids these days? Have credit cards ruined people's idea of affordability? Just because a person wants something now, does that always mean she should get it?

Exercise

What events in life have caused you to have low self-esteem?

_____

_____

What are three qualities that can lead you to a happier life?

1._____

2._____

3._____

CHAPTER 9:
MANIFESTING YOUR FUTURE

"Do not argue for other people's weaknesses.
Do not argue for your own. When you make a mistake,
admit it, correct it, and learn from it–immediately."
– Stephen Covey

Life is about experience. All your knowledge is worthless if you do not apply it in your life. Your experience is created by applying what you know.

Everything starts with an idea, which is a thought. That is why it is crucial to pay attention to your thoughts.

An example of how thoughts lead to reality is John worrying all the time about how he is going to pay his bills. It is constantly on his mind. It creates more of the same thing, since that is his thought all the time. Yes, simply because he thought about it, he created more of the same situation. Your thoughts are frequencies or vibrations that resonate with similar vibrations that already exist.

Every single person in the world is striving to be happy. Where does happiness really come from? Today, people, places and many things try to make us happy. We work at places we do not like very much in order to buy "stuff" we really do not need.

We have replaced real happiness with buying "material" things. We forget that it is an "inside job." We must start with our own happiness from within, before we can give it away to others. That is the purest form of happiness.

The Law of Attraction.

In *The Principles of Successful Manifesting*, Thomas Herold says, "The law of attraction states that you attract into your life circumstances and events that are similar or identical to what you focus your thoughts and beliefs on. Every thought has a vibration energy pattern that will resonate with similar objects and events that already exist or are coming into existence." Be aware of your thoughts.

Your energy will always match with similar energy. You will meet people who are on the same wavelength you are. You will attract circumstances in your life that will always match what you think and believe. Coincidences you may call them? Isn't it funny how many coincidences we have all of our lives? They are not just coincidences; we attracted them into our lives.

Recently, Rhonda Byrne's *The Secret* has brought the concepts of the Law of Attraction to millions of people. Byrne's book explains that you can create what you want in three simple steps:

1) Ask. You get to choose what you want from your life, but be clear on what you want. Writing down what you want can make it clear for you. Once you ask, what you want, it is on its way to you, provided you follow the next step.

2) Believe. Believe that what you have asked for is yours already. The problem is that most people ask for something, but in asking, they are thinking about how they do not have it. As I talked about in the last chapter, you have to "Act As If." You have to act as if what you asked for is something you already have. Then your vibration will act like a magnet to bring what you want into your life. As Dr. Wayne Dyer says, "You'll see it when you believe it."

3) Receive. The final step is to receive. You deserve what you have asked for. Feel joy and gratitude for receiving it. Allow it to come into your experience. Tell yourself you are receiving all things that are good for you. They are yours to ask for. If you believe, you will receive them.

Knowing What You Want from Life. A major factor to manifesting the life that you want is to think about what you really want out of life. What do you want to do with your life?

Exercise

Answer these questions:

1) What am I good at?
2) What would I like to accomplish this year?
3) What would I like to accomplish in my lifetime?
4) Where would I like to be in five years?
5) Where would I like to be in twenty years?
6) What is my deepest desire?

Now, let's look at different areas of our lives. If we have set our goals, do we spend enough time during the day working on our goals? The goals cannot manifest themselves if we have not put in the work. Rank these areas in your life in order of importance.

1 = Most Important. 5 = Least Important.

_____   Your health

_____   Your relationships

_____   Your financial situation

_____   Your profession

_____   Your fun time, vacations and holidays

You must take action to manifest your goals. They will not just come to you while you are sitting at home watching a football game. Some examples of taking action might be:

- Taking tennis lessons or tennis classes
- Attending a workshop that focuses on your interest
- Doing a weekend boot camp to help your fitness
- Taking a class on how to cook healthier for you and your family

There is an important aspect of manifestation that requires consistency. You must be in emotional agreement with your goals. They must feel right to you, or you will have a hard time achieving them. We need to put our attention into making our goals a reality.

You need to spend a good part of your day working on your most important goal. You will not achieve your number one goal on this list if you only spend ten minutes a day working on it. It is an ongoing process. Do not get discouraged during the process. You may be having changes occurring in your thinking or your behavior that you are not aware of so you do not see it.

If one way does not lead to success, do not give up at that point; simply try another. If you stick to a goal, you will reach it.

If Manifesting Is Not Working

Soon after watching the DVD, *The Secret*, millions of people were very excited about this newfound information. We re-focused our minds, re-declared our intentions to the Universe and waited for the results to happen. We waited and we waited...and nothing happened. Every day we expected to see dramatic changes in our lives, and it n-e-v-e-r happened. What went wrong?

Three possible things could have gone wrong:

1) You tell yourself you are waiting—telling yourself you are waiting causes frustration. Again, you need to believe you already have what you want or it will not come into your life.

2) You are focusing on lack. When you ask for something because you are feeling you are lacking it, rather than acting as if you already have it, you trigger the lack so that the lack of what you want grows stronger. This feeling of lack is a signal to you that you need to align with your true goals and desires and Act as If.

3) You have stopped living a life of manifestation. In other words, you gave up. What you wanted did not come—maybe you never believed it could, or you did not believe hard enough. You may have been focusing on lack. As I've said before in this book, NEVER give up.

To reshape your thinking, come back to the present moment and stop those negative feelings. Start thinking about what you really want to attract.

In the 2008 Olympics, how many Olympic records and World records were shattered? Look at Michael Phelps breaking Mark Spitz's record with eight Olympic gold medals. Look at sprinter Usain Bolt. No one had really heard of him before the 2008 Olympics, yet he shattered three Olympic & World records in the 100-meter, the 200-meter and the 400-meter relay. Look at the records set by Dara Torres, forty-one years old, the oldest woman to win a medal. It's amazing just that she was still competitive at her age, and it was her fifth Olympics, and she won three silver medals and then had to have shoulder surgery right after the Olympics were completed. So, she was injured while winning all of her silver medals. All these examples are powerful mindsets for manifestation.

In a tennis match, most people learn more by losing than they do by winning. When you lose, you go back and re-think what you could have done better and why you lost. You replay what strategy worked and what did not work, so you can do better next time you play that person, or that team.

Life is a matter of making mistakes and learning from them. We are a "work in progress." It seems like if we make mistakes and have not learned the lesson yet, then we keep repeating the same mistake repeatedly.

One of the biggest mistakes we make is not taking the time to learn from our mistakes. Many people work at jobs they hate, but they complain they are too tired after work to look for another job or start their own business. That's a mistake that doesn't leave room for the situation to get better. Thinking we do not have enough time, and not making time, is never going to let us manifest anything.

Exercise:

Make a list of what you want to achieve in the next few years.

_____

_____

_____

_____

_____

_____

Make a list of your innermost desires and dreams.

_____

_____

_____

_____

_____

_____

MANIFESTING WEALTH

Doesn't money seem to be the biggest issue when it comes to manifesting? Isn't household debt at an all-time high? Personal bankruptcies have at least doubled in the last decade. Foreclosures on houses are at an all-time high. Never before in history have people had so much stuff and so little freedom.

> *Too many people spend money they haven't earned, to buy*
> *things they don't want, to impress people they don't like.*
> — Will Smith

We have to change our thinking when it comes to money.

In a 2003 study by Merrill Lynch, personal wealth within the United States alone had climbed to $27 trillion dollars. However, 90% of the wealth is owned by only 10% of the people! What knowledge do the wealthy 10% have, that the other 90% are missing?

Exercise:

Write down all the beliefs you have about money, whether or not they make sense. Just write them down off the top of your head.

_____

_____

_____

_____

_____

Now, write down any new ideas you may have after understanding how believing can help you attract the wealth you want to have.

_____

_____

_____

_____

How does it feel to be a millionaire?

- How does it feel to have abundance in your life?
- How does it feel to give to others?
- How does it feel to buy something without having to look at the price?
- How does it feel to have more money than you can spend?

The more you think and feel about this, the more you train your mind to think in a new way. This new way will lead to living an abundant and prosperous life!

Intention: Aim for Your Goals

Intention refers to what a person plans to do or achieve. By setting and realigning your intentions, you will achieve your goals and fulfill your dreams. What is the difference between setting a goal and having an intention? You can set as many goals as you want; however, if you do not have any intention to achieve them, they will never happen. An intention is much more powerful than simply setting a goal. Intentions will allow you to reach any goal. A goal is a subject; it is something that is happening in the future. What is your goal? What are your intentions to do what is needed to achieve that goal?

Exercise:

Creating Your Intentions Worksheet

Write down your intentions in each of these areas of your life. Be specific.

1. Personal Development: _____

2. Health: _____

3. Relationships: _____

4. Career: _____

5. Financial and Wealth: _____

6. Sports and Hobbies: _____

7. Community and Charity: _____

Attitude Makes a Difference

This is the basic principle of looking at the glass half full or half empty. It is your viewpoint of life that determines your attitude. Have you ever gotten up in the morning and stubbed your toe on the bed? Then your shower ran out of hot water? Then you stepped in dog poop getting in your car and by the time you went inside to clean your shoe, you were late for work? Now that you were late for work, you got stuck driving behind the little ninety-year-old lady, who can barely see over the steering wheel, who is driving twenty mph UNDER the speed limit on a one-way street.

With all that good luck on your side, you miss every green traffic light before you get on the freeway and now you are really late for work. To make matters worse, you get on the freeway, there is an accident ahead of you and now traffic is completely stopped. What will your attitude be at this point? Some people call it road rage, cursing at anyone who will listen, even cursing at the radio. Then, you have some people who are grateful they got stuck behind that little old lady who made them late because otherwise, they might have been in the freeway accident. Which person are you?

When you stay in gratitude, you will have a good day. When you stay in gratitude, it will always help your attitude. Focusing on who you are and what you have will shift your attitude and make you more humble. Recognize what you do have in life. Go out in nature and recognize the beauty of life. Pick a flower, smell a rose, pet an animal, watch and feel the peace of it all.

Having a positive attitude helps in every aspect of your life as we have discussed in this book. It helps with getting to your goal weight, it helps with pursuing your fitness goals, and it helps in your tennis game. That is why you can make a comeback in a set even if you are losing 5-2. If you have the positive attitude that you can come back and play every point as if it is match point, then you will win more of those matches than you will lose. If you lose one set, do you have the right attitude to stay on the tennis court to win in three sets?

Have you ever noticed that many times after a really close first set, either 7-5 or 7-6, the next set isn't close at all? Why is that? If the first set were so close, shouldn't the second set be just as close? Often, the next set is 6-2 or 6-1. What happened? One player didn't have the positive attitude to stay out there for two more sets, so he gave up his tenacity and fight.

Playing tennis teaches us to keep a positive attitude, which is mentally hard for our opponents when they see we are not giving up. Also in doubles, you can help your partner have a good attitude by talking and being your partner's cheerleader, even if he is not having a good day. Your partner feels your attitude, too. So, be the best you can be by always having a positive attitude, no matter the score.

The Art of Manifesting

Let's summarize everything we have talked about in this chapter. Know that fulfilling your dreams is the purpose of your life. It is exercising your strengths and talents to contribute to the greater good of all. Know that fulfilling your dreams is your destiny. Never ever give anybody permission to take this power away from you. Thomas Herold, in *Dream Manifesto,* states:

"Decide what you want in life. This may change during your life, so evaluate your goals and dreams every few years. Align with your long-term goals and adjust your short-term goals. Know your strengths, talents and gifts. Also, know your weak areas, exercise your strengths and get help from others for your weak areas. Understand that you have unlimited attention. Decide where you want to put your attention. Limit the areas where you waste your attention. Increase the areas where you want results. Use your imagination as a virtual playing field. Imagine what it feels like to have reached your goals. Imagine what it feels like when you live your dreams. Contemplate your beliefs. Your beliefs create reality. Replace non-supporting beliefs with beliefs that support your goals and dreams. Create powerful intentions that state your life dreams. Understand that what you hold in your consciousness attracts similar circumstances in your life."

Use A Vision Board to Manifest Your Dreams

You hear this from every person who has studied how to succeed in life so your dreams come true. Just do it! What do you have to lose?

Buy a large corkboard or a large poster board and start pinning or pasting up your dreams. Use words and pictures that show exactly what you want in life. Put this board in a place where you can see it every day. Spend some time every day and let any imaginative thoughts and feelings flow through you. Dreams will come true!

Some of the dreams you might illustrate on your Vision Board include:

- being healthy and feeling vital
- being happy from the inside out
- having a more positive attitude toward life
- going on vacations
- living your passion
- having money in abundance
- living in your own house
- having more control over your life
- being fulfilled in your work
- having rewarding and joyful relationships
- feeling bright and alive

Gratitude and Helping Others

One great way to help your manifestation is by getting out of the way of it. Shift your focus from your own life (or what you are lacking in your life) and help others—it will make you grateful for what you already have and help you to attract more good to yourself. Plus, you will help someone else.

If you are ever in a bad place in your life, volunteer at a school, a hospital or a retirement home. Make a phone call to a friend just because. Make a phone call to a friend who is having a hard time in life right now. The more you serve others, the more you get out of your own way. You will always feel better after your act of kindness.

Seven years ago, after September 11, 2001, we held a charity event at our tennis club. It was a potluck dinner; drinks were donated and everyone who came to play tennis that night donated money that went directly to help the families of 9/11 victims. More than 150 people participated. We had a silent auction and a live auction, a band and food and drinks to raise money for such a good cause. Every person's feeling that night was that it felt so good to be doing something worth-while for people less fortunate than ourselves. We did it as a community, joining together and helping others after the losses we all felt on that day. We sent more than $10,000 from our one-night event. Giving back and serving others is a process that we should do, not just when tragedy hits us, but throughout the year. When was the last time you served someone else?

Stories About Manifesting

Five years ago, I was teaching at the Calabasas Tennis and Swim Center, as I have for twenty-five years. I kept having this feeling inside of me that I needed to make a change in where I was living. I was very happy with where I was living, but it was not my dream house. I was in a very spacious condominium in Calabasas, very close to where I worked. I went to a few open houses in my condominium complex and the condominiums that were for sale were small, not clean, and I thought expensive for a condominium.

On the other hand, my condominium was beautiful, with lots of windows, custom-painted walls, high ceilings and it was an end unit. Still, the thought was so strong in my gut that it was time for me to sell my condominium and see where that was going to take me. At that time, I really had no idea where I was going to move. I knew I needed to sell my condominium because I wanted a dog, I wanted a yard and I wanted a swimming pool. Not too much to ask for, right?

If I stayed where I was living, I knew I could not reach my goal, or my full potential. I had to trust what my instincts were telling me. I knew that if I did not find somewhere to live, I could move back in with my parents for a month or two. Boy, weren't they lucky to have the empty nest full again?

I really thought I was losing my mind, making a decision like this, with virtually nowhere to go. It was one of the first times in my life I totally trusted without knowing that I would be taken care of. I am usually very methodical about planning everything out to the very last detail. Now I was flying by the seat of my pants. Was I having a mid-life crisis? I didn't have a need to go out and buy a fast little sports car, but I had never made a decision like this. This was one of the first times in my life where I trusted my instincts.

I put my house on the market for the highest price in the complex. It was actually much higher than any other residence there. I didn't want to sell it for any less; it was beautiful and I had nothing to lose. I didn't have to move, and remember, I really did not have anywhere to go, except for my parents' house.

Well, my condominium sold within one week. See, I should have put it on the market for a higher price! Now I was nervous. I put most of my furniture in storage to wait for the right house to come along. I somehow knew it was going to happen.

I moved back with my parents (it was great to have dinner cooked every night and goodies in the cupboard). I was there for about a month and a half. I had made a good profit from my condominium and ended up buying a house in Encino, California. It had a swimming pool, a great entertainer's backyard, a separate yard for a dog and it was twice the size of my condominium. My dreams had come true.

I now have the sweetest German Shepherd dog named Chase. He is named after the little boy who died back on January 27, 1992, who helped me become sober. I wanted Chase's name to live on, since he meant so much to me in his short three-year lifetime. I've also found the love of my life, and I have a six-year-old stepdaughter who makes my life complete. I am grateful for my life every day when I get up. Before my feet hit the floor in the morning, I thank God for all my gifts. I am an entrepreneur and I have my own businesses as a tennis professional, coach, consultant for other tennis professionals, personal trainer, author and speaker. I have talked to thousands of people in speaking engagements and want to keep growing my business in that arena.

I am able to control my time and have the freedom to make a schedule that works around my family's schedule. I am blessed for the life I now have because of manifesting my future. You can have the same success if you follow the steps we have described.

Knowledge is power. Now you have the knowledge.

A client wrote me a letter about how her life has changed since she started playing tennis. This is one of the reasons I love my job. I love doing what I do. I can help change people's lives so they can live up to their full potential. Here is her story:

"It felt like a kick in the stomach, as if someone pulled the rug from under me. I felt hurt and imbalanced when I found out eight years ago that my husband had been living a double life. I filed for divorce, and we both agreed that we would keep it as civilized as possible. We both did not want to hurt our three amazing boys in the process. Meanwhile, I was trying so hard to be strong, but the pain of being deceived and lied to for so many years is a direct attack to one's self-esteem. You feel so ashamed and stupid for not knowing what was happening around you.

"This was unbearable for me when I was by myself. I cried for hours when the boys went to school. I cannot describe the pain I was feeling, and I could not find a way to cope with all of these feelings.

"One day a very close friend of mine suggested that I visit our local Calabasas Tennis Club and that changed everything. I remember the first day I walked onto the court. I did not even know how to hold the racquet properly. After waiting a couple of months, and taking classes from a female coach I did not learn very much from, there was an opening in Mary Pat's drill class. She finally accepted me as one of her students. I was so excited, since everyone talked about how amazing she was. I joined all of Mary Pat's drill classes and signed up for private lessons.

"I found myself playing two to three hours a day, simply because if I did not play, I felt very sad. However, when I did play, not only did it feel amazing during the game, but it carried into the rest of my day. I did not feel any pain, as if I were in my own little world.

"Playing tennis helped me to create a positive environment to focus on myself, which I had not done for years. By playing, I felt happier; it boosted and healed my injured self-esteem. I felt positive. It helped me focus better in all that I had to do for the rest of the day.

"I was so nervous at first, I could hear my own heart beat; I started winning several matches. With Mary Pat's help, I now was among the better players at the club, and my children were very happy to see me now winning tennis trophies.

"I consider myself to be so lucky and blessed to have such an amazing coach. She is my tennis doctor. She helps me with my nutrition and answers all my questions. The lessons I learned from playing tennis were used in not only my matches, but have carried on into my personal life.

"I have taken lessons when I go on vacation and I have watched all of the other tennis pros teach throughout the years, and you would have to take at least twenty-five lessons from any other pro for what Mary Pat can teach in two lessons. If you have a specific problem, she will fix it in fifteen minutes.

"I now honestly, feel that the sky is the limit and my mental and physical health and outlook on life have never been stronger. You focus, you believe in yourself and you have a plan of action that you carry forward. Go for it and you will surprise yourself as to what you are capable of accomplishing!" — Claris Jeknavorian

In closing, here are some final thoughts to help you with Winning In Tennis and In Life.

Mary Pat Faley's Seven SUCCESS Accelerators

1) **Simplify**. Keep it simple.
2) **Unwavering Values**. Know what the truth is for you and believe it.
3) **Clarify**. Be very specific.
4) **Change**. Change is inevitable and fast. It takes more energy to resist change than it does to accept change.
5) **Excel**. Excel at learning and learn to excel.
6) **Serve**. The fastest path to success is to help others succeed.
7) **Stick to it**. Never give up. Adopt the attitude of "I think I can. I think I can." Follow your dreams.

Mary Pat Faley's "Just for Today" Thoughts

Use the "just for today" approach to changing your habits. Here are some ideas:

Just for today, I will become challenged when problems come my way. Today I will be a great problem-solver.

Just for today, I will love the battle. I can create my own state of enjoyment. I will accept the hand that is dealt to me. No complaining!

Just for today I will exercise, eat, and train right. Self-discipline will bring the confidence I search for.

Just for today, I will take charge of how I feel. I am not at the mercy of my emotions.

Just for today, I will set aside some time to relax and simply let go. Relaxation is an essential part of training.

Just for today, I will have a plan to follow. The plan will keep me focused and organized.

Just for today, I will stop saying, "If I had time." If I want time, I will take it.

Just for today, I will find humor in my mistakes. When I can smile inside, I am in control.

Just for today, I will do things the best that I can. I will be satisfied with what I have done.

Just for today, I will do the ordinary things in my training extraordinarily well. It's the little things that make the difference.

Just for today, I will choose to believe that I can make the difference and that I am in control of my world.

Just for today, the choice is mine.

Mary Pat Faley's Favorite 1, 2, 3 Things Lists

Three things in life that, once gone, never come back:

1) Time
2) Words
3) Opportunity

Three things in life that can destroy a person:

1) Anger
2) Pride
3) Unforgiveness

Three things in life that you should never lose:

1) Hope
2) Peace
3) Honesty

Three things in life that are most valuable:

1) Love
2) Family & Friends
3) Kindness

Three things in life that are never certain:

1) Fortune
2) Success
3) Dreams

Three things that make a person successful:

1) Commitment
2) Sincerity
3) Hard work

A FINAL NOTE:
GETTING TO MATCH POINT!

Never give up, until you win. — Author Unknown

As long as you believe in yourself, the sky is the limit. On the other hand, maybe not even that—just look at Eileen Collins, the space shuttle commander. You never know how far you can go unless you attempt to get there. The key is to believe in yourself, believe that it is possible, and believe that you can do it.
— Martina Navratilova

Martina Navratilova believed this philosophy and it has been my own belief system since I started playing sports. There have been many adversities along the way. Adversities teach you how strong you really are. The best way to shape your future is to create it yourself. Make things happen. Take all of the strategies you have learned in this book and start making things work for you.

You now have added numerous tools to your toolbox. You have the blueprint and you have the strategy. Now use all of these new tools to create a better life for yourself and those around you. Improve your tennis game, improve your self-confidence, increase your self-esteem and understand how to be a better leader.

To succeed in life and reach your destiny, you must develop BELIEVE and TRUST in yourself.

This book reflects what I have learned and experienced in more than thirty years of teaching tennis. I want to help you bridge the gap between what you have learned in tennis and in life so you know what to do when it actually counts. I have worked over the years with thousands of people, worked through my own trials and tribulations, worked as a coach, a mentor and a competitor, so I can share my stories with you to help you on your journey to become the best you can be at anything you want to be.

I hope you will find success in these strategies I have mapped out...from eating healthy, to getting fit, to singles and doubles strategies, to learning how to focus on and off the tennis court, and finally, to creating strategies to follow your hopes and your dreams.

> *The one thing that separates winners*
> *from losers is, winners take action.*
> — *Anthony Robbins*

I've never expected overnight success and neither should you. I encourage you to keep on trying. Remember, "If at first you don't succeed, try, try again." What I have learned is to keep following your goals and your dreams, and I hope you will.

If I had listened when someone told me I started too late playing tennis to get a scholarship to college, I would have missed my true calling. I just kept following my heart's goals and desires. It has taken me beyond all of my wildest dreams. I went to college on a full tennis scholarship, and I have been doing what I love to get up and do every day—sharing my passion with others. Now I am passing on the great concepts I have learned along my journey.

Now that I have given you the knowledge and the material, I challenge you to put them into action.

Execute the following:

- Take care and be in charge of your own overall health.
- Eat a well-balanced and healthy diet. Know what you are eating.
- Exercise daily. Make it your goal to be more physically fit.
- Improve your tennis by implementing, "Tennis is as easy as 1, 2, 3."
- Develop your winning strategies in singles, doubles and life.
- Learn the "secret" of how to focus, for tennis and life.

- Embrace change, no matter what form it comes in.
- Develop better leadership qualities and improve your self-confidence and self-esteem.
- Manifest your future. The sky is the limit!

Starting today, I challenge you to implement your goals and dreams.

Do not just read about these lessons, but learn and apply them on the court and in your life.

Martina Navratilova's advice to you is, "Look for the openings, and even if you do not 'win,' you will have a lot of fun trying. There are opportunities for victory in your life. Be adventurous. Make the necessary changes; do not be afraid of them and what might happen. Once you try something different, you will realize how easy it really was to change. Who knows? You may just turn your life around for the better and experience a quality of life you never knew existed."

As you strive to change, caring for yourself, doing for others, and becoming better than you are right now, know that you will have good days and bad days. Just take it one day at a time. If you have a bad day, know that tomorrow will be different. Nothing worth having is a simple climb to the mountaintop. Some days you will feel like you are pedaling and pedaling, and there is no end in sight. Nevertheless, my advice is...keep pedaling. There will be some setbacks along the way. Some days may feel like you cannot go any further; the pain and the frustration is too great. Just remember that those days will pass. Life goes on; therefore, you get up and keep going in the direction of your goals and dreams. Obstacles will arise, and you will rise above those.

When you get to the top of the mountain and
think you are done, you then go down to the bottom;
there's always another mountain to climb.
— Charlie Brown

The rest of your life is in front of you, so you might as well give it your best shot. You have nothing to lose, and everything to gain! Let today be the beginning of a fresh start.

It is my hope that this book helps you break through your own personal barrier. I hope it inspires you to take more risks and play the game on your own terms. I want you to be able to say you are the kind of player who plays better when the pressure is on, that you have learned to love the game even more than before. Also, that you cherish the opportunities that are brought before you.

My hope is also that this book has touched your life in a positive way. I want you to take charge of your health, your fitness, your nutrition, your tennis life that is really supposed to be fun, and to win at the game of life! Get out of bed everyday for a fresh start and a new beginning. Let today be the beginning of a new you—for the rest of your life.

Today, I live to make a difference in people's lives.

First, think.
Second, believe.
Third, dream.
And finally, dare.
— Walt Disney

To further your continued success in *Winning in Tennis and Life*, you can reach me at:

www.WinningInTennisAndLife.com
Or www.MaryPatFaley.com

I am available for tennis lessons, teaching tennis professionals my "secrets," tennis consulting, speaking engagements, life coaching and personal training.

Remember:

Plan with your head; play with your heart.

MARY PAT FALEY'S
1, 2, 3 CHEAT SHEETS

These "cheat sheets" are good to keep in your racquet bag. To save you from having to tear them out of the book, I've made them available for you to download and print when you visit my website. If you're losing or want to stay focused and keep your committee in your head quiet (or at least in agreement), then read these little reminders while you are switching sides of the court. They are guaranteed to help you regain your focus.

So many times, we need to remember the little things when we're in the middle of a match, don't we? These "cheat sheets" will be your reminder, or your private coach, while you are on the tennis court playing your match.

You can also review these cheat sheets quickly before you start playing tennis, as a mental practice before you even hit one tennis ball. This will get your mind focused on what you're going to work on that day, either while playing the game or practicing. You will enjoy your tennis game so much more. You will play freely, without "over-thinking" about how to hit a shot. You won't beat yourself up every time you miss a particular shot, because you will have the "tools" to fix it – a cheat sheet (plus what you've learned in this book)!

There's nothing more frustrating than making the same mistake over and over again. Don't you hate hitting the same forehand long, just past the baseline, more than half the time? This "cheat sheet" will give you the knowledge you need to fix your mistake right away. It's hard to see what you're doing while you are the one playing the game. However, if you were able to stand outside and watch the game, you could probably analyze and fix the problem right away. That's why these "cheat sheets" are every tennis player's answers to improving every time.

Remember, ***knowledge is power.*** You have the knowledge to fix, change or focus on what is wrong while you are still playing the game on the tennis court.

I recommend using a few of the focus techniques first. If you are struggling with one particular shot, then go to the section that talks about that shot to get more specific.

FOCUS TECHNIQUES

Remember, there are nine focus techniques. There is no one right or wrong way. Be sure to visit my website to learn more *advanced* focus techniques to take your tennis game to the next level. Over the years, I have found that students pick certain focus techniques they find very helpful for their game. Sometimes, that technique doesn't work as well as it did when they started using the technique. That's when they pick another focus drill and work on that. Sometimes just changing things up will keep your mind fresh. These are the main techniques that seem to work best for most people:

1) Say "Bounce, hit."

Watch the spot that the ball actually bounces; and say the word, "Bounce."

See the ball actually hit your racquet, or at least see the blur of the racquet, and say the word, "Hit."

2) Watch the seams of the ball.

Do you see the ball more clearly coming toward you before you hit the ball, or do you see the ball more clearly after it leaves your racquet? Pay close attention to how much more the seams of the ball move after the bounce. This is when it's most important to watch the ball...especially the seams of the ball.

3) "Track it to the racquet."

Make sure your eyes are tracking the ball when your opponent hits the shot, all the way to seeing the flight of the ball over the net. Then have your eyes track the ball to your racquet. So, you are tracking the ball from your opponent's racquet, through the air, to your racquet.

Mary Pat's 1, 2, 3
Quick-Fix for All Strokes

With every stroke in tennis, as soon as you miss a shot, you can name probably 10 different things that you did wrong within that ONE individual stroke. However, the problem is you go through the gamut of all of the instructions you have received over the years, and you have the entire "committee" talking to you about what you did wrong. Most people tell themselves at least 4-6 different things they did wrong on that one particular shot. To me, that is too much thinking...stinkin' thinkin'...or just plain circuit overload. Your brain cannot remember all these things and hit the ball at the same time. It is impossible.

In analyzing a shot you miss, there might have been 10 things that you did wrong in that one shot. But, to correct the problem, you cannot possibly think of all 10 things that you did wrong. If you fix the #1 problem, all of the other nine things will probably correct themselves automatically. This means you do not have to think about all 10 things you might have done wrong - just fix one problem. It is like dominos; if you hit the first one down, the rest will automatically follow. Here's the main problem that is usually wrong when tennis strokes are missed.

So, let's "Keep It Simple, Silly... K.I.S.S."

1) If you:

> MISS: The forehand or the backhand GROUNDSTOKES go LONG, past the baseline,
>
> RESULT: You are hitting the ball too late
>
> FIX: Turn your shoulders sooner; therefore, you will hit the ball earlier, at the #1 hitting spot.

2) If you:

> MISS: The forehand or the backhand GROUNDSTROKES into the NET,

RESULT: You are not using your legs.

FIX: Bend (your knees) on the bounce.

1) Bounce

2) Bend

3) Balance

FIX: Aim two racquet-lengths above the net.

FIX: Finish over your shoulder with your racquet.

3) If you:

MISS: The forehand or the backhand VOLLEY goes LONG, past the baseline.

RESULT: You are hitting late.

FIX: You are not straightening your elbow soon enough. Start straightening your elbow when the ball is crossing the net.

4) If you:

MISS: The forehand or backhand VOLLEY goes into the NET.

RESULT: You are hitting too early or too soon

FIX: Set your racquet first. (You are probably skipping that step).

1) Set the racquet

2) Step at the same time you make contact with the ball. Squeeze and freeze. Hold finish for one second.

3) Now, go back to ready position with racquet and foot.

5) If you:

MISS: The forehand or the backhand APPROACH SHOTS go LONG.

RESULT: You are hitting the approach shot late, or behind your body.

FIX: You need to turn your shoulders earlier, so that

1) You will hit the ball in hitting spot #1, which is in front of your body.

2) You will slow down when hitting this shot, not stopped, not running full steam ahead, but rather, slowing down.

3) If it is the high shot above the net, remember to roll over the top half of the ball.

6) If you:

MISS: The forehand or the backhand APPROACH SHOTS go into the NET.

RESULT: You are not following through.

FIX: Use your core to turn your body; you will automatically follow-through.

1) Use your legs to bend, which will also help you follow-through.

2) Shorten your backswing a little and have a full follow-through. Most people have a big backswing and no follow-through. That is when it goes into the net.

3) Think of the back of your hand going all the way to your opposite ear.

7) If you:

MISS: The OVERHEAD goes LONG.

RESULT: You are hitting the overhead late.

FIX: Turn your shoulders earlier, as soon as you see the ball coming off your opponent's racquet.

1) Use your left hand to turn your shoulders, which puts the racquet in the proper position.

2) Use your left hand to sight the ball as if you are going to catch the ball with that hand. Your left arm is always in front of you and to the right (if you are right-handed).

3) Always get behind the ball with your feet as quickly as you can, then try to step in and hit it.

8) If you:

MISS: The OVERHEAD goes into the NET.

RESULT: You are dropping your head down too soon.

FIX: Stand up really tall, especially from your waist up and hit the overhead feeling like you are stretching up as far as you can to hit the ball. Make sure you watch the ball to your racquet.

9) If you:

MISS: The SERVE goes LONG.

RESULT: You are hitting the ball too late.

FIX: Move your toss more in front of your body.

1) Release the ball at eye level. Do not let go of the ball when it is above your head, or the toss will always be too far behind your body, or the baseline.

2) Make sure that you feel the "snap" or the "pronate" from your forearm.

3) Make sure that you see contact to your racquet...assume the serve will go in.

10) If you:

MISS: The SERVE goes into the NET.

RESULT: You are hitting the ball too soon, or the toss is too low.

FIX: Toss the ball a little bit higher.

1) Again, release the ball at eye level, not earlier, or the ball toss will end up too far in front of you.

2) The toss should be a little higher than the racquet when it is at full extension.

3) Hit the ball at the peak, which is at the moment the ball stops; right after it gets to its highest point, and before it starts its decent.

11) If you:

MISS: The SERVE is erratic.

RESULT: You are double faulting

FIX: You must take your time before each and every serve.

1) Look at the spot where you want the serve to land in the box on the other side of the court.

2) Watch contact point when you hit the serve.

3) Guide the ball with the palm of your hand where you want it to land. Remember to aim one racquet-length above the net if you are missing too many into the net.

12) If you:

MISS: You always feel rushed and are playing defense instead of offense.

RESULT: You are getting to the ball a little late.

FIX: Make sure you are watching your opponent when they are hitting the ball, and right before they hit the shot. You want to **SPLIT-STEP**, which will land you on your toes and have your weight forward, so your first step to the ball will be much quicker.

Be sure to visit my website: www.WinningInTennisAndLife.com to get more FREE TECHNIQUES about how to hit other kinds of "specialty shots", which include how to hit a swinging volley, or drop shots and how to hit the perfect short angle passing shot.

I also am available for consultation, speaking seminars, tennis seminars, group lessons or private lessons.

Take your tennis to a new level. Be the greatest champion that you can be!!!

BELIEVE IN YOURSELF...

PLAN WITH YOUR HEAD.

PLAY WITH YOUR HEART.

ABOUT THE AUTHOR

Mary Pat Faley grew up in Chicago. When she was 15, her father's company transferred the family to California. She was a good athlete in all sports in Chicago. However, when they moved to California, she started focusing on tennis. Being a great athlete did not earn you a college scholarship, which was her goal.

She received a full tennis scholarship from the University of Alabama in Birmingham, a Division I school. She has been sectionally and nationally ranked.

She has coached high school tennis teams and was also a collegiate tennis coach. She has coached thousands of students, over the past 30 years. She started coaching them as beginner juniors, and they continued climbing upward through the ranks, becoming highly ranked junior players. She has traveled all over the United States coaching, and being an inspirational mentor. Hundreds of her players have gotten scholarships to college, and then advanced on to playing on the ATP circuit, and the WTA circuit. Many students have also become full-time tennis professionals at various clubs around the country.

She has developed her own teaching methods, such as:

- Playing tennis is as easy as 1, 2, 3.
- Tennis strategies, both singles and doubles are as easy as 1, 2, 3.
- "Tennis by Numbers," if you can count, you can play tennis.
- "TNT, which is a program designed for Tennis and Training."

She has had years of experience being a speaker and positively influencing people's lives. She is USPTA (United States Professional Tennis Association) certified, still teaches at Calabasas Tennis & Swim Center in Calabasas, California, and she is available to teach other tennis professionals her "secrets" to her success as a tennis consultant. She was a real estate broker, is a professional speaker, is a life coach, and is a NASM certified personal trainer. Her spirit is one of boundless energy. She resides in Encino, California with her family.